DELIVERING
EXCEPTIONAL
PERFORMANCE

◆

"This book offers a wake up call to people and organisations. It provides a theoretical framework which works in reality and is a must for all organisations and individuals who wish to succeed in this era of constant change and rapid technological advance."

Sue Tomlinson, Director, Career Action Centre Cable and Wireless

"If you are concerned about the performance of your organisation, your team, yourself, this book is for you. It will make you think and probably help you change. If you only read one book this year make it this one."

Peter Cole, SBC Warburg

"The hard part of strategy is implementation because it usually requires changes in the way people work. *Delivering Exceptional Performance* will help managers at all levels to accomplish this most difficult of tasks with its clear ideas and practical examples."

John Constable, Consultant and Professor of Business Strategy

An ideal book for helping managers understand how to deliver exceptional performance. Case examples illustrate how differen companies are tackling the issues facing them as they work to manage performance in the changing social and economic environment.

Harald Wilkens, Group Training and Development Manager, Bayer Group UK

DELIVERING EXCEPTIONAL PERFORMANCE

◆

Aligning the Potential of Organizations, Teams and Individuals

◆

Pam Jones

Joy Palmer

Carole Osterweil

and

Diana Whitehead

London . Hong Kong . Johannesburg
Melbourne . Singapore . Washington

PITMAN PUBLISHING
128 Long Acre, London WC2E 9AN
Tel: +44 (0)171 447 2000
Fax: +44 (0)171 240 5771

A Division of Pearson Professional Limited

First published in Great Britain 1996

ISBN 0 273 62498 9

British Library Cataloguing in Publication Data
A CIP catalogue record for this book can be obtained from the British Library.

1 3 5 7 9 10 8 6 4 2

Typeset by Pantek Arts, Maidstone, Kent
Printed and bound in Great Britain by Biddles Ltd, Guildford and King's Lynn

The Publishers' policy is to use paper manufactured from sustainable forests.

658.402

About the authors

Pam Jones BA (Hons) MBA

Pam is Director of the Ashridge Performance Through People Programme. She
works as a consultant, teacher and coach
to organizations and individuals in order
to help them develop and excel. She works
internationally and has spent three years
in the Asia pacific region with Hong Kong
and Shanghai Bank. Her experience spans
a range of organizations in both the public
and private sector and this experience has
stimulated the development of *Delivering
Exceptional Performance*.

Joy Palmer BA (Hons), DPM, FIPD, MIMC

Joy established her own business consultancy, Interactives, ten years ago, having
previously worked internationally in HR
departments in the high technology
industry. She now works with multinational clients in diverse industries,
including energy, finance and telecommunications, in the area of people and
organization strategy, performance management and business change.

Joy became an associate of Ashridge
Management College in 1995 and is a regular contributor to the Performance
Through People Programme. In addition, she works at various business
schools throughout the UK with managers at varying stages along the
transition into the knowledge era.

Carole Osterweil BSc (Tech), MBA

Carole is an Assistant Director of Studies at Ashridge, where she specializes in integrative approaches to help people move from functional to project and process-based working. She works extensively with organizations which are undertaking major change programmes, often associated with business process reengineering and empowerment. The key facets of this work are: a strong focus on translating ideas into action; the alignment of structural and cultural changes; and recognizing people as the key resource.

This builds on her own experience as a leader of multi-disciplinary project teams at Glaxo and Lucas, and as an internal consultant at Unisys.

Diana Whitehead BA (Hons), TEFL (RSA), MBA

Diana first joined Ashridge in 1994 to undertake a research project. As well as working on *Delivering Exceptional Performance* she has carried out several research projects and taught on a number of open and tailored programmes. Prior to joining Ashridge, Diana worked in Switzerland and Germany for ten years. She spent four years in personnel with Bosch, where she specialized in assessment centres for graduate recruitment and also ran her own company specializing in language training and translation.

Diana is currently working with Woolworths plc, London, managing their graduate recruitment and education, and putting *Delivering Exceptional Performance* into practice.

CONTENTS

◆

"All changed, changed utterly:
A terrible beauty is born"

W B Yeats, Easter 1916

PREFACE

◆

This book developed out of our experiences of working with managers from many different types of organizations, all facing similar challenges and struggling to make sense of them. As our own imaginations were fired by the opportunities we could see, we decided to research the area more thoroughly so that we could test our ideas and find new approaches to help. This, above all, is what we wanted to do with this book: to offer managers new insights into the challenge which faces them, to inspire and to guide them by showing the exciting possibilities that lie ahead and by offering practical ways of moving down the road to the era in which human brain power plays center stage.

We're not saying it is easy; nor is it accomplished overnight and there certainly is no panacea for a quick fix. But if this book leaves you feeling inspired, feeling that you can really start to contribute to your organization's future and feeling that you have now got some tools to get you started, then we have accomplished our goal.

We wish you *bon voyage*.

INTRODUCTION

By Richard Pascale

◆

"Be all that you can be" – a simple statement, yet compelling enough to shift the recruiting ground for US soldiers from the street to the high school, thus ensuring that the quality of young men and women recruits steadily climbed through the 1980s.

What this statement, of Major General Maxwell Thurman, Head of Army Recruiting Command in the late seventies and eighties, did for the US army was to create a future which inspired and captured the enthusiasm of the people needed to make things happen.

This need to harness and mobilize human talent is blindingly obvious – yet there is often an alarming disconnection between this obvious need and the way businesses set out to manage and deliver performance. As we face an ever-intensifying back-drop of competition and change, this disconnection needs to be addressed. We must move beyond many traditional boundaries; boundaries which have typified the industrial age. Not only boundaries of markets and competition, of organizations and work, but also boundaries of authority, of time, of experience and of control.

At the same time as the future becomes harder to predict, the past and our familiar responses to the problems we face become less reliable indicators of our continued success. We operate with mental maps and tend to see the world through these, rather than seeing these maps themselves. Hence, our familiar ways of operating are often invisible to us. We see only too late the seeds of destruction, sown by our own hands.

To break out of a potentially downward spiral of performance, businesses must be able to reinvent themselves – they need a capability for transformation and renewal. This leads to a search for new insights, new thoughts, new approaches which force us, not only to examine and challenge existing ways of operating but also to generate the essential breakthroughs which will enable us to get beyond what we currently do. We have to be able to see the box we are in and open it, before we can get out of it. A capacity for renewal in your business means you are more likely to make something great happen, rather than sit back and have something happen to you.

The search for new ways of stealing an edge is evident in the management fads that quickly find their way into the language and tools of organizations. Over the last 15 years, we have seen TQM, Excellence, One-Minute Managing, Intrapreneuring, BPR, Benchmarking – to name but a few. The trouble with these new approaches is that for many organizations they are easy come, easy go. Why is that so many of them miss their target? In part it is because what they offer is not readily accessible to the managers who have responsibility for day-to-day performance. Many good concepts and frameworks never take root in people's action frames because they seem neither relevant nor readily put into practice.

This presents a challenge to leaders and management thinkers whose agendas include business strategy and the change implementation that frequently accompanies it. We can only get beyond the boundaries of our present world if we take people with us. Sustainable change requires engagement and commitment not from a few but from the many different people involved.

Delivering exceptional performance takes people and puts their energies and talents at the heart of the business system. It asks "How can managers, when all that is familiar seems to be disappearing, latch on to and learn from new approaches, using them to guide their own and others' actions?". The authors of *Delivering Exceptional Performance* provide a comprehensive treatment of the essential elements of a high performing organization. A particular strength of the book is the assessment and consulting tools which accompany each chapter and ground concepts in the real world of "how to do." *Delivering Exceptional Performance* is an accessible and useful handbook for the practitioner.

ACKNOWLEDGEMENTS

◆

As knowledge workers we have come together as a virtual team to write this book. We all hold a number of professional roles as teachers and consultants, and it is through these roles that we have been able to access our wide network of contacts. They have provided us with ideas, research agendas and case material for which we are extremely grateful. The Ashridge Performance Through People Programme has also provided us with inspiration and ideas, so many thanks to all those who knowingly or unknowingly stimulated our thoughts.

Our reality, as many professionals are finding, is one of constant juggling of roles and contracts, and achieving the balance with our personal lives. This book reflects the lives we lead. Without the support of our partners and children, it would have been harder still.

We extend our appreciation to the often invisible team, K, Louise, Brian, and to Stuart Crainer for his editorial contribution, to all at Pitman Publishing, and to the people in the Ashridge Learning Resource Centre, who on-line have accessed the databases of the world. And finally, our thanks go to Deana, who as much as anybody on this planet knows what it means to have linked herself to the soul of the new machine.

"Man is still the most extraordinary computer of all."

John F Kennedy

Chapter 1

◆

PERFORMANCE THROUGH PEOPLE

In an era of unprecedented change, organizations must be rebuilt. If they are to succeed, their new foundations will be their greatest resource: people. Utilizing and fulfilling the potential of all of their people, all of the time, is the organizational and managerial challenge of our times.

UNLEASHING THE POWER OF PEOPLE

Disaster, devastation and destruction haunt our lives. In January 1995, the Japanese city of Kobe was torn apart by an earthquake. A modern, sophisticated city was thrown into chaos. Later in the same year, one of the worst storms this century swept up the Atlantic coast of the United States leaving a trail of death and destruction. Twelve states declared a state of emergency as heavy snow and hurricanes killed at least 66 people. Gusts of up to 70 mph whipped around the skyscrapers of New York; Hurricane Allison swirled in from the Gulf of Mexico and buffeted the north-western coast of Florida; a tornado ripped through suburbs in Philadelphia; in Kentucky a "twister" ripped the roof from a school.

Though we expect and are accustomed to a life of clinical efficiency, at any moment we may be confronted by the twin forces of chaos and uncertainty.

Chaos and uncertainty inevitably bring change. Everything familiar is destroyed or altered beyond recognition. Amid the chaos, the human and material destruction, people start anew. Disasters are a fact of life, but so too is the ability of people to rebuild their homes, lives and communities. Time and time again they dramatically demonstrate an ability to work together to push themselves to exceptional limits.

And yet, it invariably takes disasters of such magnitude for this innate human energy to be unleashed. In their ordinary lives – at home and at work – such strength, ingenuity and vigor largely lies dormant and untapped. *Delivering Exceptional Performance* is about unleashing these forces in the organization of the late 1990s and beyond.

A NEW APPROACH FOR THE INFORMATION AGE

As we enter the information age, in which knowledge is the key organizational resource, the pace and the scale of the change demanded of organizations and those who work within them is enormous. Just as agricultural era processes, systems and attitudes had to be rebuilt to capitalize on the new industrial era, so industrial era skills and techniques must be rebuilt to take advantage of the opportunities offered by the information age.

The organizations we see around us have not been laid waste by a natural disaster. But they are afflicted by change, coupled with the twin forces of chaos and uncertainty, which always accompany such disasters. They, too, need to be built anew – and their people must be the builders.

The new era demands a fresh, innovative and radical approach. Building on existing processes, structures and ideas simply produces more of the same – it is akin to rebuilding a city which has been destroyed by an earthquake using the same foundations. Organizations must start from scratch. They must start again, but without forgetting what is valuable from the past. They must look at every aspect of what they do in a holistic way. Charles Handy provides the example of the destruction of the library at the University of Dubrovnik. It was rebuilt, not as a carbon copy of what had gone before, but with computer equipment and links to global databases instead of the books and journals it had previously housed. [1]

We have left the age of capital-based assets and entered the information age. Proof of this is nowhere more obvious than in the cars we drive. The electronic technology installed in a luxury car is now worth more than the steel the car is made of. A television advertisement claims: "There is a BMW with more computing power than it took to send a man to the moon."

The new world of management and organizations is powered by Information Technology (IT). In the rush of enthusiasm for IT during the 1980s, we were told that IT could – and most certainly would – replace us. It would cut a swathe through the world of employment, wiping away our jobs. Computers were smart and getting smarter by the day. Inadequate and fearful, we would be cast aside as the new machine set about ruling the world.

The hyperbole appeared to be matched by changes in corporate reality – in the US, a research project estimated that between 1972 and 1978, each 10 percent increase in computer power was associated with a 1.8 percent decrease in the employment of clerks and a 1.2 percent decrease in the employment of managers. [2]

However, the blind enthusiasm, and the feelings of inadequacy and fear it engendered, has proved to be largely misplaced. For all the wondrous technology now at our disposal, no computer will ever match the human brain for its sheer complexity. And no computer will ever be able to design itself, build itself or operate itself.

No computer can smile a welcome "hello," or deliver the kind of personal service that keeps customers coming back for more.

There are many examples of companies which have become disillusioned by the failure of technology to deliver its promise of massive productivity gains.

In the early 1980s, the UK engineering company TI invested heavily in automating its procurement department. As a result, the department worked much faster, but everyone else had to fill in the paperwork and it took much longer for the company to purchase anything.[3]

Similarly, banks have spent heavily on IT over the last 25 years, but few are truly satisfied with the results so far – not least because recent deregulation, coupled with the lower barriers to entry that IT offers, has enabled many non-bank competitors to muscle in.[4] You now have upstart banks which do all their business over the phone, and even retailing groups moving into areas once the sole domain of the big banks.

Technology is miraculous, but it does not solve all of our problems. One American phone company admits that its computerized billing system is a disaster, producing errors on three quarters of its orders for new phones.[5]

The Barings Bank collapse happened despite all the technology available to managers – a report by the Singapore authorities blamed institutional incompetence and a total failure of internal controls by senior management.[6]

Organizations are realizing that people, not technology, are the crucial differentiators in business success. Technology alone is not the route to competitive advantage. More usually, competitive advantage comes from having an organizational structure geared to innovation, or one which enables technology to be put to work more effectively than your competitors.

Technology provides the information; people turn that information into knowledge and use it to help achieve the organization's reasons for existing. The same information is generally freely available, so is not a differentiator.

In the information age, therefore, the critical differentiator is knowledge; the knowledge generated and utilized by people. Bill Gates of Microsoft believes we are on the brink of another revolution involving inexpensive communication, allowing computers to join together.[7] In such a technological paradise, people will continue to make the difference.

PEOPLE RULE!

Paradoxically, the new machine has ended the age of machines. "In the machine age control was everything. Managers were allergic to surprises," observes Gary Hamel, co-author of *Competing for the Future*. "The results of that obsession were painfully detailed reporting systems, endless review meetings, brusque phone calls when budget variances were spotted, a temptation to second-guess operating managers, and a seemingly unquenchable thirst on the part of HQ for more data."[8]

From controlling we have moved to enabling. If organizations are to enable people, managers must create a world in which the exceptional ingenuity and energy of people is channeled into their working lives. They must inspire people to change their mind-sets without having an obvious, immediate catalyst to accomplish this.

Delivering Exceptional Performance is concerned with how managers can return to first principles to begin the process of recreating the organization. To do so, we will argue, depends on viewing the organization as a whole, as well as each part of it.

Such change will not – and cannot – occur overnight. Managers have to expend all their time and energy keeping the business going today, as well as having to prepare for tomorrow. But, we hope to inspire you with our ideas; to challenge your way of looking at things and to help you as you take your first steps into the new world.

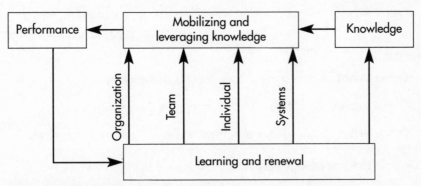

Fig 1.1 Delivering exceptional performance – leveraging the knowledge resource

5

HARNESSING THE KNOWLEDGE WITHIN

The need to maximize human resources is reshaping the world of work. Traditional paternalistic approaches – typified by security, certainty and the idea of a job for life – are giving way to a dynamic era of change, challenge and uncertainty, which focuses both on the individual and on new forms of teams. A new psychological contract is emerging to forge a very different relationship between employer and employee. Knowledge is no longer the ethereal preserve of the few, but an all-embracing corporate necessity (see Figure 1.2). We are all knowledge workers.

Inevitably, given the scale of the changes underway, there is also confusion as people grapple with the inherent anomalies and ambiguity involved. As we progress into the information age, managers will have to adjust their style to one in which leadership involves conducting, coaching and mentoring. Gary Hamel believes that the language, tools, roles and responsibilities of management in this new world are only now being invented.[9]

People are beginning to realize that a deep sense of belonging and common understanding are needed between an organization

---

Know how = skill base, for example trade secrets, engineering standards, expertise of the organization.

Know who = the people with the information, both internally & externally; the informal network that gets the work done.

Know when = sense of timing when developing new products, managing lead times, closing out old products and pacing the market.

Know what = mastery of a consistent set of meanings.

Know where = ability to identify appropriate market niches.

Know why = knowledge of context and how it relates to our efforts.

Fig 1.2: The knowledge resource
Source: Savage, C, Fifth Generation Management, Integrating Enterprises Through Human Networking, Butterworth Heinemann, Oxford, 1990

and its people in order to achieve exceptional effort and results. Former Nissan personnel director, Peter Wickens, champions the idea of an ascendant organization, involving a partnership between managers and people, in which business strategy, objectives, the organization's needs and individual evaluation and needs are integrated.[10]

Karl Albrecht first recognized the concept of "emotional labor," which he described as any kind of work in which a person's feelings are tools of their trade.[11] We would argue that a person's feelings and emotions are integral to any work or job they are doing, but especially so in the new age, where quality of interaction with others is paramount. Midland Bank's 24-hour a day banking service, First Direct, calls this the "Moment of Truth." On their 100th phone call, at the end of a busy seven-hour shift, will a person be committed enough to want to make this last customer feel special?

Achieving this level of motivation demands a new kind of leadership, characterized by guidance and support rather than rules. It must recognize that the key resource of the organization, people, are unique. Customers are people. Too often, standard systems and procedures are not personal or individual enough to recognize this uniqueness.

"Fifth generation management," the term coined by Charles Savage, formerly of Digital Equipment Corporation, to describe the new contribution of management in the knowledge era, is not something that can be taught – it has to come from within, through discovering the power of our own insights, emotions and ability to see new patterns.[12]

This presents fresh managerial challenges. Managers must focus and co-ordinate multiple-task teams; build trust and openness; learn the unique strengths of people; and engender accountability and learning. They must develop new habits, attitudes, behaviors and skills, and learn to overcome the fears which often go hand-in-hand with the loss of traditional power. Managers are no longer a protected species. They no longer control all performance decisions. New performance and people management approaches, and the rising popularity of 360 degree feedback tools, mean that they are more accountable for their actions and other people have a say in performance decisions.

In addition, managers are finding that they are often taking on greater responsibility for human resource management than ever before, including training and a whole host of activities traditionally seen as the domain of specialist or corporate HR departments. Once they have recognized the need to nurture the development of others, they are often daunted by the challenge, and frequently express concern about their lack of skills, knowledge and ability to do this with confidence.

Managers feel they are facing insurmountable challenges in pursuit of their organization's goals. They have to manage their own performance and development, as well as that of their teams. Traditional career paths have often disappeared. For many, this is uncharted and frightening territory.

The task is further confused by the fact that organizations are also changing as they recognize the need to find new ways of supporting their people through the complex maze of demands and responsibilities, which are part and parcel of the new work ethos. It is a maze in which job descriptions are being replaced by temporary roles and competencies. Flexible contracts are becoming the norm; reward and benefit systems are being questioned and sometimes revolutionized; hierarchy is giving way to flatter structures based on processes and teams.

The management of these crucial business elements is a vital part of the whole process of developing each individual to maximize their contribution to the organization's success. Where does all this leave you?

Such radical changes and new demands are not easily or instantly mastered. All of the managers we have worked with recently are in organizations that have undergone change of some kind, ranging from trying to get more from existing resources, to radical restructuring, delayering and downsizing. A few are trying to cope with a new information technology strategy or new processes and systems which mean increased workload, while familiarization with the system, itself a huge task, takes place. The majority are worried, stressed, challenged and often confused. Look at how they describe their immediate challenges:

8

"Team leadership to ensure the whole bank understands the reason and priority of the projects . . . to improve the culture so that the bank is one and not a lot of individual divisions. Need to ensure that multi-disciplinary teams work together without reverting to defending their department."

Senior manager, a leading Argentinean bank

"Centralization and rationalization have resulted in major reorganization of roles, responsibilities and the structure of the organization. This has caused a major upheaval in the way people do their jobs, and the new organization in which they operate. I need to create a team atmosphere that will be self-sustaining to improve the overall performance of my department."

Director of purchasing, electronics company

"A major change has been the flattening of the hierarchical structure, giving rise to job enlargement, enrichment and empowerment. As a result, people may feel 'put upon' and promotion prospects have been considerably lessened. I am keen to encourage and utilize team resources to produce better results."

Technical sales manager, worldwide conglomerate

"I would like a better understanding of how to motivate and influence my team."

Technical group leader, major telecommunications company

"Creating high performance teams, getting the best out of people."

Investment manager, major bank

"My organization's style is to manage complex, often intangible tasks through multi-disciplinary teams. I would like to focus on the motivation and management of such teams, the performance of individuals within teams."

Director of commissioning, UK Local Health Authority

What becomes increasingly clear is that a change in any aspect of the way performance is managed will have a knock-on effect on performance management in other parts of the organization. No manager is an island – and nor can any department, team or function work in isolation.

ACHIEVING SUCCESS

Amid this maelstrom of chaos and change, achieving high performance and helping people reach their potential no longer seems logical and straightforward. In the past, when the world was stable, achieving high performance appeared to be a simple matter of being logical, of eliminating short-term risks, and creating order for people to work in. It was about getting compliance from people, about controlling and solving problems. The emphasis was on trying to stop the bad things happening, and using energy to constrain and stabilize.

In the new turbulent world, the emphasis has changed. Managers are conjurers rather than controllers, asked to achieve high performance by helping people realize their full potential. Those who excel at this seem able to do so by magic, juggling various interests, talents, and conflicts. We believe there are common themes, and those who succeed manage to steer a clear course through uncertainty, building commitment and enthusiasm along the way. It is about motivating people to believe in and use their talent, and about inspiring others with what you yourself believe. The concentration is on human energy and enthusiasm, making the best things happen, and your managerial energy is channeled into energizing others.

Achieving such wide-ranging and bold objectives requires people management of the highest level, and an approach which is integrated and aligned: performance through people.

But what is performance through people? The IPM's 1992 report defines performance management as "a philosophy rather than a clearly defined process or set of policies . . . an approach to creating a shared vision of the purpose and aims of the organization, helping each individual employee to understand and recognize their part in contributing to them, and in so doing, manage and enhance the performance of both individuals and the organization."[13]

Delivering exceptional performance is more than philosophy, more than creating a shared vision. It involves recognizing that people can contribute intellect, imagination, curiosity, radical ideas, forsight, creativity, energy and commitment. Working relationships must be shaped to harness this power of people so that exceptional performance can be delivered at the same time as people are nurtured, developed and enthused.

Managing people's performance has often been misunderstood and overlooked. The annual appraisal, for example, has damaged perceptions of what performance management involves. The appraisal is much maligned, and rightly so – in many companies it adds no value and, worse still, creates cynicism. This justifiable and understandable cynicism has reinforced the belief that people do not matter, that the organization does not care, and that people are dispensable. In turn, this makes any changes far more difficult to achieve.

The reality is that managing results through people can – and must – be made to work. It is not a dreamy abstraction, an ideal for those on the soft side of the business, but a new competitive imperative.

PRISMS OF PERFORMANCE

With these new facts of corporate life combined with insights from managers, as well as ideas and experiences developed from the Performance Through People course at Ashridge Management College, we tried to understand the differences between organizations. Why do some implement change initiatives successfully, to emerge with a powerful and high performance workforce, while others struggle? We found that organizations which recognize knowledge workers as their major asset, which welcome the situation and are prepared for the challenge of the future, are able to successfully implement change. Organizations that cling to old ideas and beliefs, holding on to the past and failing to acknowledge the dawning of a new era, tend to struggle. In successful organizations new attitudes, values and skills are all-encompassing. There is no hiding place.

Source of competitive advantage

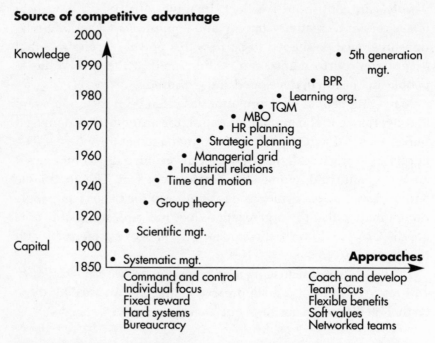

Fig 1.3 Leveraging performance – the development of management ideas over time

As Figure 1.3 demonstrates, ideas about performance management have evolved. Evolution now needs to give way to more revolutionary interpretations. To help managers with the complexities and uncertainties involved in managing performance through people, and to illustrate the key inter-relationships, we have developed the image of a prism (see Figure 1.4).

Light passed through a prism divides into the colors of the spectrum, but if the sides of the prism are not aligned, the light will not be split. In our use of this image, the base of the prism represents the organization, while each side represents a different facet of managing performance. Like a prism, if one of these facets of people management is not accurately aligned, the outcome or performance may not be optimal, but risks being faulty, incorrect or stultified in some way.

The four sides of the Prism present a holistic, integrated approach to the challenge of delivering exceptional results through people.

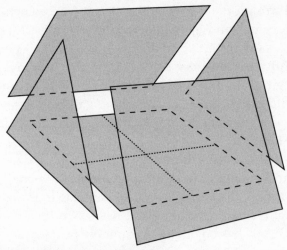

Fig 1.4 The Performance Prism image

As a prism is capable of splitting light into the colors of the spectrum, it provides a powerful image of the potential of harnessing people's performance for delivering exceptional results.

Some organizations have achieved more alignment than others. Some are still struggling to ensure that all the facets work together to support the purpose, or intent, of the organization (see Figure 1.5).

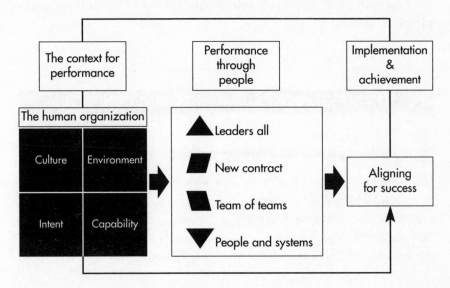

Fig 1.5 The Performance Prism

13

Working through the Performance Prism framework, with its various dimensions and elements, can help you explore the full impact of any new initiative to ensure that you are operating in alignment with your purpose and goals. It also provides a useful way of testing the alignment of existing performance management initiatives with other dimensions in the organization, and it may cast light on why they are not producing the desired results within the expected timescale.

As well as being a useful model for those who are developing the policies and initiatives to create alignment and manage change in the organization, the Prism is equally valuable to those working in, or leading, teams. Although the Prism is an image of a solid structure, each side has one thing in common: people.

Often we approach people management in a clinical, dissociated way which ignores the fact that the people who work in the organization and who implement change have talents, aspirations and resources that cannot be tapped in a controlled, clinical, standard way. In our framework, people are the light passing through the framework. Managers must be able to step outside the Prism, to take a helicopter view, side views and views looking up from the bottom of the organization, while recognizing that they too are an integral part of it. What is a prism without light? What is an organization without people?

THE PERFORMANCE COMPETENCY QUESTIONNAIRE

Do you deliver performance through people?

Many managers have become familiar with the behavioral competencies approach which gained popularity in the late 1980s. This identifies specific competencies considered necessary for superior performance. We use this approach at Ashridge to help managers identify their own strengths and weaknesses in relation to performance through people.

This abridged version of the Ashridge Performance Competency Questionnaire will help you begin analyzing your own competencies for each facet of the Performance Prism. Your score will indicate your level of competence, and point to areas of the Performance Prism which you may need to develop further. The appropriate chapter will assist in this development, providing you with a holistic view on how to deliver exceptional performance through people.

You can use this as a self-completion questionnaire, or your colleagues can complete it on your behalf to provide you with some feedback on how they see your strengths and areas for development.

Think about each statement and rate yourself accordingly, using the five-point scale described below:

1 = NOT COMPETENT   An unused or untested area

2 = SOME COMPETENCE   A slight ability demonstrated in this area

3 = FAIRLY COMPETENT   An average ability demonstrated in this area

4 = VERY COMPETENT   An above average ability demonstrated
                           in this area

5 = EXTREMELY COMPETENT   Regarded as an expert in this area

- Try to be as honest and objective as possible
- Circle one response for each item on the scale
- Take your time with each item and think about specific examples or situations where the competency is demonstrated.

QUESTIONNAIRE

1	Adapts leadership style to the current situation	1 2 3 4 5
2	Provides a clear picture about what is required of others	1 2 3 4 5
3	Encourages others to seek new opportunities for their development	1 2 3 4 5
4	Measures team's performance in terms of output	1 2 3 4 5
5	Conveys a positive attitude towards change	1 2 3 4 5
6	Encourages others to perform to the highest level	1 2 3 4 5
7	Produces individual development plans with each team member	1 2 3 4 5
8	Recognizes and credits contributions of team members	1 2 3 4 5
9	Measures team performance in terms of quality	1 2 3 4 5
10	Creates a clear vision of change	1 2 3 4 5
11	Has a clear focus of own direction	1 2 3 4 5
12	Identifies the aims, aspirations and motivations of team members	1 2 3 4 5
13	Helps foster collaboration amongst team members	1 2 3 4 5
14	Has a clear understanding of the organization's performance management systems	1 2 3 4 5
15	Takes a strategic view of the business environment	1 2 3 4 5
16	Takes responsibility for own development	1 2 3 4 5
17	Treats team members as individuals	1 2 3 4 5
18	Involves expertise and knowledge of all team members	1 2 3 4 5
19	Uses both formal and informal systems for recognition and communication.	1 2 3 4 5
20	Understands the competitive environment in which the organization operates	1 2 3 4 5

21	Shares information freely with all members of the team	1 2 3 4 5
22	Deals with performance problems in a constructive manner	1 2 3 4 5
23	Encourages teams to take responsibility for achieving their goals	1 2 3 4 5
24	Reviews performance of team members at least twice a year	1 2 3 4 5
25	Knows what to do to "get on" in the organization	1 2 3 4 5
26	Recognizes the imaginative and creative ideas of others	1 2 3 4 5
27	Sets achievable milestones for others to improve performance	1 2 3 4 5
28	Demonstrates trust in the team and its members	1 2 3 4 5
29	Provides open honest feedback to all team members	1 2 3 4 5
30	Is sensitive to organizational issues and politics	1 2 3 4 5
31	Is able to deal with pressure and still function well under stressful conditions	1 2 3 4 5
32	Is committed to developing the skills and abilities of team members	1 2 3 4 5
33	Cascades the organization's business plan or strategic goals to team level	1 2 3 4 5
34	Sets objectives which are aligned with the wider business objectives	1 2 3 4 5
35	Communicates clearly to the team where the organization is going	1 2 3 4 5
36	Handles criticisms or setbacks in a constructive manner	1 2 3 4 5
37	Uses a range of opportunities to develop team members	1 2 3 4 5
38	Creates an atmosphere where team members can contribute ideas freely	1 2 3 4 5
39	Sets challenging objectives	1 2 3 4 5
40	Ensures the team is aware of the organization's purpose	1 2 3 4 5

Scoring

Transfer your scores for each question onto the score sheet. Then add up each column to obtain a total score.

Q	Score A	Q	Score B	Q	Score C	Q	Score D	Q	Score E
1		2		3		4		5	
6		7		8		9		10	
11		12		13		14		15	
16		17		18		19		20	
21		22		23		24		25	
26		27		28		29		30	
31		32		33		34		35	
36		37		38		39		40	
Total A		Total B		Total C		Total D		Total E	

Plot your scores on to the radar diagram in Figure 1.6. Joining up the points will give you a pictorial representation of your performance management competency profile. The radar diagram is particularly useful if you are asking others to fill in the questionnaire on your behalf. You can also plot their scores so that you can get a clear comparison as to how others see your performance.

UNDERSTANDING YOUR PERFORMANCE MANAGEMENT COMPETENCY PROFILE

Your A score refers to the leadership competencies required to achieve exceptional performance. They are concerned with your leadership style, your ability to create a positive climate, your approach to self-development and your ability to demonstrate emotional resilience. All these issues are developed further in Chapter 3, where there is also a more detailed leadership questionnaire.

Your B score refers to the competencies required to achieve exceptional performance by clearly understanding and balancing the requirements of the organization with the expectations and potential of your team members. It is concerned with your ability to communicate the requirements of the

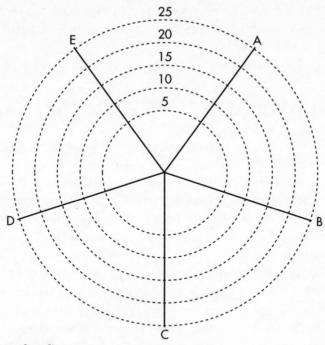

Fig 1.6 Radar diagram

organization, understand the expectations of others, manage performance difficulties and coach effectively to achieve good results. These issues are discussed in more detail in Chapter 4.

Your C score refers to the competencies required to build and maintain high performing teams. It focuses on the ability to motivate others, develop high performing teams, ensure effective team communications and encourage empowerment amongst team members. These issues are covered in detail in Chapter 5.

Your D score refers to the competencies required to measure performance effectively. It particularly focuses on measuring and reviewing performance, setting clear objectives which are aligned to the wider business, and understanding how to get the most out of the performance management systems in your organization. These issues are covered in Chapter 6.

Your E score refers to your competence in understanding the organization as a whole. It is concerned with managing change, understanding the wider business context in which you operate, understanding the organization's culture, and creating a sense of direction for those you work with, which will help in achieving exceptional performance from others. These issues are covered in detail in Chapter 2.

HOW TO GET THE MOST FROM THIS BOOK

Delivering Exceptional Performance is for managers responsible for achieving results through people, the people who will use their abilities to generate wealth in the 1990s and beyond. It looks at how they can develop their full potential in order to achieve exceptional performance for themselves and others. The book follows the Prism framework, and each chapter focuses on a different facet of performance.

The focus of this book is on self-development; providing practical and accessible means by which you can find your own way of maximizing the power of performance through people. At the same time, the book offers solutions to managing performance in the new era. It examines innovative concepts and styles of releasing the full potential of people for steering organizations through uncertain times. It is not a leap into the unknown – though it may seem so.

Each chapter takes on a practical focus with case examples, exercises, and checklists to illustrate the way in which managing performance has shifted. It provides you with the tools and insights to facilitate this shift in your own thinking and actions, as well as in others, so that you can take exceptional performance off the wish list and make it a reality. Finding your way around the chapters is easy using the various icons illustrated below to guide your interest.

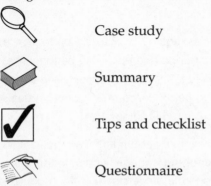

Case study

Summary

Tips and checklist

Questionnaire

Change is the unifying theme of this book. It pulls together all sides of the Prism in a dynamic way, recognizing that there is no stable base on which it stands. There are always new pressures and shocks to the business equilibrium, like the shifting ground in an earthquake, the rising waters of a flood. We cannot control the force of change any more than we can in these kinds of natural disasters, merely learn to ride on the crest of the wave.

Hopefully what you discover on your journey through this book will influence the choices you and your organization make today, preparing you and your people to embrace and surmount the challenge of tomorrow.

A wide variety of case studies have been selected to represent different industrial sectors, many with global operations and global perspective. They include organizations such as: Avon Cosmetics, American Express, Avon Tyres, Bayer plc, Lloyds Bank, Nissan Motors and Swiss Bank Corporation. They have been selected to provide an up-to-date insight into the different ways organizations are tackling the issue of developing high performance.

Delivering Exceptional Performance aims to help avert disaster, by taking the mystery out of performance management and putting it into people. The time for lip-service has passed: the new agenda must be driven by the needs, aspirations and potential of people. Only if this is achieved will individuals and organizations fulfill their long dormant potential.

PERFORMANCE THROUGH PEOPLE

The knowledge age is upon us. We can embrace it, have the vision to understand and contribute to its potential, or we can deny it and remain trapped in our boxes. We can experience the new challenges of working together as equals, of truly valuing each other's contributions, or we can stay locked up in the cultures of distrust, built by yesterday's managers. It will be easier, in the short term, to stay locked up. To break free requires a change of mind-set which is not for the weak-hearted.

Organizations must at least start building the foundations for the information age now if they haven't already started. They must provide the kinds of culture, structure, and style of management in which teams of knowledge workers can flourish, and their contribution be harnessed. New ways of working and new contracts must be established jointly, with a developmental approach to managing performance, which involves coaching, mentoring and providing multiple feedback and open exchange. Incentives, rewards and other motivational programs must be developed to align with the new forms of working. Investing in the continued development of talent is critical to achieving competitive advantage.

References

1. Handy, C, "Trust and the vital organization", *Harvard Business Review*, May-June 1995.
2. Scott Morton, M S (ed), *The Corporation of the 1990s*, Oxford University Press, Oxford, 1991.
3. *The Economist*, 1 May 1993.
4. *The Economist*, 3 October 1992.
5. *The Economist*, 1 May 1993
6. *The Times*, 20 October 1995
7. Gates, B, *The Road Ahead*, Viking, London, 1995.
8. Hamel, G, Foreword to *The Financial Times Handbook of Management* (editor: Crainer, S), FT/Pitman, London, 1995.
9. Hamel, G and Prahalad, C K, *Competing for the Future*, Harvard Business School Press, Cambridge, Mass., 1994.
10. Wickens, P, *The Ascendant Organization*, Macmillan Press, London, 1995.
11. Albrecht, K, *Service Within: Solving the Middle Management Leadership Crisis*, Dow-Jones–Irwin Inc., USA, 1990.
12. Savage, C, *Fifth Generation Management,* Integrating Enterprises Through Human Networking, Butterworth Heinemann, Oxford, 1990.
13. *Performance Management in the UK – An Analysis of the Issues*, IPM, 1992.

"Tomorrow's effective organization will be conjured up anew each day."

Tom Peters[1]

Chapter 2

◆

THE HUMAN ORGANIZATION

There is a tendency even now, to think of organizations as fixed, stable and unchanging. Rarely do we see them as part of the dynamics of the operation itself, impacting on our performance for better or worse. However, we can broaden our understanding about the influence of the organization on performance, by seeing it not just as the stage for performance, but as a vital and integral part of the performance. From being inflexible and mechanical the organization must be reconfigured as flexible and human.

YOUR ORGANIZATION NEEDS YOU

The abstract world of organizational dynamics is not the natural home for many managers, whose operational realism, pragmatism and ability to solve problems in the present has been the basis for their career success. Yet, by becoming bogged down in the moment, managers can easily take the future for granted, or overlook it entirely. In *Competing for the Future*, Gary Hamel and C K Prahalad estimate that managers spend less than 3 percent of their time on the long-term future.

Meeting the increasingly sophisticated needs of customers, adapting to new technologies and achieving more with less, requires the ability to anticipate the future, challenge the status quo, help others through the change process and, finally, to have the emotional resilience to cope with the resulting increased work pressures.

The ever-present dilemma is to achieve or manage change, while maintaining enough stability to continue to do whatever the organization is supposed to be doing now. Planning and preparing for success in the future demands achievements in the present.

Many organizations, faced with these factors, have responded with relatively easy short-term measures to cut costs, to stay profitable. As the payroll is most often the biggest overhead, this inevitably means cutting people numbers – downsizing, delayering, reengineering – to eliminate layers of management and delegate responsibility to those at the sharp end. The resulting organizations are often perceived as more flexible and more entrepreneurial. Appearances can be deceptive. In fact, more fundamental changes are required to create new ways of organizing and mobilizing those who remain, in order to achieve the performance improvements that managers expect and need. Fewer people doing more of the same is not an adequate or even appropriate response. Achieving change demands a broader perspective and a more imaginative outlook.

KNOWLEDGE AND THE HUMAN ORGANIZATION

"Tomorrow's economy will revolve around innovatively assembled brain power, not muscle power. Microsoft's only factory asset is the human imagination," says Tom Peters.[2]

We are in the midst of a dawning new age, in which brain power plays center stage. The mechanical organization is giving way to the human organization; acceptable performance must give way to exceptional performance. As organizations begin to adjust to the demands and potential of people, we need a more holistic and humanistic view of managing people's performance and capability. This is at the heart of our concept of the human organization.

As Geoffrey Colvin, Executive Director of *Fortune* magazine recently said: "It helps to think of business today as going through a humanist revolution. The change is from the physical to the intellectual and from the mechanical to the human."[3]

Revolutions in the business world are never instantaneous. There is no instant panacea, as every organization is at a different stage of transition. There is no archetypal case study or inspiration. Best practice has to be drawn from a variety of sources.

THE HUMAN ORGANIZATION AND THE PERFORMANCE PRISM

With the old certainties removed, and traditional approaches no longer providing answers, the managers with whom we work are often overwhelmed by the complexity of managing performance. Struggling to meet the demands made of them, they know that they need a more holistic approach. Yet they find it difficult to understand what this involves at an organizational level. We define this level as the overall context of performance, and use the four quadrants in the base of the Prism as a guide to what this involves, as shown in Figure 2.1.

1. Environment in the Performance Prism

The environment is usually portrayed as something external to the organization: as an interplay of random or uncontrollable forces, such as exchange rates, interest rates, and demand cycles, against (or with) which the organization must react as best it can. If you accept that external environmental pressures, like those illustrated in Figure 2.3, drive the business, the role of managers is to

THE HUMAN ORGANIZATION

Culture	Environment
Intent	Capability

Fig 2.1 Prism base

ensure fit between the organization and its operating environment.

More recent views identify multiple relationships between the organization and its environment, blurring the boundaries between the internal and external world. Environment becomes something for managers to influence and shape, rather than something to react to.

A number of sets of relationships exist between organizations and their environments, as shown in the framework developed by Allaire and Firsirotu (see Figure 2.2).[4]

In the first scenario, **Harmony and continuity**, the organization's strategy is well adjusted to its present environment, resulting in sound performance. The future is an evolutionary and predictable version of the present, for which the organization is able to prepare and change in an incremental manner.

In the second scenario, the organization has a strategy which is inappropriate for the present situation, and results in poor performance. However, it is anticipated that the future will be fundamentally different from the present situation and will suit the existing strategy. At this stage in the future, the firm will reap the benefits. As a result, this is a case of **Pre-emptive adjustment or Temporary misfit.**

In the third scenario, the organization is well adjusted to its current environment and enjoying success, but predicts that in the future the environment will radically change. To meet this challenge the organization must change and this is where planned, fundamental, organizational change, and development becomes essential. This scenario is one of **Transformation or reorientation.**

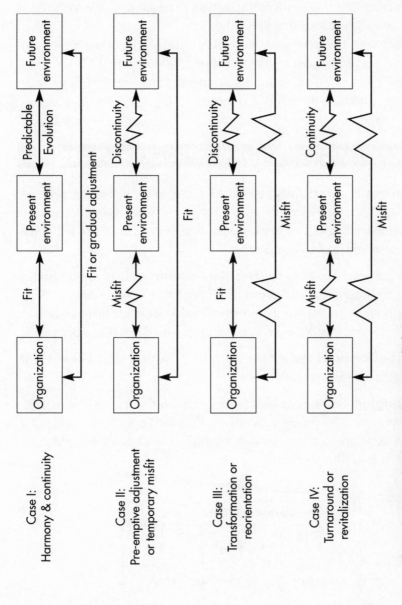

Fig. 2.2 Organization-environment linkages
Source: Allaire and Firsirotu, 1985

Finally, the worst scenario is where the company is misaligned with its current environment and the future appears to be more of the same. If the situation is one of loss of performance and declining market share, then **Revitalization** is needed. If bankruptcy is imminent, **Turnaround** is needed.

Whatever the scenario, sustainability in the long term will depend on more than a plan for immediate survival. There must also be a strong focus around the direction for the future to energize and mobilize the people involved.[5]

ORGANIZATION AND ENVIRONMENT: EXTERNAL DRIVERS

- **Economic uncertainty**, increased competition, increasing customer demands, political changes and exchange rate movements directly affect profitability and loss of market share if the company stands still and is not prepared for the change.

- The pace of change in the **IT environment** leads to rapid obsolescence of assets, but also opens up fantastic new opportunities. In 1992, one company estimated the potential market for information services in the home, via interactive TV, to be worth at least $120 billion per year.[6]

- **Global markets** mean increased competition, and require new skills in order to maintain competitiveness.

- **Changing demographics** have increased the demand for flexible, part-time and temporary jobs. Women are playing a larger role in the workplace due to changes in the age and structure of the population, as well as the structure of work.

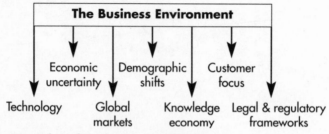

Fig 2.3 Examples of environmental forces

- The new **knowledge economy** means that 70 percent of all jobs in Europe will require brain rather than manual skills by 2000, and this will have implications for the available skill base, possibly leading to skill shortages.[7]

- **Legal and regulatory frameworks** can have profound effects on how business is organized. For example, deregulation in the banking industry during the 1980s unleashed enormous competition from around the world. In the USA and UK, controls on capital movements were abolished or rewritten, and banks were exposed to the rigors of the marketplace.

2. Intent in the Performance Prism

In recent years we have been bombarded by a host of terms, used in peculiar ways by companies and management commentators, to describe the response to the environment. There is talk of vision, mission, purpose, strategy and, more recently, strategic intent.[8] As these terms proliferate in the language of management, so too does the confusion with which they are received and used. Whether we use these terms to assert why the company exists, where it is going, what it aims to achieve, or how it is going to achieve it, we are seeking to describe a web of relationships between organizational ends and means.

Ask yourself, why does your company exist? Many managers, who see themselves struggling to deliver results under day-to-day pressures, respond to the question with comments such as "to generate revenue," "to make a profit," to "deliver shareholder value," "to maximize benefits to customers." Undoubtedly this is important, but by itself it is not enough. Andrew Campbell of Ashridge's Strategic Management Centre, says: "These objectives are commonly found in mission statements. Yet, they are little more than a reiteration of the rules of the economic game companies are playing."[9] Companies who describe themselves in these terms are like politicians who are driven to win votes. Votes are the entry ticket to the game, but without a manifesto behind them, such politicians are unlikely to be in the game for long.

In creating a human context for performance, we must push beyond a purely economic expression of what we aim to achieve.

"The principal purpose of a company is not to make a profit, full stop. It is to make profit in order to continue to do things or make things, and to do so ever better and more abundantly. Profit has to be a means to other ends rather than an end in itself," says Charles Handy.[10]

We choose the term *intent* in the Prism because it implies a link to motives, to the will and drive to focus on and achieve our goals. However elegant or economically precise we make our objectives, it is human talent and energy which delivers them. The performance context managers define must appeal to the human need for endeavor. Having an aim is one thing; making it a reality is quite another.

The people who are most successful have a drive to make things happen, to push beyond the boundaries of what is already possible. Mountaineer Chris Bonington says that successful climbers usually have strong egos, wanting to be the first person to stand on a summit. But there is more to it. "It's also the great drive to find something in yourself, or a curiosity of finding whether this can be done," says Bonington.[11]

Nolan Bushnell, who created the first electronic game, thinks it is about a can-do attitude: "I always feel like there is a solution. I believe that there is a truth. It's not always obvious what that truth is and it's not always obvious how to get to it, but if you keep searching, you can figure it out."[12]

Declaring intent

The same sort of drive can be translated into organizational terms. "Strategic intent implies a particular point of view about the long-term market or competitive position that a firm hopes to build over the coming decade or so. Hence, it conveys a sense of direction, a sense of discovery . . . a sense of destiny," say Gary Hamel and C K Prahalad. [13]

The defining feature of strategic intent is that it positions the company relative to others operating, or intending to operate, in the same domain. It clearly signals the nature of the value proposition you are offering, to everyone you deal with. Delivering exceptional performance through people extends this idea to the point where all efforts are aligned to this value proposition. This is when intent permeates and is adopted as part of the intentions of everyone involved, guiding the performance delivered by each individual.

To translate strategic intent into everyday terms, many companies publish a simple statement which can be easily expressed and is meaningful. Sun Microsystems' network vision is about the idea that you can only realize the true value of computers when they work together in networks. Rather than communicating this in complex terms it is captured by a simple statement: "The network is the computer."

Successful statements of intent capture the hearts and minds of people, individual managers, employees, customers; everybody who is involved. They are neither lofty nor grandiose, nor are they plain vanilla, failing to differentiate your company from others. A well-formulated and communicated statement of strategic intent, translated into shared objectives for implementation, forms a common managerial frame which guides both thought and action. If shared, intent will be the lens through which forces or drivers in the environment will be interpreted, and through which decisions about how to respond will be made, at every organizational level, by all the people involved.

Framing and reframing strategy

Strategy is a fairly recent construct in the language of management. Even so, it is cloaked in enough mythology and confusion to persuade many managers that it is something that distracts, rather than focuses, performance.

Well-formulated intent is the crux of strategy. It establishes direction, forming a reference point from which to evaluate all information and action, for establishing whether ideas or proposals are onside or offside, whether activities are core or a distraction. Having said this, no direction is certain; intent is not so precise that it needs to lock a company into a particular strategy. It is a mistake to wield strategy as an absolute or unquestionable truth. In today's business world, nothing can be written in tablets of stone, and the growing emphasis is now on "business re-scoping," the essence of what framing and reframing strategy actually means.

Re-scoping is more dynamic than conventional notions of laying down an unbending strategy. But attitudes must change if strategy is to become a main artery in the decision-making process.

Many organizations avoid tinkering with strategy because of the confusion and ambiguity it creates in the minds of senior managers, and because it takes the focus away from sorting out today's problems. Yet this year's revenues are no indication of tomorrow's survival. It is a bit like the man who says "don't confuse me with facts, my mind is made up."

Often, people who interface daily at the boundary of the organization and its environment are highly receptive, while senior managers are more remote, unwilling or unable to listen, treating strategy as a read-only file. As managers, we are taught the benefits of control; we strive to create an equilibrium in the factors of production at our disposal. Yet organisms adapt when they mutate – equilibrium can only deliver more of the same. Responsiveness precedes response. Sun Microsoft's CEO Scott McNealy says his organization needs to be controversial: "If everybody believes in your strategy, you have zero chance of profit."[14]

3. Culture in the Performance Prism

At the mention of purpose, mission and values, many people's response is cynical. Accusations of companies developing elaborate and costly mission statements to no visible or worthwhile effect, are often true. What goes wrong?

Strategy and values

Ultimately strategy implementation is about human behavior, which is influenced by organizational values every working day. Strategy and values cannot be disentangled, nor can they exist in a vacuum from what people actually think and do. Most people think of culture as the "way we do things around here." More broadly and accurately, culture can be described as "a set of visible beliefs which are known, understood and shared by most people in the organization."[15]

Often the company's cultural legacy is less than ideal for where it is aiming to get to. When acquisitions take place, there is often the need to assess and integrate or renew a number of different cultures. The majority of acquisitions in the 1980s failed to deliver intended synergies, and conflicting corporate cultures is one of the top five reasons why mergers fail.[16] Between 1984 and 1987, £1,160 billion was spent on mergers and acquisitions. The frenetic activity cannot disguise the fact that around three-quarters of the mergers and acquisitions failed to bring greater returns than bank deposits.[17]

Shifting mind-sets

The key to successful culture management has been close to the heart of those involved with the many changes taking place in all kinds of organizations. The challenge for those facing the "compete or die" scenario has been how to create an environment in which strategies for improving performance, productivity or quality will take root and thrive. When the UK Institute of Personnel and Development carried out research into performance management and quality management, the message was that if these kinds of strategies are to have any hope of success, first the culture has to be right.[18] Follow-up research concluded that in many cases, too little emphasis is placed on the role of people in the cultural change process, with the result that people management practices have often presented barriers to change, rather than facilitating it.

The influence of culture, whether positive or negative, tends to be self-perpetuating. It is hard to change culture because people are the custodians of organizational beliefs, and people do not like their beliefs to be challenged. Our actions are framed by beliefs which dictate what is possible and what is impossible. In this sense, strategy and performance are inevitably culture-bound.

Throughout the 1970s and 1980s, IBM believed unequivocally in mainframe computing. During the early 1980s, this internal view of the world led to many decisions aimed at perpetuating the company's position in mainframes, at the expense of other options. Blinkered by their long-held views, managers could not see that changes in the external world were making this position unsustainable. Sooner or later, the evidence builds to reveal that our beliefs are at best only partial perspectives and at worst, may be completely out of date and wrong. Often, by the time we realize, it is too late to change.

This is undoubtedly a performance management failure. Each of us must learn the skills that enable us to step outside of and see back into the culture to which we belong, to transcend culture and see it as a dimension of managerial influence, a part of what is to be performed.

"Changing mind-sets" is now common parlance. This means being aware of your own mind-set and knowing how to influence the mind-sets of others. In this way, you will be able to create meanings which harmonize with strategy and which energize strategy through mobilizing people's commitment and talents.

BAYER'S VISION 2000

Bayer is a diverse company, with 30,000 people working from its headquarters in Leverkusen, Germany. It comprises 21 business groups or Geschaftsbereiche (GBs).

Against this background in the UK division, Bayer plc, with 1,700 people, is relatively small, yet its structure is complex with seven key divisions, including Pharmaceuticals, Polymers and Industrial Chemicals (ICD). While the Pharmaceuticals Division operates as part of a European organization, the other divisions are far more fragmented.

For example, in the Polymers Division, the GB structure means that each product group, such as rubber, plastics and polyurethanes, presents a different face to the market, and follows a strategy set by its own GB in Germany.

Given the demands of the local UK marketplace, there are inevitably some tensions between the HQ's desire to exert control and the desire for divisional independence. In the UK these differences have become more apparent with the launch in 1994 of the Vision 2000 initiative.

Vision 2000 is a totally new approach to how the business is managed, embracing a fundamental change in the way that people see and develop their role within the company. All members of the Bayer team are encouraged to take personal responsibility for their performance and development, though each division has the freedom to decide how to communicate and implement the initiative. Vision 2000 is being supported by a competency initiative, identifying key roles and 18 core competencies. The reward and review system is to be aligned with the competency framework, to enable people to develop and move between roles. A 180 degree feedback mechanism is now also being developed.

Bayer is deliberately attempting to go beyond merely communicating the vision. It aims to change performance and reward systems which influence culture and behavior and help develop the commitment needed to realize Vision 2000.

This emphasis on building teams and increasing openness across divisional boundaries is quite contrary to the culture of independent, and in many ways competing GBs, which characterizes the headquarters in Leverkusen.

4. Capability management in the Performance Prism

Aligning opportunities and resources

Managing exceptional performance at the organization level is about alignment of opportunity and resources, trying to match perceived opportunities in the environment with the resources at the organization's disposal.

Ideas about how to manage capability, the organization's resources, and the way these are configured, have gathered ground in recent years, evident through the notion of core competencies and the resource-based view of organizations. Many companies now see and make much more explicit links between their strategic aims and the capabilities they require to achieve them.

Most of us would expect strategic intent to be translated into business strategy or marketing strategy and, in turn, for this to be linked to R&D activities, to production plans and programs for new product development or new service provision. Unfortunately, people can be regarded merely as a means to an end in these strategies – another legacy of the industrial age. The inclusion of capability management in the Prism framework is recognition of a new relationship between people and what is produced. The relationship sees the knowledge and skills, the "brains" of people, as the base of the organization, the primary source of value creation.

Knowledge, skills and people

In the human organization, people must be considered as a part of an organization's overall capability. It is not enough to manage people on a day-to-day basis. Nor is it enough to simply identify and link people's objectives to the business plan. Managing the performance of people at the organizational level also means managing the knowledge base as a whole. Skills, know-how, ideas and the more subtle array of human talents, are the organization's finite elements which can be grouped together, clustered and managed to deliver either poor, mediocre or exceptional results.

Knowledge and value

Human capital is knowledge with the potential for value. If knowledge is not effectively created, integrated and shared, it remains unexploited. It is the conversion of "raw" knowledge, sometimes called human or intellectual capital, into new technologies, processes and products that transforms "latent" know-how into capability. This is when we can speak of the conversion of knowledge into structural capital and assets – smart processes, smart technologies, valuable assets which are the core of the business, the source of sustainable advantage.

We use a simple framework to demonstrate the links between knowledge and value. Figure 2.4 shows three phases of capability to be managed.

Organizations which are successful at building and sustaining strong market position manage these layers of capability in an integrated and coherent way. Companies like 3M, Xerox, Canon, Honda and Intel have consistently outpaced their competitors, precisely because of the known links between capability and value, and the way they are able to quickly focus their core capabilities on new areas of opportunity.

3M, for example, is undoubtedly one of the world's most enduringly successful innovators, having leveraged a portfolio of 100 technologies into some 60,000 products. The pace of innovation has always been tough, measured by an objective of generating 25 percent of sales from new products introduced in the last five years. Rather than becoming complacent, 3M CEO Desi DeSimone has recently increased the target to 30 percent of sales from products introduced in the past four years. 3M has also made the essential decision to focus on its core areas of expertise – for example, leaving the market for magnets by divesting itself of a $6 million business which was losing millions of dollars a year.

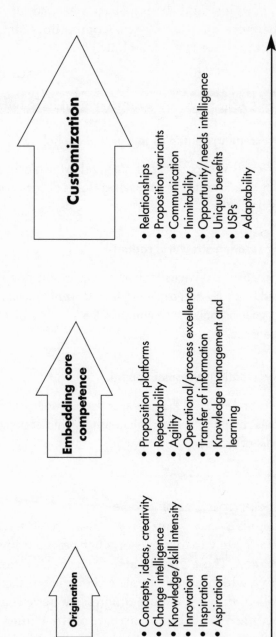

Fig 2.4 Leveraging capability

Similarly, Intel continues to go from strength to strength in the highly competitive, volume-driven semiconductor market. It manages to maintain margins and boost sales because of the sophistication of its operational processes. Competitors simply cannot get chips out of the door faster than Intel. [19]

THREE LAYERS OF CAPABILITY MANAGEMENT

Originating capability: creating human or intellectual capital

The base layer, from where new capabilities emerge and existing ones can be developed. This layer constitutes the basic building blocks of capability – ideas, concepts, knowledge, skills.

Embedding capability: creating structural capital

Smart technologies, processes, services that your company is good at. What sets you apart and is readily accessible to be customized around new opportunities. It makes your organization more than the sum of individual skills, learning and experience.

Customizing capability: creating customer capital

Offering unique benefits and value to the customer through specific offerings in specific domains, built up through relationships with customers. Recognizable in the value of brands.

© Interactives 1995

Knowledge, value and perspectives on people

Managers who recognize they want to do more to "manage people's performance" have varied views of what people bring to the performance equation. These views range from the traditional accounting perspective which wants people to be efficiently cost-managed and controlled, through a more progressive perspective, which recognizes people's contribution as part of the value creation activity, to a much more future-oriented view which sees people as core to building sustainable advantage.

Knowledge and skill	People	Managerial focus	Performance emphasis
Operational cost	Overhead	Cost-effectiveness Hire-fire Headcount	Control
Added value	Contribution	Productivity Utilization Optimize contribution	
Scope of opportunity	Opportunity cost	Investment Development Return on investment	Leverage

Fig 2.5 Perspectives on people

Figure 2.5 lays out some of the main differences in these perspectives. Which one of these most closely matches your own thinking, and what does this tell you about your performance management style?

Ideas about how intellectual capital can be measured and managed have already begun to emerge, being adopted by companies like Siemens, Rank Xerox, Skandia, DEC, BP and Hoffman LaRoche. Patricia Seemann of Hoffman LaRoche says: "Knowledge management is about improving organizational productivity by focusing and accelerating knowledge creation in companies."[20]

Leading academics, Christopher Bartlett and Sumantra Ghoshal, similarly contend: "What 3M and Intel have in common is a carefully nurtured, deeply embedded corporate work ethic that triggers the individual-level behaviors of entrepreneurship, collaboration and learning, that are the foundation of organizational renewal."[21] The entrepreneurial organization, say Bartlett and Ghoshal, is the organizational form of the future.

To achieve such a bold reshaping of organizations, intellectual capital must be intimately linked to structural and customer capital.

Strategy, structure and knowledge integration

People's knowledge and skills are vitally important factors in delivering exceptional performance, but equally important are the ways in which people are grouped together into teams and units, and the way work is connected by systems and processes. Delivery excellence to the customer stems only from a competitive and agile response. Customer and market focus are important, but achieving this in practice means actively focusing many dimensions of the organization simultaneously on key areas of opportunity. Doing this well requires us to think about what many now refer to as *organizational architecture*.

Much of what is written about markets and strategy is written in a vacuum from organization design. The classic view, expressed by Alfred Chandler and Peter Drucker, is that structure follows strategy. This has led to the over-simplistic view that organizations create structure simply to co-ordinate activities and to regulate the actions of people.

A more contemporary view expresses the relationship between strategy and structure as much more inter-related. Tom Peters extends this to the extreme when he says structure determines rather than follows strategy. In this, the organization's architecture is part of the capability, integral to the strategic response.

We usually picture buildings and cities when we think of architecture. We look at their overall structure and infrastructure, and comment on how well-suited these are for the wider environment in which they must stand. Some buildings are inspiring, others are efficient, some are just plain difficult to navigate, and some take their toll on the human soul. A house is not a home, and so it is with the architecture of organizations. Things like structure, systems and processes, how activities are configured, how information flows around and across the parts, can all make us feel alienated or, alternatively, provide a sense of belonging. They can pull the organization together, making it a stimulating and productive place to live and work in, or they pull the organization apart, unnecessarily draining the energies of the people involved, making our performance not better, but worse.

While there is no one optimum organizational architecture, there have been more or less dominant types at different times. These different types have developed because they have been suited to different environmental conditions, to different strategic responses. Figure 2.6 summarizes the organizational types prevalent during this century, including the network organization which has started to emerge in response to the way work will need to be organized in the post-industrial age.

Network organizations

Many corporations are delayering, as they recognize the energy-sapping effects of top-heavy management. Better work methods and automation mean that companies are producing more with less direct labor. However, organization flattening only treats the symptoms – it does not re-define relationships between people and functions in the organization.

The steep functional hierarchies to which we have grown accustomed actively promote fragmentation, cultures of distrust, "not invented here" thinking and the acceptance of minimal accountabilities by giving people safe boxes from which to declare "not my problem." If we can switch to see ourselves as knowledge contributors in a network, our starting point for effective performance can be co-operation and collaboration rather than avoidance, indifference and distrust.

Networked organizations are emerging because the classic command and control hierarchy of the bureaucratic model is slow to respond to change. By design, the hierarchy is a fixed rather than flexible architecture.

Network architectures have two key dimensions.

- **Information architecture** – the links between IT systems, processes and people.

- **Social architecture** – human processes of working with and sharing knowledge with other people.

However, networks are not easily constrained or explained. The idea of the networked organization is of an organization almost without structure. Dynamic processes and fluid teams replace rigid organizational lines. In the network model, activities need to be highly integrated, but this integration relies on knowledge and relationships and a clear common sense of purpose. This has led to

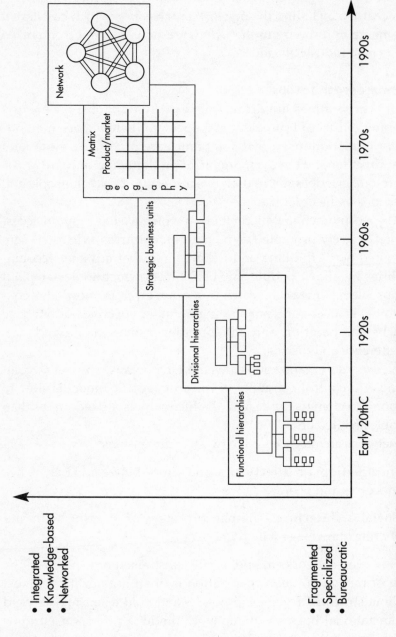

Fig 2.6 An historical perspective on organization design

ideas about "work as a network of conversations"[22] and the "hyper-text organization made up of interconnected layers or contexts: the business system, the project team, and the knowledge base."[23]

Suddenly, the props we have come to lean on as managers seem to have been entirely removed. How can people work without a clear organization chart? How can people be expected to perform without a clear boss directing and controlling what they do? How can I as a manager be successful when I am no longer the control point for all information, resources, actions, functional priorities, because they have been devolved throughout my team? How can people operate in more than one team? How can I be successful when knowledge, not position, is the basis for business decisions? Given these apparently imponderable questions, it is little wonder that, for many managers, it is the changing shape of organizations which looms like the threat of a natural disaster.

DO YOU BELIEVE IN HIERARCHY?

Which of the following statements rings most true to you?

- Hierarchy is for managing predictable events; it is not adaptable to the need for rapid change.

- Breaking organizations into departments overly fragments the diversity and clusters of competence needed to develop solutions to complex business problems.

- Management behavior must change, relying more on collaboration than control.

- Low formalization of structure gives freedom and enables creativity.

- People can manage their own performance through autonomy and feedback from colleagues, customers and others.

- Information systems will remove the need for formal, narrow communication channels.

OR:

- Winning in global markets demands the resources and management only to be found in larger stable organizations.

- People like security and predictability and to know which manager to look to.

- Managers must control performance, otherwise projects go off the rails.

- Information systems are oversold, networks are a remote ideal.

- Structure reduces ambiguity and the chance of things going wrong.

(To analyze your organization in greater depth refer to the organization profile on page 70.)

Managing performance in the network

To shift from rectangles and lines to circles and nets in a drawing is easy. Intellectually and emotionally, it is much harder to accept the changes this implies. Giving up the comfort of known job boundaries and established reporting relationships is hard. But amid the vulnerability, there is also challenge and excitement.

The central problem for performance management in the network organization is to reconcile commercial effectiveness with the flourishing of human talents. The emphasis on influencing relationships requires us to abandon the ideas about productivity, based on the division and sub-division of labor pioneered by Frederick W Taylor, and to develop more subtle approaches. These need to be based on a deep understanding of the factors which affect the performance of the most talented of our people and how to unite these together in creative, collaborative constellations.

Networks of networks

From the organizational standpoint there are a number of levels of network to be managed:

- the network team or virtual team, formed around individual contributions of knowledge and expertise

- the network enterprise, made up of cross-business teams of teams

- the virtual or extended enterprise, comprising strategic relationships, alliances and partnerships.

Partly due to enhanced access to and investment in computer network infrastructures, many companies are already operating some kind of network arrangement. Companies like ABB, Digital Equipment Corporation and the World Health Organization are some of the most well-known pioneers of this. ABB speaks of the global exchange of technology as part of its commitment to industrial and ecological efficiency worldwide. ABB uses "tiger teams," made up of engineers and technicians from around the world, to enable rapid transfer of know-how across borders and to allow it to deliver its objectives of being globally strong and locally flexible.

At the extreme of the concept of the network organization is the virtual enterprise, in which companies temporarily combine to share costs, risks, skills and access to global markets. It has been described as the "pick 'n' mix," best of everything company, with each player bringing its core competence to the table.

Proof that many companies are starting to think along these lines is the growing number of strategic alliances. For example, AT&T used Japan's Marubeni Trading to link up with Matsushita Electric Industrial to produce its Safari notebook computer. MCI Communications uses partnerships with as many as a 100 large companies to win contracts with large customers.[24]

Benetton, Italy's largest textiles company, is a family-run network. The Benetton Group is the core company, and the network is created by a system of different companies in manufacturing and retailing. Downstream there are independent entrepreneurs called agents and store owners. Such is the fluidity and efficiency of its systems, Benetton can process 80 million garments a year through just three factories, employing only 300 people.

In parallel with the growth of strategic alliances, many companies are demerging their large-scale, vertically integrated and divisionalized operations, and there are signs of a trend towards demergers of large conglomerates. Hanson, the $17 billion giant, saw share prices tumbling in 1995, after years of growth. This led to its split into four parts, enabling each business to concentrate on its core activities. This was also the logic behind the demergers of AT&T, ITT and ICI.

HUMAN ORGANIZATION MANAGEMENT

Shifting the performance context

How can you, as a manager, build on these ideas and use them in practical ways, to help deliver exceptional performance?

Aligning the various elements of the Prism and managing organization as a continuous design process require particular skills, techniques and processes. Managing the necessary shifts in the overall context for performance can become part and parcel of the manager's toolkit for delivering extraordinary performance.

Many of the frameworks about organizational performance, like the base of the Prism itself, describe important performance variables. What they rarely offer is a systematic process for auditing the health of these variables, for creating sustainable improvement plans, and for making these plans come alive as part of a constant process of review and organization renewal. Very often, senior managers, top teams and various special task forces and working groups, spend several traumatic days together diagnosing problems and developing plans, only to find there is no momentum to achieve implementation back in the workplace.

Throughout the remainder of this chapter we will take you through a process for managing at the organizational level. It involves building a network of performance intelligence and using this intelligence to change the organization in an iterative, dynamic way, emphasizing the human, as well as the intellectual, activities involved.

The circle of review and renewal

The circle of review and renewal is a process which incorporates the four elements – environment, intent, culture and capability – from the base of the Prism, into a process framework for assessing and developing the organization's performance. It integrates the "what" and the "how" required for coherently managing the many factors involved.

Because we may not be used to "owning" the problem of performance at the organization level, we can make the mistake of thinking it is someone else's problem. We say these things should be sorted by HQ, senior management, the corporate center. But we can take ourselves out of the box and not wait for others to do it for us or to us. The review and renewal process can be tackled either by individual managers and a single team, or by a group of managers across several areas of the business. It does not always mean starting at the top of the business, reviewing the whole at once, but wherever you do start from, you will need to take a helicopter view.

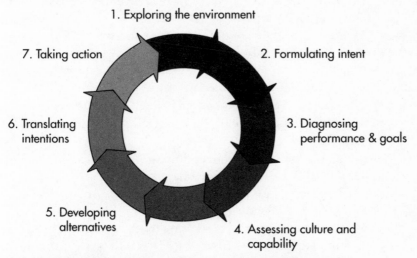

Fig 2.7 The circle of review and renewal in practice
Sources: ©Interactives 1991 as used in "Beyond the Boundaries of HRM – business integration in practice," IPM National Conference, Harrogate 1991 with Peter Cole of Swiss Bank Corporation

SWISS BANK CORPORATION

REVIEW AND RENEWAL IN PRACTICE

Swiss Bank Corporation, now SBC Warburg, was faced with a depressing business environment at the end of the 1980s. The industry as a whole was in decline and the role of banks was under question. The traditional strengths of banks as providers of capital was being undermined by the ability of borrowers to access capital markets direct. The emergence of non-bank stand-alone competitors increased the risk and reduced the profitability of many commercial banks, and equity values suffered as a consequence. In the US, the value of the bank's stocks fell by 60 percent between mid-1989 and mid-1990. In the UK throughout 1990, the *FT Banks Index* under-performed the *FTSE 100*. Customer requirements were changing, but the financial services industry generally was suffering from a lack of marketing experience and talent in the field.

At the same time, technology was advancing very quickly. Unit costs for sophisticated financial computing decreased from the mid-1960s to the mid-1980s by close to 100 percent. Unit costs for transmission of such data decreased by about the same in the same period. According to Peter Cole, Human Resources Director, the low productivity of the gigantic investments being made in technology would not have been tolerated in other more financially and managerially disciplined industries.

There was also deregulation and globalization to contend with – significant barriers to entry had given way to significant barriers to exit.

These external problems were compounded by internal ones, including a lack of general management skills, marketing skills and a weak culture. High levels of compensation combined with an acceptance of mediocre performance standards, low yields on investment in technology and marketing expenditure meant that overall quality suffered. The cost base of the industry needed to be brought into line and managed with a genuine adding of value. Management behavior and values needed to change substantially. Those responsible for running the business needed the means to apply the knowledge, technologies and methods which relate to managing human performance. "More from Less" became the theme of the change initiative at SBC.

Senior management accepted the dilemma between expedient short-term actions and the need to build competitive advantage for the future; they accepted that change was vital. The effective management of this change was critical to ensure future survival and profitability. Ironically, some of the very psychological and cultural characteristics of the banking industry that had helped in the past, were now a potential hindrance. Factors such as conservatism, prudence and caution could manifest themselves as resistance to change and the inability or unwillingness to experiment with new ways of doing things.

The cost analysis for 1990 showed that the single largest item of expenditure in the organization was for people – 40 percent of the total. Also SBC was significantly higher than the industry average for the ratio of support people to revenue producing people. So improving employee performance was seen as a major challenge for the immediate future. As human resources (HR) were rapidly replacing capital assets as generators of income, the HR function initially provided the catalyst, drive and methods for the changes. Later, the change process was able to be transferred to line management, as were many of the day-to-day organization and people processes.

"Change management is not for gifted amateurs. It requires a methodology and a technology to achieve it. Change is forever; even the nature of change changes," says Rudolph Bogni, Chief Executive of the bank's London office.

People add value by being effective, and they do this by applying their skills. This implies a need to manage the corporate portfolio of skills and to create skill intensity where it is lacking. Management information on the skill inputs for different business functions is required, together with how to source and deploy these cost-effectively. It means knowing the requirements for converting these skills to adequate outputs, and it is here that it is necessary to assess return on skill through many layers of business performance at the individual or business unit level.

This need to develop solutions that made a real contribution to business performance, presupposes some mechanisms for measuring how well we are doing. SBC recognized the need to move away from crude, superficial quantitative analysis, towards an in-depth picture of what was going on and how productive the organization was. There was a need to quantify or graphically represent what it had previously supposed to be purely perceptual or qualitative measures. In doing this, it pinpointed the cause of inefficiencies and specific quality and performance problems.

Using the Organization Review process outlined in this chapter, SBC set about achieving a detailed understanding and analysis of their business objectives and plans in organizational terms. In this context, organization means organizing principles, structure, systems, processes, management practice, culture, skill, demographics and all aspects of performance. Review means the systematic analysis and diagnosis of these elements in relation to the current business environment and future business goals. A diagnostic framework was applied to this analysis and business-specific initiatives were developed. All actions have a quantifiable outcome, and all outcomes are related to the achievement of a specific business goal.

The result is a coherent program for managing change, in which all actions are integrated and relevant to business needs. The process establishes the relationships and inter-relationships between various organizational factors, and allows an identification of the impact of these on business performance.

At SBC, systematic initiatives were implemented to address four key business issues:

1. **Profitability** – the need to secure sustainable revenue streams with adequate returns for the future.
2. **Productivity** – the focus of the skill intensity project which enhanced the bank's ability to develop and deliver improved products and services.
3. **Managing** – the need for a flat, non-hierarchical structure with a responsible and disciplined leadership; a clear vision, understood and shared by all and translated into actions; the right culture, with emphasis on new values and ways of doing things.
4. **Clients** – internal and external, the need to be a customer-facing organization, with a relationship-centered approach to doing business.

The measures taken were being achieved by managing both qualitative improvements and quantitative reductions. Revenues increased by more than 30 percent per employee during 1991 and in 1991 and 1992 record levels of profitability were reached.

"There has been a major blood transfusion here: 350 people have left and 250 people have come. We have got rid of the cynics and gained switched on people, who have taken ownership of the bank," said Rudolph Bogni, Chief Executive at SBC's London office.

Since the transformation, the company has successfully acquired the O'Connor Partnership in 1992, Brinson and Partners (a leading US-based fund manager) in 1994 and SG Warburg in 1995. SBC Warburg is now established as the pre-eminent European-based global integrated investment bank, as highlighted in *Euromoney's* 1995 Poll of Polls, in which the company held second position.[26] As Peter Cole says: "Within SBC Warburg, we have continued to demonstrate not only our ability to initiate and manage continuous change, but we have proven that it is essential for the future viability and success of the business. By every measure of performance and productivity, the bank has been turned round. But we cannot afford to become complacent. SBC is now very strongly positioned to build on its successes and continue to improve."[27]

THE CIRCLE OF REVIEW AND RENEWAL

Phase 1: Exploring the environment

We step into the Circle at the place most pertinent to survival – the chaotic and uncertain world of competition, customers and choice. The focus of this phase is on gathering and revamping intelligence on what we have earlier referred to as the organization's environment.

There are many simple techniques available. One of the most commonly applied is a SWOT analysis. This technique, shown in Figure 2.8, is used to develop an overview of the company's prospects in terms of its strengths and weaknesses with regard to various opportunities and threats.

Examples of these potential threats could be the increasing obsolescence of the firm's production technology, increasing tariff barriers or new entrants to the market. Potential opportunities could include trade agreements which open up new markets, declining competition in specific markets, favorable exchange rate movements or the need for alliances because of market convergence across industries.

Strengths

- _____
- _____
- _____
- _____

Weaknesses

- _____
- _____
- _____
- _____

Opportunities

- _____
- _____
- _____
- _____

Threats

- _____
- _____
- _____
- _____

Fig 2.8 Template for conducting a SWOT analysis

The SWOT analysis takes into account the kinds of environmental variables shown earlier. The wider environment in which the organization and its industry are located can be subdivided into four sectors:

- **Political** • **Economic** • **Social** • **Technological.**

STEP or PEST analysis (acronyms for the four sectors) is useful in encouraging us to think in a more focused way about environmental influences on the organization. The environmental forces shown in Figure 2.3 are very similar to this.

EXPLORING YOUR ENVIRONMENT

- How frequently do you think about the forces which are impacting your business most heavily today?
- How well are you managing these?
- Can you identify the key drivers relevant to your business?
- Which of these will be impacting your business heavily tomorrow?

Another highly influential technique is Michael Porter's Five Forces Model, which determines the extent of competition in the industry. The rationale behind this model is that industry profitability is not determined by what a product looks like, or what kind of technology it uses. Instead, it is determined by the structure of the industry. The five forces are: threats from potential entrants, the power of buyers, the power of suppliers, threats from substitutes and competitive rivalry. If all five forces are strong, industry profitability would be expected to be low, regardless of the products. Weak forces, however, allow higher prices and above-average industry profitability. Organizations can influence the five forces by the strategies they pursue.

Such techniques are often criticized for being restrained to rational analysis, and for not pushing thinking beyond existing industry structures. Rationality can seem ill-suited to the irrational turmoil facing managers every day of the working week.

Recently, the concept of "stretch" rather than "fit" has gained ground in the way managers think about their strategic response to the environment. This means reaching beyond what you can obviously deliver and thinking about new ways of exploiting capability and creating new opportunities with different relationships in the marketplace.

For this, managers need more than knowledge. "Stretch" also requires aspiration, vision, imagination and ingenuity. It asks managers to think about core competence in different ways and to look at new configurations of industry players. Techniques like visioning, and other creative exercises are useful for this kind of future-focused thinking. They deliberately take us out of the box in which we ordinarily see what is possible for the organization, so that we may not only see different things, but more importantly see things differently. Imagine what would have happened if IBM had moved out of its box in the 1970s.

BACK FROM THE FUTURE

Imagine it is ten years from now. You have just attended a shareholders' meeting which has reported outstanding results for the fifth year running. You think back over the last ten years:

- Was this success easy to predict?
- What were the important strategic choices that had to be made?
- How easy was it to foresee the major opportunities and threats?
- What purpose has been driving the business, and how have you influenced or created new markets for realizing this?
- How has the shape of competition changed?
- What major alliances did you need to form?
- What was your biggest surprise?
- What were you most prepared for?
- What were you least prepared for?

Exploring the environment can be tackled in a loose, qualitative way, by collecting management opinions, or it can be more structured and formalized, involving workshops and interviews conducted by professional business facilitators, using data supplied by research and intelligence bureaux. The most important things to achieve are first, a window to the world outside and second, a dialogue between the people who need to do something about what this window reveals.

WHAT ARE THE KEY BUSINESS DRIVERS?

- What strategic options are available?

- What is our position in the face of these options?

- How do we fare against our competitors?

- How is the competition changing?

- How is the competitive domain changing?

- What opportunities are there to shape this domain to advantage?

Phase 2: Formulating intent

The evidence, insights and inspirations gleaned from investigating the environment feed into stage 2 of the process, where they are used in the formulation of strategic intent. Different styles of strategy formulation often mean bringing key groups together.

NUCLEAR ELECTRIC: POWER TO CHANGE

Nuclear Electric was created in 1990, following the privatization of the UK power generating industry. It now operates six nuclear power stations in England and Wales.

In 1990, the company faced a new competitive enviroment. Business reality meant that output had to be increased by 38 percent, while also reducing headcount by 25 percent. These ambitious targets could not have been achieved with the existing bureaucratic culture, so in association with Ashridge Management

College, the company embarked on a radical program of cultural and structural change.

The result was the delivery of several management development programs, including "Implementing Strategy for Senior Managers," targeted at the 100 senior managers responsible for converting the company vision into action, and beginning with a workshop to identify learning needs.

This demonstrated just how strongly the old company's highly centralized culture had formed thinking and behavior – there was a great deal of stress among the managers, who were used to working in an environment where strategy was directional and gave clear priorities for implementation.

The situation had to be challenged by the learning program, as the company's vision was still evolving and could not give the managers the kind of direction they were seeking. They needed to understand that those formulating the vision needed feedback from those implementing it, in order to develop it further.

The resulting learning program consisted of a two–week residential course, followed by two to three months of project implementation. This culminated in a project review meeting with the chairman, CEO and members of a strategy group. Throughout this time, the managers worked on a strategic project of their choice.

Various frameworks and concepts were introduced, to give them a different perspective of their role, increasing their ability to think strategically, and to structure their work as a series of open projects which they could then delegate without fear of losing control. The necessary skills to help them achieve corporate objectives could be identified, and once back in the workplace, they could focus on the high-level view rather than project details.

HOW GOOD IS YOUR INTENT?

- Why does the organization exist?

- Why will it exist in the future?

- Is this clearly communicated?

- Is it expressed in terms that individuals can identify with?

- How well formulated is the strategic intent of the business?

- What is distinctive about the offering?

- How clear is your position relative to others?

- Are you sure? How do you know?

- How defensive are senior management (or you) in response to strategic challenges from people in the organization?

- How dynamic are processes for strategy formulation?

- How open are these processes to input from others operating at the edge of the organization?

- How quickly can your organization respond once the need for change in direction is recognized?

Phase 3: Analyzing current goals and performance

Understanding current performance in relation to business goals is what many managers see as the heart of their management role. Organizations often have systems for this which generate copious information: five-year plans, yearly plans, quarterly reviews, monthly reports and so on. This information usually tells us where we stand financially and what performance is like in key areas. Often the key indicators of performance are purely financial, but improving financial results requires organizational action and change. Simple cost-cutting or playing with the numbers can take a company out of an immediate crisis, but this is rarely enough. Taking action which will genuinely improve business performance requires an understanding of the links between the numbers and the use of capability in the business.

Numbers, people and performance
To achieve change we have to identify the underlying reasons for performance – what factors are contributing to success or failure,

and how is this related to what people are doing? Yet surprisingly, business management and financial systems are frequently disconnected from human performance management systems. Delivering exceptional performance through people necessitates links to be created between such systems. Business performance is people-dependent. Figure 2.9 shows a simple framework for creating the links. How complete are these linkages in your business?

Creating linkages

Performance through people does not imply humanism at the expense of commercial realism. Too often these are seen to be mutually exclusive, but such polarized perspectives are not sustainable in the knowledge era. The links between performance and people need to become increasingly transparent.

Nordstrom, the US specialty retailer, pays its sales people entirely on a commission basis, linked to revenues and growth in sales, and drives exceptional performance through a culture of accountability and open recognition. Sales per hour per sales person are not only always known by managers at Nordstrom, they are also openly published. There are consequences for good and poor performance. Moreover, there is ownership of targets because sales people are involved in the target-setting process. The links between revenues at a macro-level, and performance at the individual level, are tight. Nordstrom has developed a culture of customer service which is infectious, but it knows that achieving service and growth in such a highly competitive market, where it is hard to steal a lead depends on committed and high-performing people.

Look at SBC which needed to drastically revitalize performance. To increase both awareness of, and accountability for, what needed to change, a simple profitability/productivity chart was used to plot desired and actual improvements at business level. These goals were translated to a per person average so that actual performance at individual level could be tracked against these targets. In turn this financial framework for improvement was linked to a clear action framework showing the areas of performance which needed to be developed if these improvements were to be achieved.

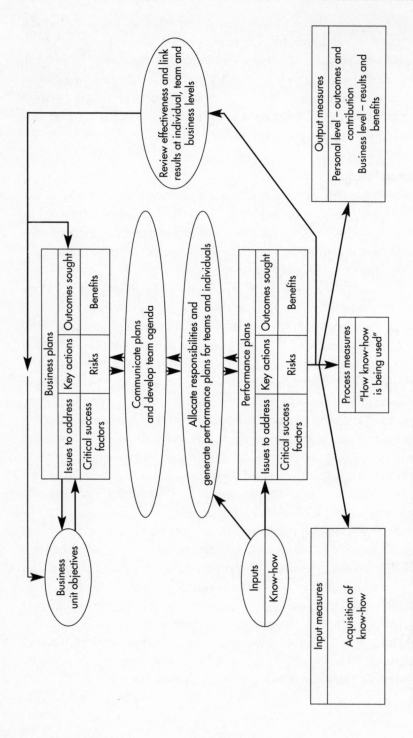

Fig 2.9 Turning intent into a performance agenda

KEY QUESTIONS

- What are the key indicators of performance in the business?
- Do these need review and change?
- What types of information do these indicators yield?
- Is it balanced or financially biased?
- How well-developed are links between financial reporting systems and other parts of the performance management process?
- Does it provide a front view or rear view of performance?
- How clear are the links between the performance of the business as a whole and the performance of sub-units, teams and individuals?
- How fully integrated is information about performance?
- Is information reported functionally, by department or horizontally around critical cross-business activities?

Phase 4: Assessing culture

We often think of culture as external to our influence, something that affects us rather than the other way round. Yet one of the strongest influences on the culture of any work group will be the managers responsible for the group's performance. While we may feel unable to change culture at the macro-level, or at least recognize that this will take time, there is much we can do, with quick results, much closer to home.

SURFING THE CULTURAL NETWORK

To find out what is going on, and to be able to take steps to change and improve culture with confidence and without suspicion, you will need to be invited to belong to the informal network of the groups you wish to influence. Where do you stand on the following?

- Do you recognize the network's existence?

- Do you believe it is important, or do you feel that managers must not associate with informal "gossip"?

- Who do you regularly talk to?

- Who do these people talk to, and how quickly does your word get around?

- How often do you spend time chatting?

- Do people seek you out to let you know what is going on?

- Do you ask your contacts for the names of others to talk to. Do the same names recur, a small set of key influences?

- Have you cultivated your relationships with these key influences, letting them carry your news and feed back their news on events?.

- Do you feel irritated or excited when you get caught up in conversations shooting the breeze?

- Do you seek a low profile, or seek out and cash in on situations where a story about you could emerge?

- Do you maintain contacts for reasons of support rather than expertise or shared working?

- Are the bulk of your communications informal and verbal?

The more times you have answered the questions above positively, then the more on-line to the network you are. Check where you said "no," and see if you can start to change this. Observe the difference it makes to the kind of information you can get hold of and the speed at which your ideas and thinking start to have an effect.

Developing a wider view of culture

If you want to understand the nature of culture around you more fully, then try to produce a picture of the culture of your organization, unit or team, using the template in Figure 2.10. Ask others to complete it too, or use your contacts in the network to help answer some of the questions raised. What does it tell you about your culture, the beliefs and the behaviors it supports, the people who are successful and unsuccessful, the lessons of the past and the hopes for the future?

Once you have completed this use the checklist below to think back to the organization's purpose and strategy. Are there healthy links, or does something need to change? What can you learn about the links between performance and culture?

THE LOW-PERFORMANCE VIRUS

Unhealthy, low-performing cultures are afflicted by the corporate equivalent of a virus. Look at the statements that follow. Do they ring true or false for your own organization?

- The purpose and intent of the organization are vague and fuzzily articulated.

- Beliefs and values about what is important are confusing or unclear.

- Beliefs and values about success and failure are not explicit.

- There are strongly conflicting beliefs and values about what is important.

- There is emphasis on the internal organization rather than customers, competitors, trends.

- Customers are on the edge rather than the center of the organization's performance.

- There is emphasis on the short term rather than the sustainable future.

- There is more glory in yesterday than tomorrow.

- Key people work personal agendas and this is undiscussable.

- Key people have a time orientation to today rather than tomorrow.

- Key people have stakes in the status quo that cannot be challenged.

- Different values and behaviors are important at the department or team level rather than of the organization as a whole.

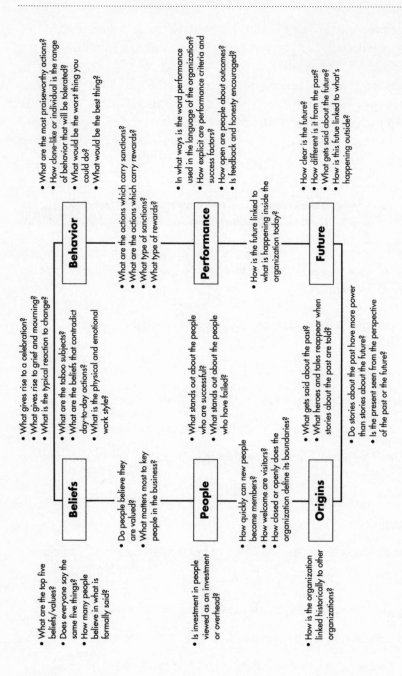

Fig 2.10 Culture map

- The heroes are outside the system.

- The heroes disrupt rather than build common understanding.

- Day-to-day activities are disorganized and ad hoc.

- Day-to-day activities are contradictory.

- Behaviors that are rewarded contradict what is formally stated as rewardable.

- Celebrations focus on internal rather than external happenings.

Symptoms of cultural viruses

Confusion

- People are confused about who is doing what and why.

- It seems unusually difficult to get things done.

- People seem awkward and unwilling to co-operate.

- Mistakes are frequent and people want to apportion blame.

Despondency

- Persistent complaining or pleas for an end to confusion.

- People leaving or talking about leaving.

- People blocking and being unco-operative.

Emotional attacks

- People are worried, insecure, frightened and express this in emotional outbursts.

- Denouncements about strategy, policy, plans.

- Denouncements about people, particularly those driving the organization forward.

Phase 4: Assessing capability

Earlier we divided capability into the resources in the organization and the way these are organizationally configured. We looked at ideas about knowledge as a key resource, and at the organizational architectures best suited for harnessing and leveraging this. In this next phase, we look at ways of assessing this capability in the circle of review and renewal.

Leveraging knowledge for performance

One useful way of thinking about knowledge management is to think of two basic types of know-how – specialist expertise and business management. These can be blended in terms of both concentration and mix for different types of results.

Stereotypically, knowledge work is confined to organizations populated by a high proportion of professionals, with high levels of expertise, working together in a fairly free and creative manner. We imagine the creative start-up, whether this is in computing, advertising or consulting. In such companies, traditional management skills and disciplines are deemed counter-cultural by the professional majority. Gray suits and bean counters cramp creative style.

And once the gray suits take over, the company is liable to lose its way. Apple Computers sought to institutionalize its start-up culture once the organization grew and became more mature. *Business Week* recently waxed lyrical on the rise and fall of Apple: "The year was 1984. Apple Computer Inc. was the Magic Kingdom. It was the hip, young heart of Silicon Valley – the place where America was showing the world how the combination of technology and entrepreneurship could make a revolution. Apple created the legend of two kids in a garage inventing a computer – and then building a New Age company where the old corporate rules were scrapped. No dress codes, no formal meetings – nothing to get in the way of what really mattered: creating computers that, Apple promised, would change the world.

"Today, Apple – the very icon of a post-industrial high tech America – is barely recognizable in the troubled $11 billion company that bears its name. Years of overlooked opportunities, flip-flop strategies, and a mind-boggling disregard for market realities have caught up."[28]

In the absence of business building and business management, companies eventually flounder or stagnate, not being robust enough to survive changes in key people, or organized enough to build sustainable advantage. If Apple can get it so wrong, anyone, and any organization, can.

The trick in leveraging knowledge for performance is to create a whole which is more than the sum of the parts, yet leaves the parts free enough to continue to change and grow. This means investing in the business expertise required to embed specialist expertise. Some organizations rely on relatively low levels of know-how in the professional or technical sense, relying primarily on business expertise to generate returns: McDonald's is a good example of this.

Managing two types of know-how no longer means two families of jobs and dual career structures. Flatter, networked organizations require that know-how is combined, blurring the boundaries of management and professional jobs. The concept of "T-shaped skills" – deep expertise in one discipline combined with breadth in other areas – has gathered ground in a number of companies, precisely because professionals are now expected to understand the context in which their know-how is applied (see Figure 2.11).

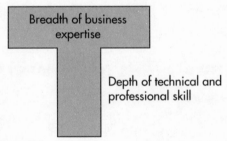

Fig 2.11 T-shaped skills

With business perspective, professionals and specialists can become self-managing and self-directing; more flexible teams can be created, and the organization can be more responsive in positioning the business idea in the marketplace

During the last three years, the New Technology Group in Courtaulds Coatings Division, part of the international Courtaulds chemical and industrial products business, has faced pressures to introduce a set of changes which re-orient the group from research towards technology and product development.

Dr Tim Handyside, the group's Manager, says that people are under more pressure to perform across disciplines. He encourages people to invest in the development of technical and business skills which complement their existing skill set. "This does not mean generic "multi-skilling," but focused "hybrid-skilling," geared to the Coatings business technology base," comments Dr Janice Light, who works with Tim. In the R&D environment, this extends the technical reach of the group, and is resulting in a stronger base where neither skills nor people are pigeonholed.

Peter Drucker, who comprehensively described the tasks of the manager in the era of the bureaucratic organization, has recently said: "The essence of management is to make knowledge productive."

In practice, this means:

- understanding and creating the right quality of leadership and business know-how for your organization;

- building and leveraging the core and peripheral specialist know-how vital to your success;

- developing, in people and systems, the perspective needed for knowledge to be smartly applied;

- keeping knowledge up to date and transferable, tying it to learning and change.

SYNTEGRA: AIMING FOR T-SHAPED SKILLS

Syntegra is the systems integration business of BT (British Telecommunications). As a prime contractor, it orchestrates all the information and communications systems needed to enable its customers to make fundamental changes to the way their businesses work, so they are more effective and competitive. The organization is a catalyst: a combination of consultant, integrator and change manager.

As part of the training and development initiative, which also includes computer-based training, self-managed learning and "on-the-job assignments," Syntegra has developed a skills effectiveness program. This describes the skills required to add value in the business, and is the method through which investment is focused into skill development. Skills effectiveness feeds into a sophisticated resource management program that informs project staffing, personal development, regular skill reviews and personal development planning.

The demands of the marketplace and customer-focused project business, mean that most people have some degree of customer contact and considerable business responsibilities. Interpersonal, communication and commercial skills are highly desirable. The requirement is for the continuous development of a blend of technical, professional and business skills; in other words, T-shaped skills, where the vertical is technical and professional skill, and the horizontal cross bar represents general business skills such as interpersonal, influencing and leadership skills. As most people did not have skills profiles which match the T-shaped model, this was a major goal of Syntegra's skills effectiveness program.

As the business environment becomes more turbulent and complex, companies will need high levels of perspective and adaptability in greater numbers of people to interpret events with the foresight required to deliver a pre-emptive response.

Profiling organizational architecture

Organizations which are moving closer to the networked model have often been described as task-based. There is a high sense of overall purpose and commitment to goals, and a corresponding looseness in the distribution of authority. Teams form around key tasks and have the freedom to make decisions in relation to these tasks. Managing such an approach demands integration. As we progress into the knowledge era, we need to move beyond structure and formal systems as the primary means of co-ordinating activities. Formal reporting lines are being replaced by softer, but more sophisticated and effective ways of ensuring coherence in the way the organization holds together.

Some primary examples of this are: commitment to purpose, the sharing of strategic intent, and a common understanding of what needs to be achieved. Local decisions and actions are taken from a wider frame of reference. Less structure and less control, more sharing of information, more understanding of the big picture, more cross-linking of activities and leaving more up to people to make decisions. Is this your organization?

ORGANIZATION PROFILE

HOW IS YOUR ORGANIZATION CONNECTED?

Thinking back to the discussion on pages 42–46, find out the profile of your own organization on the dimensions of integration (insert I) and control (insert D) by completing the Organization Profile Questionnaire below.

Here are some statements about some aspects of your present work organization and your experience of it.

Please read each statement carefully and decide whether you **agree** or **disagree** with the statement in terms of your own work experience and employing organization. Then put a **cross** in the appropriate box alongside. There are no right or wrong answers, and this is not a test of ability or intelligence. So work steadily through it, and give honest responses.

ORGANIZATION PROFILE QUESTIONNAIRE

		Agree	Disagree
1	Everyone in the organization generally knows what contribution they make to the whole.		
2	Management are not very approachable.		
3	Loyalty to one's own department tends to come first.		
4	Everyone is pleased when the organization is successful.		
5	People spend a lot of time blaming others for their own mistakes.		
6	I generally know where to go when I want help.		
7	They tell us we are here to carry out instructions.		
8	I am proud of the success of my organization.		
9	Decisions always seem to come down from the top.		
10	There seems to be quite a lot of friction and not so much co-operation between departments.		

		Agree	Disagree
11	Managers encourage discussion of new proposals with their people.		
12	People normally consider the effect of their actions upon the whole organization.		
13	The only way we learn of changes is by the grapevine.		
14	It is not uncommon here to get conflicting orders and instructions.		
15	On the whole, people do not feel very free to speak their minds.		
16	People seem to prefer to get on with the job by themselves.		
17	One's job depends not so much on titles or activities, but on what sort of position you can carve out for yourself.		
18	Normally staff are expected to accept orders without question.		
19	People in the organization only get together when there is a crisis.		
20	Managers place value on the opinions of people.		
21	In my job, I am rather unclear about what goes on in other functions.		
22	I don't think many people below senior management really understand the organization's objectives.		
23	I often find it difficult to know who to approach for information.		
24	Managers seem more concerned about the narrow interest of their department rather than wider organization objectives.		
25	Managers are pretty intolerant of error and are not very good at listening to explanations.		
26	On the whole, communication in the organization seems to be pretty full and free.		
27	In our organization, people are not afraid to say what they think.		

		Agree	Disagree
28	Wider participation in management is seen as a desirable objective by the organization.		
29	All too often, no one knows what his/her counterpart in another part of the organization is doing about things that affect them both.		
30	Managers tend to use their power to coerce people.		
31	In our organization, I think people exercise quite a lot of influence on their managers.		
32	Most people feel pretty good about the organization.		
33	Managers are pretty good at discussing its proposals with people.		
34	People do not seem very involved in decisions related to their work.		
35	It is only by experience that you get to know the right people to go to.		
36	Bosses seem to keep changing their minds without consultation.		
37	Better results, it is felt, are obtained by involving everybody in the problems.		
38	The general direction of communication seems to be downward.		
39	Teamwork is a feature of everyday life.		
40	There seems to be a lot of informal and voluntary co-operation amongst people in our organization.		
41	You are not paid to think in our organization.		

Scoring

For each question, circle the number (or *pair* of numbers) in the column which matches your "agree/disagree" decisions. For example, if you agree with Q1, circle 2I; if you agree with Q4 circle 1I + 1D.

Q	Agree	Disagree
1	2I	
2		1D
3		1I
4	1I + 1D	
5		1I
6	1I	
7		2D
8	2D	
9		1D
10		2I
11	2D	
12	1I	
13		1I + 1D
14		2I
15		1D
16		1I
17		1I
18		2D
19		1I
20	2D	
21		2I

Q	Agree	Disagree
22		1I + 1D
23		1I
24		2I
25		1D
26	1I + 1D	
27	1I + 1D	
28		2D
29		2I
30		1D
31	1D	
32	1I + 1D	
33	2D	
34		1I + 1D
35		1I
36		1I + 1D
37	1D	
38		1D
39	2I	
40	1I + 1D	
41		1D

Now add vertically the circled numbers:

Is   [I]   [I]   [I]   [I]
Ds   [D]   [D]   [D]   [D]

Total I score (add all I boxes)   [   ] I

Total D score (add all D boxes)   [   ] D

Next plot your I (integration) and D (control) scores on the grid shown in Figure 2.12.

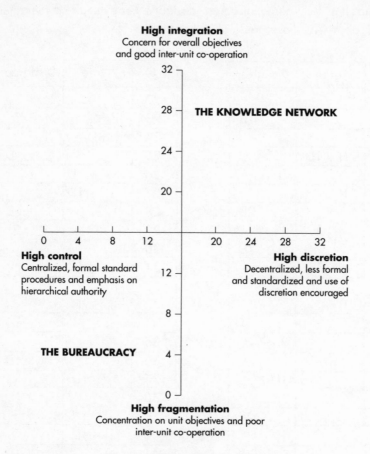

Fig 2.12 Organization profile grid for plotting scores

The further you are to the right of both dimensions, then the closer your organization is to the knowledge-network-type of achitecture most suited to a rapid and reconfigurable response.

When you have plotted the position of your organization today, think about the organization tomorrow, and plot the picture you would like to see two or three years from now. Make a list of the things that need to change. What can you and others do to take these changes forward?

Phase 5: Developing alternatives

What you have discovered from looking at culture and capability, together with what is now known about issues in current performance, leads to conclusions about the organization today. When these conclusions are put together with outcomes from the exploration of the business environment and the formulation of strategic intent, a picture starts to emerge of what needs to be done to move forward.

In one sense, the circle of review and renewal enables managers to conduct classic gap analysis on the organization as a whole. This covers both macro- and micro-elements of the organization's contextual design and the interplay of some key performance variables. What this provides is the information to pull together a blueprint for change, for developing missing capability around a focus on achieving future goals.

This means going beyond identifying the constraints to success and explicitly **defining** the conditions required for success.

KEY QUESTIONS

- What do we need to do to be successful?

- How do we move from where we are now to where we need to get to?

- What are the critical success factors?

- What are the risks versus the benefits?

- What will be the key indicators of our progress?

Phase 6: Translating intentions

Once a clear and communicable blueprint for the future has been established, it can be used as a template for translating intentions into specific change objectives and accountabilities for revitalizing and enhancing performance. The SBC matrix in Figure 2.13 shows a coherent approach to this, as do the key ideas in the American Express program, shown on page 225.

	Organization audit	Organization change	Managing the bank	Increasing skills intensity	Manage for better results	Syndicate the vision
Increase revenues		✔	✔	✔	✔	
Reduce costs		✔	✔	✔	✔	
Deploy resources for maximum return	✔	✔				
Increase high-quality resources	✔	✔		✔	✔	
Decrease low-quality resources	✔	✔			✔	
Improve utilization	✔	✔	✔	✔	✔	✔
Customer-facing organizations	✔	✔	✔		✔	
Informal structures	✔	✔	✔		✔	✔
Responsible leadership	✔	✔	✔	✔		✔
Clear vision		✔			✔	✔
The right culture	✔	✔	✔	✔	✔	✔

Fig 2.13 SBC matrix showing a coherent approach

Phase 7: Taking action

As every manager realizes, knowing what you want to change is one thing; changing it is quite another. Unfortunately for those who wave the banner of change, the present has a momentum all of its own. This momentum is driven by one overarching instruction: repeat. The action phase of renewal means breaking through the repeat barrier, the inertia of the present, so that we can take important first steps away from what we are doing today.

One way to approach it is to chunk down what the organization is trying to achieve, into bite-size pieces of "desirable difference." This can be as simple as putting small stakes or flags in the ground, which signal where you need to get to, and represent small aiming points which people feel are do-able. Often these stakes or flags become anchors for change, and help to pull bigger or further change through. This action phase brings us into the whole arena of managing organizational change. (This is covered more fully in Chapter 7, when we look at ways of aligning all facets of the Performance Prism.)

What you do need to recognize at this stage, is that even starting a review may be the first step toward change. It will certainly be perceived as such by others. How well you are able to move to the renewal actions will be influenced by how well the review phases are carried out. We have not been describing intellectual activities; we have been involved in a human process.

Involvement and commitment or exclusion and resistance begin to develop the moment the first questions are posed. Asking questions about performance is a fundamental challenge to the status quo, and the status quo is made up of individuals or groups of stakeholders, whose various interests will be threatened, or at the very least disturbed, by an activity of this kind.

Working out how to conduct a review, is a design activity in its own right. Think about who to involve, how to run it and what techniques to use. The aim is to pre-empt the disturbance you will create.

THE HUMAN ORGANIZATION

Managing performance at organizational level means managing the organization itself as a key part of business performance. There is increasing recognition that in turbulent and intensely competitive world markets, organizations are platforms of global capability, which need to respond quickly and variously to narrowing windows of opportunity. This capability will increasingly consist of resources that are knowledge-based. Thinking of organizations in a new light as human organizations and managing them accordingly will be an important success factor in the years ahead.

We have used the Prism image to stress four important elements in the human organization: environment, intent, capability and culture, which interrelate to form a dynamic context of performance. Thinking in terms of the human organization is a way of framing this context, a frame which is humanistic rather than mechanistic. It is this context itself, as well as concrete things within it, that organizations now have to create and manage to enable exceptional performance. Without a backcloth of meaningful and compelling contexts, human confidence flounders. Our energy begins to dissipate, rather than gathering momentum and power. Without confidence and energy, the challenge of the unknown makes us feel vulnerable instead of excited, and it is through our fears, rather than our hopes, that we turn and face the uncertainties of our world.

References

1. Peters, T, *Liberation Management*, Knopf, New York, 1992.
2. Quoted at *Opportunity 2000: Towards a Balanced Workforce*, a conference run by Knowledge Era Enterprises, Inc., London, 21 November, 1995.
3. Colvin, G, "What your computer can't do for you", *Director*, February 1996.
4. Allaire, Y and Firsirotu, M, "How to implement radical strategies in large organizations" *Sloan Management Review*, 26, 3, Spring 1985.
5. Deal, T and Kennedy, A, *Corporate Cultures: The Rites and Rituals of Corporate Life*, Addison Wesley, Reading, Mass, 1982.
6. Hamel, G and Prahalad, C K, *Competing for the Future*, Harvard Business School Press, Cambridge, Mass., 1994.
7. Handy, C, *The Age of Unreason*, Business Books, London, 1989.
8. Hamel, G and Prahald, C K, *Competing for the Future*, Harvard University Press, Cambridge, Mass., 1994.
9. Campbell, A, "Mission, Vision and Strategy Development," in *The Financial Times Handbook of Management*, FT/Pitman, London, 1995.
10. Handy, C, *The Empty Raincoat*, Hutchinson, London, 1994.
11. De Bono, E, *Teaching Thinking*, Penguin, Harmondsworth, 1978.
12. De Bono, E, *Teaching Thinking*, Penguin, Harmondsworth, 1978.
13. Hamel, G, and Prahald, C K, *Competing for the Future*, Harvard Business School Press, Cambridge, Mass., 1994.
14. Hof, R D with Rebello, K and Burrows, P, "Scott McNealy's Rising Sun," *Business Week*, 22 January 1996.
15. Deal, T, and Kennedy, A, *Corporate Cultures*, Addison Wesley, Reading, 1982.
16. Zweig, P L, "The case against mergers," *Business Week*, 30 October 1995.
17. Clark, P J, *Beyond the Deal: Optimizing Merger and Acquisition Value*, Harper, New York, 1991.
18. Baron, A and Walters, M, "The Culture Factor," *Corporate and International Perspectives*, UK Institute of Personnel and Development, 1994.

19. Hof, R D, and Port, O, "Silicon Goes from Peak to Peak," *Business Week*, 8 January, 1996.
20. Conference: *Leveraging Knowledge For Sustainable Advantage*, 26-27 March 1996, Business Intelligence & The Strategic Planning Society, London.
21. Bartlett, C A and Ghoshal, S, "Rebuilding Behavioral Context: Turn Process Re-engineering into People Rejuvenation," *Sloan Management Review*, Fall 1995.
22. Pascale, R, *Re-inventing the Orgainzation*, Conference, London, 1995.
23. Nonaka, I, The Hypertext Organization, Conference: *Opportunity 2000: Towards a Balanced Workforce*, Knowledge Era Enterprises Inc., London 21 November 1995.
24. Byrne, J A, "The virtual corporation," *Business Week*, 8 February, 1993.
25. © Interactives 1991 as used in "Beyond the Boundaries of HRM – business integration in practice," IPM National Conference, Harrogate 1991 with Peter Cole of Swiss Bank Corporation.
26. Poll of Polls, *Euromoney*, January 1994.
27. Pickard, J, "At the heart of the business," *Personnel Management*, March 1994.
28. *Business Week*, 5 February,1996.

"People you lead have to recognize that they too have power. The aim is for people to say: 'The leader did nothing, we did it ourselves.'"

Steve Shirley, life President of FI Group[1]

Chapter 3

◆

LEADERS ALL

L eadership is critical to the achievement of high performance, no matter what your business or area of responsibility. It is also essential in helping others aspire to and attain high levels of performance for themselves and the organization. Today we are all leaders. This chapter will help you understand the process of leadership and the consequences of your actions as a leader of others.

LEADERSHIP THROUGH PEOPLE

Traditional views of leadership conjure up pictures of generals bravely leading their troops to battle or, on the organizational front, charismatic executives responsible for huge resources, both human and financial. Many of today's leaders are very different. With flatter structures increasingly common, and the move to project and matrix management, we are all leaders, even if we do not hold formal leadership roles.

As one CEO pointed out: "The traditional organization asked maybe 5 percent of its people to do 95 percent of its thinking. What we have tried to do is get 100 percent of the people to do 100 percent of the thinking."

The harsh and sometimes unacknowledged reality is that organizations can no longer survive if leadership remains the responsibility of a few individuals.

As James Kouzes and Barry Posner argue, in a productive work community, leaders are not commanders and controllers, bosses and big shots. Instead, they are servers and supporters, partners and providers.[2]

In the report *Making Quality Work*, George Binney and Colin Williams describe how Nissan Motor Manufacturing (UK), based in Sunderland, realized that central to the success of its quality initiative was the enhancement of the role of the supervisors. Instead of being by-passed and undervalued, they became recognized as the leaders, guides and mentors of the team.

They were made responsible for:

- selecting the people who worked for them
- communicating face-to-face to their teams
- on-the-job training
- balancing the work of the team
- ensuring high levels of attendance and time keeping
- solving problems and maintaining equipment
- quality (there are no inspectors).

Similarly, at Grundfos, one of the world's leading pump manufacturers, Quality Director Finn Moller recalls how "one MD in an assembly plant abroad protested to me about the end of inspection." I said, "No, we haven't stopped inspection, we've moved from 50 to 2,000 inspectors."[3]

Many managers we meet have little traditional authority, perhaps no direct reports and few resources. Yet they are managing a number of significant projects and are having to lead and motivate project teams to achieve results within tight timescales. These men and women have to demonstrate considerable leadership qualities and skills, as do all employees, as they continue to take on greater responsibility.

So how do we define leadership? How does it differ from management? What is the most effective way to lead for performance? How can managers craft a style appropriate to their own particular circumstances?

Before looking at these issues reflect on your own approach:

- **What does leadership mean to you?**

- **How would you describe your leadership style?**

Apparently simple questions, but managers typically do not spend much time reflecting on how they do their job, what the secret of their success is and where they need to improve. The initial question – "What does leadership mean to you?" – is one we have asked many managers. The range of different responses is huge – perhaps not surprising if you consider there are over 400 definitions of leadership.

What does leadership mean to you?

"Having a clear focus, communicating it to others and giving them the space to develop"

"Bringing people with you – engendering commitment and enthusiasm"

"Setting strategic objectives, being creative in helping others achieve against those objectives"

"Being accountable and responsible and ensuring financial profitability and success"

"Providing direction and achieving goals"

"Being able to make things happen"

"Inspiring the best performance out of the individual"

"It means planning and motivating, taking risks and making decisions, not being afraid to face challenges and changes."

The list is broad and reflects the different priorities and styles of individual managers. It also indicates that the pendulum has swung from a directive, autocratic approach to one which is more enabling, seeking to engage the hearts and minds of others in pursuit of a common goal.

These various styles are, in part, formed by the culture of the organization and a person's previous experience. Individual leadership styles are continually being reshaped by the demands faced now and anticipated in the future. Leaders need to be able to change and adapt to the demands of the situation. Leaders who fail to adapt, perish.

Look at the decline of Apple Computers, once the showcase of Silicon Valley. Steve Jobs, one of the Apple's co-founders, created the company's distinctive culture, which inspired the creativity and dedication required to bring the Apple Mac to the market. The trouble was that the culture was "unharnessed and uncontrolled" and failed to recognize the growing competitive threat. Had Jobs changed his leadership style, he may have avoided being ousted from the board in 1985, and may have been able to help the organization mature and sustain its initial success.[4]

YOUR LEADERSHIP STYLE IN CONTEXT

The following questions will help you to see your leadership style in the broader context of the organization and reflect on how it may have changed over the years, or may need to change to meet future demands:

- **How is leadership defined in your organization?**

- **How do people become leaders in your organization?**

- **What are the skills necessary for leaders in your organization?**

- **What do future leaders in your organization need to be able to do?**

LEADERSHIP FOR THE 1990s AND BEYOND

Leadership is not static. It is a dynamic process which continually needs to be crafted and changed to ensure high performance. Figure 3.1 provides a concise overview of the radical changes which the practice and theory of leadership has undergone in the last decade.

The roots of modern leadership can be traced back to the work of James McGregor Burns and, in particular, his 1978 book, *Leadership*. Burns introduced the notion of *transactional* and *transformational* leadership and these remain the most popular and appropriate leadership models.[5]

Transactional leadership is built on reciprocity, the idea that the relationship between the leader and their followers develops from

From	To
One leader	All leaders
Assessors of performance	Coaches and enablers of performance
Emphasis on giving instructions	Emphasis on communication, feedback and involvement
Hierarchical implementation	Cross-business project implementation
Emphasis on monitoring and evaluation	Emphasis on managing boundaries and focusing on the wider vision

Fig 3.1 The changing nature of leadership

the exchange of some reward, such as performance ratings, pay, recognition and praise. It involves leaders clarifying goals and objectives, communicating to organize tasks and activities with the co-operation of their employees to ensure that wider organizational goals are met. Such a relationship depends on hierarchy and the ability to work through the mode of exchange. It requires leadership skills such as the ability to obtain results, to control through structures and processes, to solve problems, to plan and organize, and work within the structures and boundaries of the organization.

Transformational leadership, on the other hand, is concerned with engaging the hearts and minds of others. It works to help all parties achieve greater motivation, satisfaction and a greater sense of achievement. It requires trust, concern and facilitation rather than direct control. The skills required are concerned with establishing a long-term vision, empowering people to control themselves, coaching and developing others and challenging the culture to change.

In transformational leadership, the power of the leader comes from creating understanding and trust. In contrast, in transactional leadership power is based much more on the notion of hierarchy and position. In essence, the two styles are the yin and yang of leadership.

While transformational leadership is popular, creating a high performance culture requires elements of transactional leadership to ensure a clear focus on the achievement and measurement of results. The secret of good leadership lies in combining the two, so that targets, results and procedures are developed and shared.

A commissioning editor we interviewed described how she could be leading 20 teams working on different projects at any one time. "I see myself as part of the team," she said. "I obviously have a leadership role. They, as editors, have been given responsibility, though I am happy to take tasks from them. In a sense, it's an inversion of roles, it gives them a sense of power and control."

True transformational leadership requires that others are empowered, yet, as the editor points out, elements of transactional leadership are essential to the success of her role. As a result, she now places more emphasis on objective-setting – "I appreciate that it is a good way of focusing and acts as a basis for evaluation."

The practice of transformational leadership and the advent of empowerment means that the notion of leaders and followers is gradually dissolving. Indeed, at times, leaders need to take on the previously unfamiliar role of followers. As the French statesman Talleyrand said: "They are my people. I must follow them because I am their leader."

ADAPTING TO THE SITUATION

Theories and models of leadership are alluring. However, the reality of practising transactional and transformational leadership in the right place at the right time is very different. Employees have varying skill levels. Some have performance difficulties; some need more direction and encouragement; some relish the chance for greater responsibility, and love challenge and change; some fear it. Combined with this variety of individual needs and behavior, leaders have to work in the broader organizational and environmental context. This may mean operating in situations of uncertainty, low morale and ever-decreasing timescales in which to achieve goals.

Transactional leadership	Transformational leadership
Clarify goals and objectives to obtain immediate results	Establish long-term vision
Create structures and processes for control	Create a climate of trust
Solve problems	Empower people to control themselves; manage problem-solving
Maintain and improve the current situation	Change the current situation
Plan, organize and control	Coach and develop people
Guard and defend the culture	Challenge and change the culture
Power comes from position and authority in the organization	Power comes from influencing a network of relationships

Fig 3.2 Transactional and transformational leadership

Given that leadership is a highly complex and difficult process, how can you best develop your skills and abilities to be more effective? There is no instant solution. There is no formula. Leadership demands flexibility. However, it is possible to break leadership down into a range of activities, attitudes and behaviors, some of which you may already use effectively, while others you may need to develop.

The Leadership Competencies Questionnaire will help to identify your own leadership strengths and areas for development.

LEADERSHIP COMPETENCIES QUESTIONNAIRE

Please indicate the extent to which each of the following competencies applies to you. Think about each statement and rate yourself according to the five-point scale below. (You can always give this questionnaire to others to gain their perception of your leadership competencies.)

5 = Always
4 = Often
3 = Sometimes
2 = Rarely
1 = Never

QUESTIONNAIRE

1 Listen carefully to others	1 2 3 4 5
2 Give people responsibility for tasks and projects	1 2 3 4 5
3 Challenge the rules and conventions in the organization	1 2 3 4 5
4 Have a clear vision for the team	1 2 3 4 5
5 Have a clear perception of your strengths and weaknesses	1 2 3 4 5
6 Encourage ideas from the team	1 2 3 4 5
7 Demonstrate trust to others	1 2 3 4 5
8 Anticipate and adapt to changing conditions	1 2 3 4 5
9 Communicate the vision and ideas clearly to others	1 2 3 4 5
10 Spend time keeping up to date and developing new skills	1 2 3 4 5
11 Motivate and encourage others	1 2 3 4 5
12 Provide training to enable people to work effectively	1 2 3 4 5
13 Help others to manage change	1 2 3 4 5
14 Demonstrate a high level of commitment to your work	1 2 3 4 5
15 Manage time well	1 2 3 4 5
16 Develop a good communication network throughout the organization	1 2 3 4 5
17 Provide support for people when needed	1 2 3 4 5
18 Manage stress well	1 2 3 4 5
19 Focus on achieving results	1 2 3 4 5
20 Have a positive attitude towards yourself	1 2 3 4 5

Scoring

Transfer your scores on to the chart and add them up.

Q	Column 1 Score	Q	Column 2 Score	Q	Column 3 Score	Q	Column 4 Score	Q	Column 5 Score
1		2		3		4		5	
6		7		8		9		10	
11		12		13		14		15	
16		17		18		19		20	
Total		Total		Total		Total		Total	

The leadership competencies contained in this questionnaire cover skills and behaviors associated with modern leadership, and can be classified under these headings:

Column 1 ...... **L** istening
Column 2 ...... **E** mpowering
Column 3 ...... **A** dapting
Column 4 ...... **D** elivering
Column 5 ...... **S** elf-understanding

Listening: your score_____

Listening is at the crux of any relationship. Relationships only flourish and develop where people feel they are listened to, and their contribution recognized. Listening includes not only the skills of active listening, but also having a positive regard for others, and the ability to demonstrate this by communicating on a regular basis. Through listening it is easier to understand and motivate others. Ideas and suggestions can be developed and, by listening to the wider networks within and outside the organization, it is easier to react to and influence change.

Empowering: your score_____

Empowerment requires a major leap for managers whose very existence used to rely on their formal power base. Yet ironically, giving up power through empowering others often creates more power and the freedom to really lead. There are a number of components to empowerment. The first is the ability to surrender power and give people real responsibility and autonomy to achieve their work. The second is trusting the people involved. The final component is providing the training and support mechanisms to enable people to become really empowered in the work they do.

Adapting: your score_____

More than ever before managers have to adapt and change to circumstances as they arise. Change is continual and has become part of the everyday leadership experience. This is discussed further in Chapter 7. Adapting involves challenging the status quo and trying out new ways of tackling problems. It also requires a great deal of emotional resilience to manage the stresses which are inherent in an ever-changing environment.

Delivering: your score_____

The leader may not be the person who delivers the results. If they are working in an empowered team, the team members will be delivering the results and taking the credit. The leader's role is one of facilitating the success by creating and communicating a clear vision, demonstrating commitment to everyone involved and ensuring that quality results are delivered to the customer.

Self-understanding: your score _____

Today's leaders have to understand themselves and their impact on others. They have to grapple with their own needs for control and their own fears around power and authority. They have to acquire new skills: "soft" skills, such as coaching, and facilitating, as well as the "hard" skills of working with technology and finding new ways to measure and manage performance. They have to demonstrate a positive attitude towards themselves and their work. This requires the ability to understand themselves, their strengths and how to use and develop them.

Which were your highest scoring and lowest scoring areas? This will give you some idea of which skills and behaviors you may need to focus on to enhance your overall leadership style. When you have analyzed your profile, look at the appropriate section in this chapter which describes the LEADS competencies in more detail, together with suggestions on how to develop them further.

Fig 3.3: The changing nature of leadership

LEADERSHIP COMPETENCIES

Listening

Listening is an essential quality of leadership. The leader has to listen in order to understand and motivate people. It is only by listening that you can innovate and develop new ideas. Leaders need to listen to their people and teams on a one-to-one basis. They also need to listen to the organization and wider business arena. This requires an ability to build and create the networks which are so critical to understanding the opportunities and difficulties ahead.

"Instead of putting the emphasis on strong leadership, or responding to the needs of others, successful leaders are assertive and responsive. They are forthright **and** they listen," say George Binney and Colin Williams in *Leaning into the Future*.[6] "They are determined to shape a different future **and** they keep their feet firmly on the ground, taking full account of current realities. They

lead and **learn** at the same time. Importantly, these leaders in change appear at all levels in organizations, not just at the top. Leadership is repeatedly provided not by the chief executive or senior managers but by others in the organization."

The competency of listening is made up of a number of elements:

- listening to others
- encouraging innovation
- motivating others
- networking.

Listening to others

Warren Bennis, in his research into leadership, interviewed 90 leaders from different walks of life.[7] Sixty of the interviewees were chief executives of large US companies, and the other 30 included politicians, conductors of orchestras, the founder of a ballet school and Neil Armstrong, the first man on the moon. Despite the disparity in their backgrounds, they all felt that leadership was an "essentially human business," and spent 90 percent of their time with other people.

Leaders such as Anita Roddick, Richard Branson, John Sainsbury and many more spend a lot of time listening to employees and hearing their ideas and concerns in order to improve the organization. John Sainsbury, when visiting supermarkets, always went to the people on the shop floor to identify areas where improvements could be made. Indeed, those closest to the job often have the clearest picture about how to improve quality and productivity.

It is this insight on which Avon Tyres (UK) has sought to capitalize in recent years. Avon produces over 40 different types of tire, and has 1,300 employees. It has re-structured its factory, dividing it into four separate units each concentrating on a different area of the business. Decision making and planning have been passed down the line, and gradually operators and engineers are taking on more responsibility. As one of the factory managers says: "What has changed in the culture is that people are now prepared to listen more. Managers listen to operators and involve them in decision making. They feel more involved. If they are involved, they can't use others as scapegoats and instead own and work with decisions they make."

When Colgate Palmolive began to open plants in Central Europe, it faced the challenge of how to get the best from employees in countries with which it was unfamiliar. "We could have brought in strong expatriate managers to continue the authoritarian management style," said Phil Berry, the company's Director of HR for Central Europe, Middle East and Africa. Instead, it chose to emphasize its own culture and introduce a more participative approach. Employees were encouraged to share their ideas about how to run the business, and rewarded them for doing so. Colgate also provided employees with vital information, training and clear goals to stimulate ideas and engender involvement. After three years, the results are self-evident. Job satisfaction is high, there is a high level of trust between managers and employees, and the majority of the workforce is operating at a capacity that they never before thought possible.[8]

Listening to others is all about respecting people. It recognizes that they have a lot to offer and, as these examples show, listening helps others develop confidence in their own leadership and can greatly contribute to the overall performance of the organization.

However, listening is not just a matter of spending time with people. It requires making time **and** space, not just clearing your desk and diverting calls, but clearing your mind and concentrating on the speaker or the team. It requires not interrupting, but showing attention and encouragement so that the person can fully develop their thoughts and ideas. When you are listening, focus on the way the words are being spoken and on the body language of the person. You can often sense enthusiasm, concern and a whole range of emotions which add to the spoken word. It is only when you listen to your people that you can really understand what motivates and drives them.

AN EXERCISE IN LISTENING

Next time someone needs to see you, or when you are getting ideas and views from others:

- stop what you are doing;

- show you are giving your time by sitting with them without interruptions;

- give the person 100 percent of your attention and show this by looking at them, encouraging them (verbally by asking them to expand on their ideas and non-verbally by nodding and smiling and looking involved);

- make sure you do not stifle their thinking with your thoughts, counter-arguments, barriers and "yes, buts;"
- summarize their ideas to show that you have listened;
- agree next steps.

Active listening is not a passive process with no results. It is a powerful way of gaining insight to stimulate improvement, change and involvement. Phil Eaves, Sales Operations Director of Crosfield Electronics, describes how he uses active listening: "I spend a lot of my time with the overseas branches. To sit and listen to their problems in itself is not enough. I have to demonstrate that I add value, and in doing so will gain their confidence to discuss issues openly. Creating an open environment gives people more confidence to discuss the difficult issues."

One manager we worked with said that she was really using the staff appraisal system as a way of listening to her staff: "I discovered through feedback from others that I was not giving enough support and praise to the team. I recognized the trend and talked to the people about where they would like more encouragement and in what form. Now I'm trying to close the loop and morale seems to be improving." The message is: listening counts.

Encouraging innovation

Innovation and commitment will happen only if people are able to become involved and to contribute. It is depressing to count the number of ideas lost because managers do not encourage or allow the time for others to voice their thoughts.

Tagamet was the first-ever billion-dollar drug. It was developed by James Black at Smith Kline and French. Black originally proposed the idea to ICI, where he then worked, but ICI turned the opportunity down. He went to work for a much smaller company (Smith Kline and French) because they were prepared to believe in him and give him the resources he needed.[9] The result was a hugely successful product.

Innovation need not be earth shattering. It can comprise of many small changes which together can have an impact on organizational performance. Duffy Tool and Stamping in the US set up "excellence teams" among its 300 employees. These teams meet on a regular basis and, so far, have identified and corrected more than 500 quick-success problems, ranging from dealing with shift problems, improving quality and throughput, and making the environment safer. During this period the company's pre-tax profits increased significantly every year, and managers are convinced that the "excellence team" program made an important contribution toward the cost reductions and resulting profits.[10]

The cost and quality savings from employee contributions can be enormous, and can also engender a feeling of ownership and responsibility, especially when people recognize that simple changes can make dramatic inroads into costs.

Small ideas can also lead to big changes. At 3M staff can apply for "Genesis" grants, and are allowed to spend 15 percent of their working time on projects selected themselves. This attitude inspires others to come forward believing that their ideas will be supported.

All of these examples share one thing in common: innovation is given support, and the leader's role is to encourage ideas to bubble up, and to provide the framework for them to be developed and tried out.

Innovation requires creativity. It also requires the discipline to bring the right ideas to fruition. The easy way to distinguish between the two is to see creativity as the conception, and innovation as the birth.

Innovation can be seen as a cycle. The cycle starts with a concern or need. It may be from the competition, or a suggestion from a customer or from the team. This is then formulated into a statement such as "How can we improve the morale of the team?" or "How can we improve the service we offer?"

Once this is done, the creativity stage is essential to generate a range of possible, even crazy, ideas. This requires bringing the team together and using techniques, such as brainstorming, to generate ideas in a non-judgemental environment. These are analyzed to decide which can be developed further, and an action plan is then produced. Finally, after the idea has been implemented, it needs to be carefully evaluated, so that progress can be monitored and lessons learned for the future.

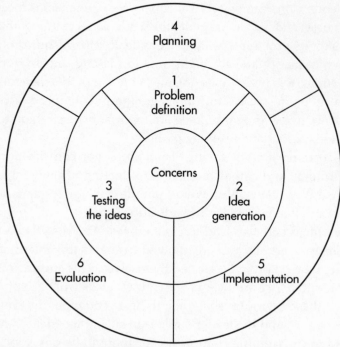

Fig 3.4 The cycle of innovation

THE BRIGHT IDEAS QUEST

If you are trying to encourage more creativity and innovation with your team, try some of these ideas.

Positive thinking

People should not waste time thinking of reasons why something cannot be done. Instead, they should think about ways to make something work, and then get it done. Ask people to think of three work-related tasks or changes they think cannot be accomplished. Then ask them to figure out ways to accomplish them. Then do the same thing yourself.

The Edison factor

Let people know that they are allowed to fail. As Thomas Edison said: "I failed my way to success." Edison conducted 9,000 experiments before he achieved a working light bulb. When an assistant asked why he persisted in this folly, Edison replied: "Young man, I haven't failed. I've learned 9,000 things that don't work."

Breaking through

If it isn't broken, break it. Test all of the assumptions about the organization's current systems, processes, methods, and products to see whether they are really necessary, and whether there might be better ones.

Brainstorming board

Put up a bulletin board in a central area and encourage people to use it to brainstorm ideas. Write a theme or problem on coloured paper and place it in the centre of the board. Provide pieces of white paper on which people can write their ideas to post on the board (you can also do this using the computer network).

Motivating others

Motivation is highly individual and explanations incredibly elusive. We are all motivated by different things at different stages in our lives. Only by listening to people and understanding what enthuses them – how they work, how they like to be managed and what their aspirations are – can you really get close to tapping into and releasing the potential and enthusiasm that real motivation brings.

TO IMPROVE THE LEVELS OF MOTIVATION IN YOUR TEAM

If you want to try to improve the levels of motivation in your team:

1 Find out what drives each of the team members. Ask them what their aspirations are, what motivates them and what demotivates them. Do not assume that people are motivated by the same things. By their very nature and their personal circumstances, their motivation will vary.

2 Do not assume that money is the only (or even the main) motivator. In Philip Sadler's book *Managing Talent*, he points out that intrinsic motivation often comes about by people setting their own goals and satisfying their own personal needs.[11] Sometimes the focus on extrinsic rewards, such as pay and bonuses, can distract people from working to their full potential.

3 Recognize that your own motivation will significantly influence that of others.

4 Remember that people will support what they helped to create. Give people variety and interest, and some control over what they do. Operators at Avon Tyres were given control over their machines. They covered all the routine maintenance jobs, with the result that the estimated downtime of the machines dropped from eight hours every ten days to four hours. Breakdowns were less frequent and oil leaks, which had seemed an insurmountable problem in the past, were completely eradicated.

5 Show trust and be open with people, keep them in the picture, not in the dark. Be clear what is expected from people – agree and review targets on a regular basis.

Networking

Networking is an essential ingredient of modern leadership. The ability to influence a network of relationships is a major element of transformational leadership, where involvement, participation and influence are important in achieving quality, decisions and results.

Some networks are formal, such as professional bodies or business networks. Others are more informal, and it is often these networks which are important in the organization when trying to listen, influence and make sense of what is going on.

It is worth spending time identifying your networks within the organization, using the exercise below. This will give you a clearer picture of how effectively you are networking, and whether you need to improve this process.

AN EXERCISE IN NETWORKING

Organization charts define the formal lines of authority in the organization. Network maps describe how things actually get done. Typically there is a relationship between the organization chart and the network map, but the network map can give you an insight into the relationships you rely on and the relationships where there might be problems.

To create a network map:

1 Put a circle to represent yourself at the center of a sheet of paper

2 Arrange around you in circles the people you associate with in order to do your job. The people you work with most frequently should be placed closest to you.

3 Reflect the formal organization structure by placing people higher in the organization above you on the map: people lower in the organization below you on the map; and your colleagues either side of you.

4 Place customers on the map in boxes rather than circles. If you think of a customer as an organizational equal, put the box on the same line that you are on. If you think of a customer as an organizational superior, put the box above you on the paper, and so forth.

5 When you have finished arraying your network around you, using frequency of contact as the criterion for where they are placed, connect each person to you using the following code:

- *Double lines* mean the relationship is very important to you if you are to do your job effectively.
- *Single lines* mean the relationship is somewhat important to you if you are to do your job effectively.
- *Dotted lines* mean the relationship is of peripheral importance to you.

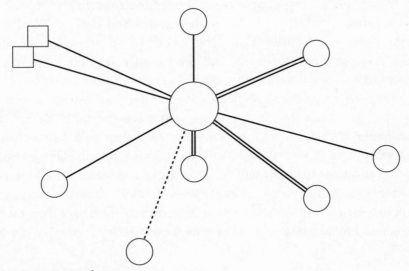

Fig 3.5 Network map

The following points will help you to "read" the "network map" (in Figure 3.5) and interpret the map you have just drawn.

1 The most important work relationships (double lines) should be the ones that are closest to the center (you). If they are not – what does this tell you?

2 Potential problems with upper management tend to be highlighted by double lines and long distances from the center.

3 Potential problems with staff tend to be highlighted by uneven distance from you: Why are some people getting more attention? Are they the right people?

4 Other potential problems with staff are highlighted when some staff have double lines, others single lines, and still others dotted lines.

5 Distance from you on the map does not always represent a problem. Sometimes people work at great geographic distance from one another, and this is reflected on the map.

Empowering

"Empowering" literally means "giving power." It is the process of enabling others. It means driving down decision making, sharing information, giving people control over their work, and thereby generating commitment. All organizations and individual managers are confronted with the need to improve levels of performance and, positively and consistently applied, empowerment can improve motivation and enhance performance.

Empowerment does not mean surrendering your legitimate managerial authority, but it does represent a leap of faith for many managers. As Gene Horan, Director of Ashridge's Leadership Development Program, points out: "You are, in fact, displaying your belief and trust that you will create synergy and increased effectiveness if you enable people at lower levels to make more decisions, to solve their own problems, to plan their own work, to set their own goals and to take responsibility for their own performance."

Empowerment is built around four elements:

- responsibility
- trust
- training
- support.

Responsibility

Empowerment requires giving people responsibility to make decisions to control their own work environment, and to make changes which will enhance the quality of the product or service offered. People need to feel a sense of ownership. They need to have autonomy to complete their work without interference. They also need to see the big picture of how their work fits into the organizational vision and goals, so that they get a real a sense of their responsibility (and value) to the organization.

At Avon Tyres, production planning has been absorbed into the individual factories. One factory Manager told us: "We began trying to empower people to do their own planning. It was hard for them to understand, even though they've actually been doing it for years. The planning department used to do the plans in minute detail and pass them on to the production department. Production would then repeat the work and re-plan because the original version was too prescriptive and did not take breakdowns into account. The difference now is that those original planners are integrated into the focus factory, they are now part of a team, and the whole factory team is responsible for the product, its quality, reliability, and timeliness."

The results speak for themselves. Since 1986, productivity and efficiency at Avon have more than doubled, and waste has been reduced year-on-year by 3 to 4 percent. These achievements have changed the perception of what can be done. When asked what has been an important factor in enabling such improvements in performance to be achieved, the Manager replied: "The changes in the management structure . . . There are no managers in key positions who are not afraid of empowering people."

PASSING ON RESPONSIBILITY

If you are looking for ways to pass on responsibility to others, ask yourself the following questions:

- What are the decisions in which people are, or would want to be, routinely involved?

- Which are the decisions on which you feel you must have the final word? Why?

- How much do you trust people to do the right things, and to do them right?

- Are you willing to commit yourself to what the team collectively decides?

- How much do people know about what is really going on in the organization?

- Do people have to put up with needless bureaucracy?

- To what extent do people have direct access to decision makers?

- Are there layers of authority in your organization which could be eliminated?

- How much discretion are you willing to give people?

When passing over responsibility you first have to consider whether you really do want to give power to others. Second, you need to think about what power you can pass on – what are the areas of your work that can increase the responsibility of others?

The list below, generated by managers, may help in compiling your own list of ideas to give more responsibility to your team. The managers were asked to think of ways they currently use power which could be passed on to others:

- evaluating others' work
- participating in hiring colleagues
- determining the pace of the work
- controlling who is chosen to succeed you
- carrying out plans in an orderly fashion
- deciding on the training others receive

- setting work priorities
- deciding (or influencing) the compensation of other people
- being involved in decisions about starting new projects
- being able to forge consensus
- adding value by being a key link in internal communications
- using discretion
- being independent.

Having identified areas where you could pass on responsibility, make a concrete plan for enhancing the empowerment and responsibility of others. Talk it over with them to gain their views and commitment, and be prepared to provide coaching and support to ensure its success.

Trust

The whole notion of developing trust through leadership is relatively new. "Dividing up labor into its various tasks fostered a basic distrust of human beings. People were not allowed to put the whole puzzle together because companies feared what people would do if they knew and saw the whole puzzle," says Charles Handy. "Managers have been brought up on a diet of power: divide and rule. They have been preoccupied with authority rather than making things happen . . . The trouble is putting faith in people is seen as an indulgence rather than a necessity."[12]

Trust is difficult to come to terms with in an environment of layoffs and uncertainty. Yet, for empowerment to work, it requires employee commitment, and this demands trust, not just trust in the leader and those being empowered, but trust throughout the organization so that employees can align themselves with its goals and vision. "Trust is the lubricant that makes it possible for organizations to work," says Warren Bennis.[13]

Trust is difficult to define. We know when it is there and we know when it is lacking. A group of course participants identified the following as the ingredients for trust:

- credibility
- honesty at all times
- willingness to admit mistakes
- openness and willingness to listen to the concerns and worries of others

- providing information when asked and keeping people in the picture about what is happening in the wider organization
- consistency
- dependability
- accurate feedback on performance.

How do you rate on this list? Would people describe you in these terms? If not, what do you need to do to help others develop greater trust in you?

Trust is something which has to be earned. Often the leader has to be the broker between the organization and a range of different stakeholders. For this reason it is important that as a leader you are seen to have a view, and be working with integrity and honesty for the good of the team.

Some organizations have transformed trust from an indulgence into a business necessity, and this has been accompanied by major improvements to the bottom line. At Semco, the now famous Brazilian company which produces pumps and cooling units, Ricardo Selmer, who heads the company, and is author of the best-selling book *Maverick!*, has put the notion of trust to the test.

As a believer in democratic management, everyone at Semco has access to the books; managers set their own salaries, productivity targets and schedules; workers make decisions, once the preserve of managers; even the distribution of the profit-sharing scheme is determined by employees. "We have taken a company that was moribund and made it thrive by refusing to squander our greatest resource, our people," says Semler. Despite hyper-inflation, recession and commercial chaos, Semco has managed to increase productivity by nearly seven-fold and profits five-fold.[14]

Training

Responsibility cannot simply be granted. People often need help in managing their new autonomy. They need new skills, and these must be provided in an appropriate and timely way. These can be technical skills, such as learning a new software package or how to manage budgets, or they may include other skills such as team management, influencing or coaching. These competencies have been referred to as *enablers*.[15]

As the matrix below indicates, empowerment requires enablement. An organization can do a lot of training to help people become more empowered. However, such training is worthless if the organization is not ready to hand over responsibility and power to its people.

Entrenched bunkers lack both power and autonomy. Like shell-shocked soldiers, they retreat to the comfort of their usual tasks when work becomes stressful or challenging.

Loose cannons are employees who are empowered but not enabled. They are eager to use authority, but lack the necessary skills and experience. In their enthusiasm, they tend to career through their organizations, leaving a path of destruction in their wake and higher levels of cynicism toward employee empowerment.

Caged eagles are able and willing to play larger roles in their organizations, but they are often thwarted by restrictive organizational practices or controlling managers. They are enabled but not empowered.

Fully empowered employees are those with both the competence and autonomy required to make greater contributions to their organizations.

Which of these are you? And which are your people? Is there anything you can do in terms of training or giving more freedom which can help people become fully empowered?

Support
The process of empowerment can be helped by providing support through spending time coaching, testing out ideas, encouraging

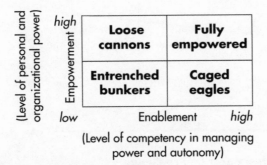

Fig 3.6 Empowerment and enablement

and allowing for mistakes. As Crosfield's Phil Eaves points out: "A good leader will recognize the impact that his decisions will have on others and support them through that change."

Support is not a passive activity. The best leaders will challenge, test ideas, ask searching questions, play devil's advocate and generally help to develop the thinking which lies behind ideas and decisions.

In contrast, a totally supportive environment provides little encouragement to take risks or meet challenges. In reality, this is rarely the case. Most managers work in the low-support high-challenge quadrant; with more and more responsibility, greater workloads and no one to look to for support. The result is burn-out, cynicism and lowering morale. The most productive environment to work in is one which provides a high degree of both challenge and support.

Penny Hughes, former president of Coca-Cola UK and Ireland, has been described as working in this way: "She is excellent at establishing rapport with people and encouraging them to be more open and challenging. To an unusual and refreshing degree she genuinely values people and is totally fair with them. She often

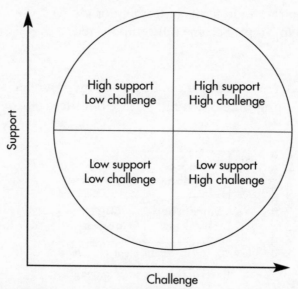

Fig 3.7 Creating support and challenge
Source: Sheperd Moscow.

walks round the office, sits on the back of a chair and shares a joke with us. There is always a lot of laughter! Within a framework of clear objectives, established annually and revisited monthly she leaves her managers to run their own show."

Such examples are a rarity. The *Ashridge Management Index*, an annual survey, draws attention to the fact that the greatest source of dissatisfaction among managers is "the lack of support and recognition they receive from their own managers. This negative factor of organizational life looms largest in managerial dissatisfaction over and above other factors such as concerns about career prospects and job security."[16]

SUPPORTING AND CHALLENGING MEANS . . .

- saying thanks

- listening and questioning

- challenging thinking and stretching ideas

- giving feedback – positive and developmental

- being open about your support to others

- visiting teams, individuals and divisions who need your support

- being honest

- recognizing milestones and results

- celebrating successes.

Adapting

Change is a constant aspect of any leader's life. Meeting the increasingly sophisticated needs of customers, adapting to new technologies and achieving more with less, requires leaders to anticipate the future, challenge the status quo, help others through the change process and, finally, to have the emotional resilience to cope with the increasing pressures.

Adapting comprises several elements:

- future scanning
- challenging convention
- managing fear
- emotional resilience.

Future scanning

The idea of gazing into a glass ball and seeing what the future brings is one we will leave firmly in the hands of fortunetellers and psychics. Yet the ability to anticipate, to scan the future, to identify areas of risk and opportunity, are open to all. By accepting that the world is constantly changing, leaders can scan the environment for ideas and trends. Liam Strong, Chief Executive of the retail chain, Sears, knows that he has to keep in touch with best practice and the latest management thinking. He does so through a network of friends and advisors scattered throughout the world, and he actively accumulates ideas. "I continuously collect them. At any given time I have a pile of cuttings and clippings. I like to stay up with what people are thinking – it is essential to have an idea of where things are moving."[17]

Organizations, such as Club Med, are always looking for new markets – as a result, it recognized the potential of Vietnam long before it was seen as a tourist attraction. Such initiatives have repercussions at team level, and by networking and keeping abreast of changes, leaders are in a position to seize opportunities and assess the risks and rewards associated with their work and that of their people.

Challenging convention

Adapting and managing the future requires leaders to challenge convention, to question the sacred cows of the organization, and to throw out rules and procedures which have been in existence for historic reasons rather than practical necessity. Initiatives such as Quality Management and Business Process Reengineering have played a major role in helping to challenge these issues.

Ford was one of the first companies to radically redesign its accounts-payable processes. It introduced "invoiceless" payment by paying suppliers when goods were received and not waiting for the suppliers' invoice as in the past. This netted Ford a saving of 75 percent. Phoenix, a US life assurance company, radically redesigned its contract processing work flow, cutting down the time to process a policy from a peak of 25 days to 24 hours.[18]

These ideas are practical, and testing and implementing them meant demolishing the sacred cows which so often hold organizations back.

Look at how Nissan dealt with the recession. Action was taken to protect the core workforce but, by the end of 1993, it was clear that the recession would continue. Most manufacturers, particularly in Germany, announced redundancies and lay-offs, but Nissan chose to challenge convention. Peter Wickens, then Nissan Personnel Director, describes how this problem was presented to the Company Council: "Operations Director, John Cushnagham and I met with the Company Council, fully explained the position and set in train a company-wide consultation process to see how we might handle the imbalance. Virtually every employee in the company was consulted, and the response which came back reflected the fact that everyone recognized that there were too many people to meet the 1994 volumes, and that the natural wastage policy would have to be accelerated. If this was done it should be done quickly, without compulsion and should be generous."

"The thing that amazed us," says Wickens, "was that given the full business information, the workforce came up with the optimum business solution. They had got there in one go and had presented a solution that management would not have put on the table, but might over the course of the several meetings have worked towards."[19]

Challenging convention means personally and remorselessly questioning **why** you and your colleagues do certain things. Is there a better way? Could you cut out processes? Do you need so many forms, meetings, structures and procedures? Challenging convention is about taking a few calculated risks and adapting or abolishing old and redundant practices, setting up new, more efficient ones in their place which enable performance to improve and develop.

Managing fear

It is one thing for a leader to demonstrate adaptability, but he or she must also be able to help people to manage and adapt to

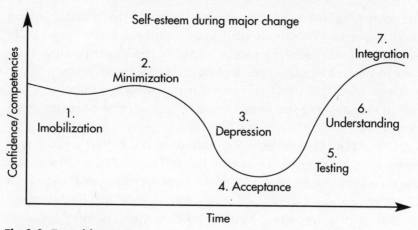

Fig 3.8 Transition curve
Source: Based on Adams, J D, Hayes, J, and Hopson, B, *Transition: Understanding and Managing Personal Change*, Martin Robertson, 1976

change. Understanding and overcoming resistance to change is vital. Figure 3.8 illustrates some effects change has on an individual's self-esteem. One of the most common fears among employees is the loss of job security. Research has shown that the survivors of downsizing initiatives not only fear for their own job security, but feel a sense of loss and guilt for colleagues who have been made redundant.[20] These fears are often expressed in different ways – low morale and other behaviours, such as working long hours, simply to be seen in the office.

Productivity fueled by fear is not usually accompanied by high performance. Zoe Thompson, Personnel Director of Anglia Railways, agrees that getting the best out of people in these circumstances is not easy, but by providing counseling, keeping staff informed and investing in training and development, her company is trying to convince employees that they are valued. Dealing with the fears surrounding "survivor syndrome," combined with the other fears in helping individuals to adapt to new changes in technology and business, is a leadership challenge in itself . It requires listening, reassurance, providing information, being honest and creating a vision of the future which everyone can buy into.[21]

Emotional resilience
It also demands what is labelled *emotional resilience*, something often now included in lists of management competencies. This is

not surprising when we consider that leaders have to take on more responsibility than ever before. FI Group's Steve Shirley says: "The constant need to rethink and relearn makes leadership a heavy strain, not least on one's natural inclination to be selfish. I've found that you need to be selfish and go beyond self. Healthy selfishness is about investing in your mind, body and spirit to ensure your own self-preservation and development. Sometimes you really have to dredge up the reserves from the depths . . . and then what frequently happens is that just when you seem to be getting over the worst a new set of problems conspire to test you again. It's rather like climbing triumphantly to the peak of a hill, only to find it isn't the top and there is a high summit again."[22]

Delivering

The "hard" side of leadership is the nitty-gritty of delivering results, achieving targets and managing resources. Delivering results means working through others, providing a clear vision and direction, communicating it, demonstrating commitment, achieving high performance and giving credit to those who achieve results.

Delivering comprises many elements:

- vision
- communication
- commitment
- results.

Vision

Creating a clear vision is often cited as one of the major aspects of leadership. A vision provides direction. It allows plans and strategies to be developed to achieve results and, most importantly, it can provide a clear picture which everyone can buy into.

IBM's definition of a vision is very clear: "In today's changing environment to have a vision is of the utmost importance. A vision shows direction, it is the lighthouse on the horizon. A puzzle is an even better analogy. You may have all the pieces of the puzzle, but without the picture of how the puzzle is supposed to look, it is very difficult to do. Action without vision is activity, vision without action is reverie, vision combined with action moves the world."[23]

The process of creating a vision requires using the right half of the brain, normally associated with creativity, music and pictures. This is not always easy when as managers we are taught to think in terms of facts, figures and analysis. Often to achieve this managers require a little help and stimulation. Many boards of directors have worked with facilitators – and with flipcharts and coloured pens – to create a picture or vision of where they want the organization to go.

AN EXERCISE IN VISION

Take a piece of flipchart paper and some pens. Decide what you want to vision about. Is it the team, the organization or yourself? Divide the page into two. On one side of the page draw the situation as you see it now and on the other side the situation you would like to see. Do not worry about not being an artist, use cartoons, shapes, diagrams, anything to represent the two scenarios. Allow yourself a chance to dream a little. Once drawn, look at the pictures. Describe what the changes are, and what the future looks like. This is your vision, and from here you can work out the details of transforming it into reality.

Obviously the dream, or vision, of the future needs to be supported by facts and arguments, and it is essential to get others to buy into it. This is where the art of communication comes in.

TIPS FOR COMMUNICATING YOUR VISION

When communicating your vision:

1 Let your feeling show. Use enthusiasm in your voice and project enthusiasm through your non-verbal body postures and movements.

2 Make liberal use of pictures, metaphors and other figures of speech to reach beyond the rational to the intuitive mind. Try to get them to add to your vision of the future.

3 Get a picture of the end-result clearly in mind: assume that your ideal outcome has in fact come to pass.

4 Find out the values, hopes and aspirations of others. You can better appeal to them if you know what "turns them on."

5 Stay with intangibles: avoid being specific, concrete or detailed at this stage.

Communication

"If the power of improved performance is to be fully released in an organization, the total workforce must be fully involved," says Coats Viyella CEO Neville Bain in *Successful Management*.[24] People have to understand the meaning of the vision in order to carry it out, and this communication must be on a macro- and micro-level in the organization. Leaders must personally communicate the vision to their people in a language which conveys enthusiasm and excitement.

Anita Roddick, founder and Managing Director of The Body Shop, believes that communication is vital. All outlets of The Body Shop are equipped with a video, and she regularly communicates with her staff about the projects, campaigns, and vision for the organization. She also visits stores, talks regularly with staff and operates a suggestion scheme. She is not just selling moisturizing creams, she is selling a global vision for a better environment, and all her employees are aware of this.

"If we want to treat customers in a way that ensures they come back and give us more business, then we have to treat our own staff in the same way," says Parcel Force, emphasizing the need for open management. Pat Hedges, Head of Internal Communications and Training at Parcel Force, describes open management as "freedom of expression between the people who work in the organization and those who manage it."

This has meant instigating such concepts as an internal communications network, new committees, training managers and attitude surveys and encouraging good relations between all levels of staff. "Now we are becoming more aware of both what they cost and what they generate. We're finding that people really love to know," says Pat Hedges.

As information becomes more readily available, communication channels will have to open up and secrecy will become a thing of the past. The benefits of openness seem to outweigh the risks and, as

Hedges says, "It's good commercial sense. Why pay managers when you can put the responsibility and authority where it should be?"[25]

However, internal PR machines will not work without the commitment of the leader to show support by communicating on a daily basis. This communication needs to be two way: top down and bottom up. Many organizations we have worked with have encouraged their leaders to communicate in a host of different ways, as outlined below.

- **Walk the talk** – be seen as someone who is ready to listen and communicate freely with others
- **Be involved with training programs** – have a slot in the day when you can to talk with the group and answer their questions
- **Have some social involvement with the organization** – be seen as someone who is approachable
- **Be honest in your communication** – do not fudge the issue or people will not trust you
- **Communicate via the organization's newsletter** – people will want to hear your views
- **Conduct site visits** – make sure you have time to talk with people at all levels
- **Set up team meetings** – help them to see the bigger picture
- **Listen well** – good communicators are good listeners. If you listen you will know just how to bring your message over
- **Adapt your style** – when communicating with different audiences.

COMMUNICATION AND YOU

Ask yourself:

- How do you communicate your vision to others in the organization?

- What opportunities could you take to improve your approach to communication?

- What benefits do you think it would bring?

Commitment

Communication and commitment go hand in hand. A leadership style which can convey commitment to others contributes hugely to achieving high performance and excellent results.

The Overseas Development Institute (ODI) when investigating the barriers to the successful implementation of total quality management (TQM) saw the absence of top management commitment as the most important barrier.[26]

Quality barriers	%
Top management commitment	92
Too narrow an understanding of quality	38
Horizontal boundaries: function and specialism	31
Vested interests	29
Organization politics	28
Cynicism	28
Organizational structure	27
Customer expectations	26
Speed of corporate action	24

Table 3.1: Quality barriers ranked in order of "very significant" replies

Jean Kvasnica, head of a multi-functional sales team at Hewlett-Packard, serving a major client, demonstrates the power of commitment. She has few traditional trappings of authority – no one on the team reports to her, so she does not formally evaluate performance or have an input into their pay levels. When asked how she motivates them, she responded: "They have to believe I know what I'm doing and won't waste their time." One of her team members commented: "Jean has vision and intense commitment to the successful outcome of the project, but the idea that makes it successful could come from anyone. She's not selfish about it."[27]

Commitment is not ownership. It is a belief and dedication which can help to empower others.

115

Results

Delivering high performance is every leader's aim. This may be performance in terms of profitability, service levels, quality or productivity. It may also be performance in terms of the development and growth of teams and their members.

Marco Landi was brought in from Texas Instruments to run Apple Europe in 1994. His overhaul of the European operation is achieving results. While the unit lost market share for the year, Landi halted the slide in the final quarter of 1995. Sales jumped 18 percent compared with an estimated market growth of 16 percent, according to research by Dataquest Inc. In the 1995 fiscal year, he tripled profits – turning in the best performance of any Apple unit in the world.

What is Landi's secret? He is reported to have a very clear focus on the basics of business, and is seen as a decisive leader, creating new structures and practices where appropriate. One of his decisions was to overhaul the Paris headquarters, replacing seven of the 12 managers reporting to him. "Apple is more and more professional. We still have fun, but we are much more customer-oriented," says Frederic Spagnou, an Apple Europe Manager. Yet, despite his drive, Landi is aware he cannot do anything by himself: "I know where I want to go, but I can't get there alone."[28]

Results are achieved by, and through, others, and leadership is about letting others share in the glory of the achievement. It is also about working with the team to set stretching and challenging targets, and ensuring that targets imposed on the team are achievable.

Phil Eaves of Crosfield Electronics was challenged with the task of turning the company's ten overseas operations into independent profit centers working within the group strategy. It was essential to develop a sense of local ownership and leadership. He worked with each of the local offices individually to develop and agree a clear operational plan, supported by a set of written objectives. These were formally reviewed on a quarterly basis. In doing so, Eaves ensured the empowerment of the local management team, and raised the profile of the goals and targets to all employees.

Self-understanding

To achieve high levels of performance and motivation from their team, leaders need to understand themselves and their impact on

116

others. They also need to be able to develop new skills and abilities, as well as juggling priorities and projects with the ease of a circus supremo. As one manager said: "I've got to set a good example to my people, and that means managing myself well. I'm now expected to coach my team and use new IT packages. I just can't afford to stop learning."

Liam Strong of Sears describes the business leader of the future: "Organizations will be more informal and workforces more challenging. One will lead from among rather than on top; it will feel more like a network than a hierarchy. Also technical skills will become increasingly more sophisticated and rapidly evolving."[29]

Leaders will have to hold their own with staff who are becoming increasingly expert. Strong goes on to advise that "leaders must be true to themselves." This means understanding yourself, your values, strengths and weakness, and learning to develop and work with them.

Self-understanding can cover a variety of elements:

- positive self-regard
- self-awareness
- self-development
- self-management.

Positive self-regard

Warren Bennis found that all the leaders he spoke with demonstrated positive self-regard. They knew themselves extremely well and emphasized their strengths. Even though they recognized their weaknesses, they did not dwell on them. Often they used others to counterbalance the skills they did not have, and refused to think of failure in a negative sense. Having made two major mistakes, William Smithburg, Chairman of Quaker Oats, said: "There isn't one senior manager in this company who hasn't been associated with a product that flopped. That includes me. It's like learning to ski. If you are not falling down, you are not learning."[30] The positive self-regard held by all the leaders provided inspiration and helped others to feel positive about themselves.

John Neal, who runs his own health and fitness company and is Fitness Conditioner for Middlesex County Cricket Club, points out

that in the sports field many of the really successful sports person-
alities have very positive self-images. Daley Thompson, the
decathlon gold medalist, never believed that he could lose. He
always thought that "when I'm competing I'm the best in the
world." If he did not win, he never felt that he had failed, but just
said: "I didn't perform at my normal level." This positive belief
that he really was the best in the world was backed up by a gruel-
ing training program. This self-belief is something which has
helped him achieve new personal bests and world records and, as
Neal points out: "It's the same with Viv Richards or Ian Botham.
When they walk out on the cricket pitch, it's not a matter of 'can I?'
But, 'How many shall I score?'"

One manager we worked with described a situation facing her.
"One day someone told me they were angry with me as they
weren't considered for a temporary promotion. We had a discussion. The fault was mine – I hadn't explained the situation to her
because I didn't feel I had time. I was quite confident that I had
done the right thing, but I felt guilty about the way I had handled
it and apologized. I wanted her to feel OK about coming to me and
expressing her views."

This manager clearly had a good image of herself. She was able
to take feedback, apologize and recognize her mistake, but equally
she demonstrated a sense of her own self-worth and certainty that
she had made the right decision

For some, developing a positive self-image is an easy concept, for
others it takes practise, recognition and real belief. In the sports field,
says John Neal, "players often use the 'Black Box' technique. A
player will initially think of all their weaknesses, visualizing each
dropped point, poor reaction, bad volley, etc. They will then put all
these pictures together and give them a shape. The shape will be put
in a black box, the lid tightly shut, and then the whole box will be
secured with chains and padlocks. Finally, the player will visualize
the box being thrown into the depths of the sea, lost for ever."

Such sports psychology can help players focus on their
strengths. In the same way leaders need to be aware of their own
strengths and abilities. They need to work with these and build on
them in a way that gives both themselves and others confidence in
their performance.

Self-awareness

Self-awareness is at the core of leadership, in terms of your own personal development and the impact and influence you have on others. As Harvard's Rosabeth Moss Kanter says: "Leaders must learn to operate without the might of the hierarchy behind them. The crutch of authority must be thrown away and replaced by their own personal ability to make relationships, use influence and work with others to achieve results."[31]

How do you see yourself? How well do you know yourself? If, like the leader in Bennis' study, you know your strengths and weaknesses and lead in a positive fashion, you will be setting the best example. Listen to yourself, analyze your leadership style and get feedback from other sources, colleagues, mentors, friends, questionnaires and courses. The more you listen to yourself – and others – the greater will be your ability to work with and understand others and bring about change.

Steve Shirley talks about how she consciously recognized her weaknesses and worked on them. "Leadership requires excellent communication skills. For a long time I was only really happy talking to people on a one-to-one basis. I had to learn the skills of talking to people in groups because it is by talking to groups that one can bring about change and get people buying in."[32]

For many people, focusing on themselves is a luxury. As one program participant said: "I've always been concerned with getting the job done. I now realize that I can get a better result if I focus on the process, how I achieve the end result, and that means focusing on myself and my impact on others.'

EXERCISING AWARENESS

An initial starting point is to list your strengths and weaknesses. Be honest and fair, and make sure that you have reasonably balanced list. Check the list out with others and add to it. A good way to do this is by taking the leadership competency questionnaire and asking some of your colleagues to fill it in for you. Make sure you sit down and get some verbal feedback from them, as the numbers alone are only part of the picture.

There is also a whole range of questionnaires and inventories which are used on development programs and in companies, and these can provide a wealth of data both about your behavior and personality. Many organizations also have their own identified list of managerial competencies, and use them to provide feedback to their staff.

The secret in using any of these approaches is to be open to the feedback. It is all too easy to be defensive or scared of the results when most inventories are designed to help you to recognize and build on your strengths.

If your organization does not have a recognized list of leadership competencies try to identify them by:

- Thinking of leaders in your organization who are successful. What characteristics, behaviors and skills do they have in common?
- Think about where your organization is heading. Will this require different sets of skills and behaviors?

Compare this list with your own analysis of your strengths and weaknesses and identify:

- What are the strengths you are bringing to the organization?
- Where can these strengths be best used?
- How can you develop them?
- What are your areas of weakness?
- Do you need to develop them? If so, how?
- Are there others in the team who have strengths you can use?

Self-development

Noel Tichy's study of transformational leaders showed that they have an enormous appetite for continual self-development.[33] Fiona Dent, responsible for self-development at Ashridge and co-author of *Sign Posts For Success – A Guide to Self-Development* agrees: "Managers have to take responsibility for honing and developing their own skills and abilities. This means taking advantage of opportunities in their whole life rather than focusing on a few days' training each year."

Sue Stevenson, Manager of Group Resources at Rank Xerox, attributes much of her success to her personal style. She has a strong network, both inside and outside the organization. She also tries to operate constantly with what she terms her "stretch zone" rather than her "comfort zone," and tries to enlarge this. She has kept a learning log for 15 years which she updates every night, learning by reflection and observation.

Another leader, Moira Holmes, Director of Personnel and Management at New Forest District Council and President of the Society of Chief Personnel Officers, looking back on her career feels that, while qualifications are important, she learns a lot more from action and that opportunities for interesting development projects are important. Holmes thinks about her development quite consciously, and realizes that an important source of learning is observing others. She acknowledges that she has had a number of influential managers and mentors throughout her career. She also identifies networking and reflection as ways in which she continues to develop herself.[34]

SELF-DEVELOPMENT CHECKLIST

- Read widely – biographies of leaders, self-development books, business magazines and journals can spark ideas.

- Keep a self-development journal – recording your progress, successes and failures can help you to keep track of what you need to do to develop.

- Watch management videos – you can pick up a lot of tips from seeing how others work and think.

- Listen to tapes – there is a wide variety of business tapes and usually ample time on the road to do some development while *en route* to your next destination.

- Attend courses/conferences. Even one-day events can provide you with a wealth of information and a network of people with whom to share ideas.

- Learn from mistakes – reflecting on why things went wrong can provide valuable insights.

- Spend time reflecting – a few minutes reflecting and conducting a personal learning review can aid the development process.

- Be curious, ask questions – learning is a life-long activity and curiosity is a valuable tool.

- Develop parallel skills – responsibilities outside work can provide leadership experience.

- Build a network of contacts who can support your development.

- Develop a mentor – spending time with someone who can act as a listener, advisor, coach and teacher.

Self-management

When managing and leading others, one of the greatest challenges is that of managing yourself. The *Ashridge Management Index* identified this as a problem for many of today's managers. Indeed, 77 percent of respondents to the survey saw work as a source of stress, 63 percent felt there was conflict between the role of parent and role of manager, and 59 percent felt under pressure to develop and learn new skills. The same report highlighted that 47 percent of the managers in the sample frequently worked more than 60 hours per week, and 60 percent frequently took work home. With such a pressurized lifestyle, it is more important than ever before for managers to manage themselves. This means managing time and creating the right balance in life.[35]

Sir John Harvey Jones recognizes the importance of managing self and balancing priorities: "I will always need to believe that my work is worthwhile and of value, but now I know that there are many other things in my life which matter more. This feeling freed me to tackle risks and to stick to my belief in ways which I now realize actually made me more likely to move ahead rather than the reverse."[36]

Stuart Friedman, reporting in *Financial Times* Mastering Management, part 3, identifies three competencies business professionals need to have in order to balance their work and their other life interests.[37] These competencies have to do with values, roles and relationships and performance and planning.

1 Values – knowing what counts and acting on it

- Clarify life priorities, purposes and values.

- Be aware of the choices you can make and the trade-offs involved.

- Act in a way which is consistent with your values.

2 Roles and relationships – getting support from others to say "no"

- Proactively build relationships, networks. Create trust, goodwill and common ground.

- Take risks by communicating your needs and feelings.

- Let go of control, delegate and develop a comfort level with ambiguity. Clarify the boundaries of your different life roles and identify areas of integration and differentiation.

3 Performance and planning – be responsible about what you can do whilst thinking ahead

- Anticipate and plan for all areas of your life.

- Identify goals for the future and select activities which will get you there.

- Recognize that you do not have to give perfection all of the time.

- Develop good time management skills.

- Remember to give time to yourself and others.

If you manage yourself, you have more chance of making your own life, and that of others, successful and fulfilling. As a leader, self-management skills are essential if you are to develop the stamina and emotional resilience now required by organizations.

Time management is a continual fight for many managers, and there are endless books, courses and videos which aim to help them find the Holy Grail. Yet the reason many managers continually fail in this area is that they fail to start by identifying their values, and what is really important to them. If you can identify your values and then bring them in to your long- and short-term goals, and then into your list of priorities and daily "To Do's," time management becomes a lot easier.

Fig 3.9 Value-based time management

AN EXERCISE IN TIME

1 Identify the things you value. You may want to take examples from the list below or add in your own:

- work
- family
- friends
- personal time
- health
- relaxation
- fitness
- learning
- career.

2 Identify a long-term goal associated with your values. For example, you might place a high value on career and learning, and want to do an MBA in the next three to five years. Or perhaps you value health, and want to lose 5kg over the next year. If you have a young family, your goal might be to see them grow up and spend time with them each day.

3 The task now is to break up the long-term goal into smaller pieces. For example an individual looking into the MBA might set a goal of collecting all the business school prospectuses over the next month. Someone wanting to lose weight could set a manageable monthly weight loss target, and the family-oriented person could find out all the dates for school holidays, plays and events for the coming year and plan around them.

4 Finally, incorporate these goals into the daily "To Do" list.

When you have identified your values, long- and short-term goals and brought them into your daily life, then it is time to pick up a time management book and adopt the most appropriate techniques to suit you.

LEADERSHIP THROUGH PEOPLE

Leadership through people is about recognizing that the boundaries between leaders and followers are becoming blurred. Leadership is spreading throughout the organization, and exists at all levels. With this in mind:

- High-performance organizations need to recognize and develop leadership as a skill.
- They need to recognize that leadership can no longer be left in the hands of a few people.
- They need to provide appropriate training, coaching and development opportunities to encourage leadership at all levels.
- They need to provide an environment which offers the right combination of support and challenge, so that people feel valued and encouraged in their work.
- They need to recognize that for successful leadership, people need to develop the whole spectrum of leadership competencies.

Leadership cannot be taught. It must be continually developed, honed and adapted to the organization and its environment. The concept of leadership and the notion of "leaders all" is crucial to the success of organizations as they move into the knowledge era.

References

1. Shirley, S, "How to give reality to vision," *Management Today*, April, 1995
2. Kouzes, J M, and Posner, B Z, *Credibility*, Jossey Bass, San Francisco, 1993
3. Binney, G, and Williams, C, *Making Quality Work*, Economist Intelligence Unit, London, 1992

4. Rebello, K and Burrows, P, "The fall of an American icon," *Business Week*, 5 February, 1996
5. Burns, J M, *Leadership*, Harper & Row, New York, 1978
6. Binney, G and Williams, C, *Leaning into the Future*, Nicolas Brealey, London, 1995
7. Bennis, W and Nanus, B, *Leaders: Strategies for Taking Charge*, Harper & Row, New York, 1985
8. Caudron, S, "Create an empowering environment," *Personnel Journal*, September 1995
9. Nayak, P R and Ketteringham J, *Breakthroughs*, Mercury, London, 1987
10. Hanks G F, "Excellence teams in action," *Management Accounting*, February 1995
11. Sadler, P, *Managing Talent*, FT/Pitman, London, 1993
12. Crainer, S, "Man of paradoxes ponders progress," *The Times*, 17 February 1994
13. Bennis, W, and Nanus, B, *Leaders: Strategies for Taking Charge*, Harper & Row, New York, 1985
14. Crainer, S, "Escape from an industrial Jurassic Park," *The Times*, 14 October 1993
15. Barner, R, "Enablement: The key to empowerment," *Training and Development*, June 1994
16. Wilson, A Holton, V and Handy, L, *Ashridge Management Index 1994/95: A survey of management opinion*, Ashridge Management Research Group, 1994
17. Tait, R, *Roads To the Top*, Macmillan Business, London, 1995
18. Omrani Danesh, "Business Process Re-engineering: A business revolution?," *Management Services*, October 1992
19. Wickens, P, *The Ascendant Organisation*, Macmillan Business, London, 1995
20. Doherty, N and Horsted, J, "Helping survivors stay on board," *People Management*, 12 January, 1995
21. Ibid.
22. Shirley, S, "How to give reality to vision," *Management Today*, April 1995
23. Quoted in Binney, G and Williams, C, *Making Quality Work*, Economist Intelligence Unit, London, 1992
24. Bain, N, *Successful Management*, Macmillan Business, London, 1995
25. Jackson, S, "Open management – empowerment to the people?," *Director*, April 1991
26. Binney, G and Williams, C, *Making Quality Work*, EIU, London, 1993
27. Sherman, S, "How tomorrow's leaders are learning their stuff," *Fortune*, 27 November 1995
28. Edmondson, G, "A blueprint from Europe," *Business Week*, 5 February, 1996
29. Quoted in Tait, R, *The Road to the Top*, Macmillan, London, 1995
30. Bennis, W, and Nanus B, *Leaders: Strategies for Taking Charge*, Harper & Row, New York, 1985

31. Syrett, M and Hogg, C, (eds), *Frontiers of Leadership*, Blackwell, Oxford, 1992
32. Quoted in Tait, R, *The Road to the Top*, Macmillan, London, 1995
33. Tichy, N Devanna, M A, *Transformational Leadership*, Wiley, New York, 1990
34. Fonda, N, "Take me to your (personnel) leader," *People Management*, 21 December 1995
35. Wilson, A Holton, V and Handy, L, *Ashridge Management Index 1994/95: A survey of management opinion*, Ashridge Management Research Group, 1994
36. Harvey Jones, J, *Making it Happen*, Collins, London, 1988
37. Friedman, S, "Developing a work life balance," *Financial Times Mastering Management*, Part 3, 10 November, 1995

◆

"To love and to work, Sigmund Freud once remarked to his disciple Erik Erikson, are the twin capacities that mark full maturity. If that is the case, then maturity may be an endangerd way station in life."

Daniel Goleman[1]

◆

Chapter 4

◆

THE NEW CONTRACT

The nature of work is being transformed and so, too, are our expectations of the relationships between people and organizations. The old psychological contract between employer and employee offered security of employment in return for loyalty. Now, with no job secure and loyalty harder to earn, a new psychological contract is emerging which places a premium on mutual support and development.

OUR CHANGING WORLD OF WORK

Expectations: The shifting scene

The changing landscape of work is beset with contradictions and paradoxes. Companies are loosening the bonds that tie them to individuals while, at the same time, taking a tighter hold. As businesses restructure, delayer and downsize, they are demanding more and more of their people. This contradiction is manifest in the widening gap that many perceive between the rhetoric of empowerment and the frustrating and bruising reality of work.

"We are demanding more loyalty and commitment from those we employ, while we undermine their support structures and job security," observed Ewart Wooldridge in a recent article.[2]

The impact on individuals of the changes that have taken place in recent years has been described as the "intensification of work."[3] Intensification brings stress and pressure. Amid the growing tension, managers must devote attention and time to the psychological impacts on those they manage – and themselves.

What is required is a new contract which addresses the present ambiguity and confusion. This calls for fresh thinking and clarification of all the unspoken expectations about work, a fundamental rethink and reframing of the many relationships involved.

These new relationships appear unclear and intangible. Traditional job definitions, responsibilities and expectations are thrown into disarray. In the words of Rosabeth Moss Kanter: "We must recognize that there is no longer the luxury of business as usual."[4]

For managers reared on a diet of clarity, the new contract is messy territory. There are neither neat legalistic solutions, nor a single standard form. Instead, the new contract deals with the beliefs people hold about what they are expecting to bring to and to take from their working lives; their implicit expectations; as well as their hopes and fears. None of us wish to engage in fruitless endeavor or inauthentic relationships, yet many of us feel this is precisely what we are involved in.

The new contract requires managers to tackle head on the issues of recognition and respect, support and security, allegiance and trust. Without trust there is no contract, yet trust is precisely what is being undermined by the changes taking place.

Facing up to reality

For many people the new contract seems not only unclear but also unfair. There is an obvious mismatch of expectations and needs which many companies and managers have yet to face up to. Given that change is now an omnipresent fact of business life, this is a startling omission.

A recent survey of 1,800 business leaders in Canada, France, Germany, Japan, the United Kingdom and the United States, found that four-fifths of all managers surveyed worked for companies that had been involved in major restructuring of some kind in the past two years[5]. Of these, two-thirds thought that the rate of change would continue at the same pace or faster into the next century. "Company reorganizations, therefore, are no longer isolated events that companies go through and put behind them. Rather, they are becoming a permanent process in businesses throughout the world," the survey concluded.

Corporate change is running in parallel with significant demographic changes. The children of the 1960s baby boom have become firmly ensconced in the working population during the 1990s. By the turn of the century, the number of potentially employable people will have risen by around one million in the UK alone. In the US, the 78 million "baby boomers" constitute the largest sector of the working population today, and experts have estimated that a proportion of these will start "retiring" (from full-time employment at least) over the next five years.[6]

Contrast with this the observation that during the same period, numbers of school leavers, in other words the next generation of potentially employable people, will have decreased by 25 percent. While this might seem at first sight to be a short-term solution to unemployment, it has deeper repercussions.

The ageing workforce, caused by roller-coaster birthrates in the 1960s and 1970s, is beginning to worry some institutions and companies. A report on the OECD countries, for example, has warned that by the year 2040, one person in five will be retired, one in ten over the age of 75, and there will be only three people of working age to support each pensioner.[7]

Some of our deepest assumptions about the ideal worker, the ideal work arrangement, the ideal career and what constitutes working life are not just challenged by these changes, they are brutally overthrown. Changes seem to be occurring at a faster rate than we can cope with. We are still working to adjust our minds, never mind being ready to introduce effective employment frameworks for dealing with them.

We have mentioned the intensification of work manifested in a number of ways – longer hours, less security, the threat of technology, career interruptions and instability, more complex relationships and tougher performance challenges. Not surprisingly, many people find this intensification alarming. They feel threatened as they watch technology arrive, functions and empires disappear, "rungs on the ladder" become fewer and careers less certain.

All kinds of interim deals are being struck as we are forced to accept the new, while desperately attempting to hang on to the old. In Germany, for example, auto-manufacturer Ford has successfully negotiated with the IG Metall (metalworkers' union) to increase the working week of its members by two and a half hours without increasing wages. In return, employees will be able to amass the time and bring forward their retirement.

Deals like this do not fully reflect the new economic realities. We cannot afford to be in both the new world and old world at once. The best of both worlds is an industrial mirage. Work is intensifying because competition is intensifying, the rules of the game are getting harder, and all parties must come to terms with the redefinition of the rules. Employers cannot continue with the heavy cost structures that they have created; people cannot expect the luxury of many of the benefits they have grown used to if the numbers do not add up. We must break away from the societal and work culture of dependency that has developed over the last 50 years to become more resourceful, flexible and creative in our response.

Embracing the new contract

Undoubtedly, many people consider the new contract a poor substitute for the traditional relationship between employer and employee. According to the rhetoric, the new contract offers flexibility, challenge and opportunity for the individual to carve growth opportunities and develop their own potential while making a measurable contribution to the goals of the organization.

In return, managers of the new contract need to deliver their part of the deal, which means not anticipating unquestioning loyalty or lip service throughout many years of service; not expecting people to put up or shut up when they believe the company is being mismanaged; not expecting people to accept being assessed by the one person who has the power to influence how much they are paid and where they can go from here; not expecting people to put in more and take out less.

If we are to create a basis for working together, and a fabric or context in which this is a satisfying experience, the new contract must form the foundations for an enduring relationship of mutual respect and commitment for however long that relationship lasts.

Embracing commitment

Bruce Tucker, an American writer on management, spent many years tracing and researching the families of the men who were featured in William H Whyte's book *The Organization Man*.[8] One story in particular caught Tucker's attention, that of Scott Myer, son of one of the "organization men." During an interview, Myer explained "that he worked in order to develop his skills and to meet personal challenges, and that when his job stopped contributing to his self-development, he would leave."[9] Indeed, he left the interviewer in no doubt, by saying: "I have no loyalty to the company. I'm in it for me."

Upon reading the article, his CEO, a member of the "organization man" generation, interrupted a business trip to phone his second-in-command and order Myer to be fired.

In the event, Myer pre-empted his dismissal by leaving to set up his own company, taking several like-minded colleagues with him. At the time, opinions were very much divided between those who thought such disloyalty inexcusable, and those who respected Myer for refusing to toe the political line and pay lip service to something he did not believe in.

Tucker notes: "In the light of that story, the differences between the generations may be summed up in two words: loyalty versus commitment. The organization man values loyalty to the company; his children value commitment to a profession. For the organization man it's 'my company, right or wrong'. For his children it's 'my company right for me or I'm gone.'"

In reality, many people are caught in the middle of these generational shifts. As a result, companies need to help develop attitudes in those who lack the confidence, experience and context to identify with something other than "the company." Embracing commitment means identifying with yourself and your profession, and seeing the world of work in terms of employability, instead of employment. To do this, individuals must have a frame of reference and a web of relationships that is wider than any single organization.

Under the old contract, the organization-employee relationship was founded on parent-child interactions, where the parent gave the orders and the child obeyed. With the new contract there is an adult-adult relationship. Both parties are equal partners, both are bringing something to the table which the other party wants. The relationship is interdependent, not dependent.

Robert Waterman draws our attention to this shift: "People mourn its passing: the long time covenant between employee and employer. We remember fondly the days when IBM could offer lifetime employment. And even if we didn't work for the likes of IBM, most of us understood that respectable companies would offer at least a measure of job security in exchange for adequate performance and some exhibition of loyalty."[10]

In Waterman's view, the new contract takes the form of a "new covenant" drawn up by employer and employee, under which both share the responsibility for improving and maintaining the latter's employability, inside or outside the company. The result, he says, is a group of self-reliant workers or a "career-resilient workforce" – employees who are not only convinced of the need to learn new skills and competencies continuously, but who are also ready to re-invent themselves to stay in touch with the changing employment market. From this can emerge independence, a necessary precondition for interdependent relationships.

Embracing independence

Many people find that professional bodies, which are increasingly encouraging career independence in their members via advice on personal networking and marketing, provide useful support. The approach has been summed up as "making yourself more memorable" and involves speaking the part, keeping in touch, being visible in the industry and taking time out to re-energize.

The brightest and the best have been quick to realize the potential opportunities the new contract provides, and are investing in making and keeping themselves attractive. Even so, the shift in attitude is significant. Charles Handy has recounted how the societal shifts, which he describes in his writing, have personally impacted him: "I was in my late forties when I realized that I was going to have to change if I was to fit the times ahead. I was, it seemed, running out of jobs. I had got as far as I was going to get in my chosen profession. Even if I wanted to mark time for 15 more years in my present role, it was extremely unlikely that I would be allowed to do so. Younger people were both cheaper and more up-to-date, and huffing and puffing about age discrimination was not going to change that basic fact. I concluded that I would have to rethink my assumptions about my career, my way of life and crucially my finances if I wanted life to go on being an interesting and rewarding experience."[11]

For those who are less confident and more isolated, a catalyst may be needed to help stimulate this new independence. Organizations can promote constant learning and knowledge-building by the training, development and career frameworks they use. They can stimulate personal networking to take people out of the box, by deploying people horizontally and putting them in touch with the outside world. These links can be essential: one manager described to us how personal networking helped her survive the loss of two jobs, one from a reorganization and the other from downsizing.

While they cannot guarantee jobs for life, forward-thinking organizations are helping to equip their people for the uncertain future which lies ahead. Of paramount importance is the need to minimize the negative impact of "survivor syndrome" which is often the result of a delayering or downsizing drive.

Companies which are serious about this are using their networks of strategic alliances and partners to practice what the Japanese call *keiretsu*, encouraging employees to seek development opportunities outside the immediate organization, through secondments, MBA sponsorship or consultancy projects. Others, such as Microsoft, McDonald's, Intel and Motorola, for example, not content with sending their high-flyers to public universities, have their own internal universities to ensure that continuing education and development is not only available to *all* employees, and relevant to their personal goals, but also tailored to the organization's strategy and the individual's workplace.

Career independence brings with it greater career choice. Companies which want to attract talent must have something alluring to offer. This requires more fundamental initiatives than brightening up recruitment campaigns – and relates back to Chapter 2, where we discussed linking the work of individuals to the aspirations and style of the whole operation. In order to attract the right people, more organizations will have to recognize that today's customer may well be tomorrow's employee. This means sharpening the way they market themselves and ensuring a consistent approach right across the board.

ADAMS UK: RECRUITING PEOPLE TO MATCH THE BRAND

In the early 1990s, staff at Adams UK, the British children's clothing retailer, like those in many other service sector organizations, were bored. They routinely stood around in dull, unimaginative stores. They were uninspired; their environment uninspiring. Facing competition from rivals like the US-based Gap Kids, it was no wonder profits were declining.

The situation was becoming untenable, and it led to a major rethink of the brand proposition and the place of people in the organization. Market research in schools revealed that, contrary to the desires of their parents, children "didn't want to go shopping for clothes at all. If they did go shopping, they certainly didn't want to try clothes on."

To make the stores a more attractive place, Adams devised a schoolroom theme. With bright colors, traditional toys and games, and kites hanging from the ceiling, the new stores are very different from the old.

Paul Wiggins, Human Resources Director, described the challenge on the people front: "We were determined to make sure that as a customer walks into the shop, everything matches and the staff match the brand."[12]

This meant running workshops to inspire and change the mind-sets of existing staff. One-third have embraced the new concept with gusto, one-third are learning fast and around one-third have left.

To attract new recruits who could live the new brand, Adams' advertising uses the schoolroom theme and a blackboard motif. This has attracted high-caliber applicants. Some even play along with the theme – one drew a picture of herself on the front of her application.

Embracing flexibility

"We are all . . . the children of yesterday's times. Discontinuity in careers was not part of those times, nor were portfolios of different sorts of work," says Charles Handy.[13]

He estimates that by the year 2000, less than half the potential workforce within the industrialized world will hold full-time positions within companies. The rest will be self-employed, part-time or temporary workers. Even now, a mere quarter of those involved in making a product or producing a service are actually employed by the organization.

In itself, of course, the concept of temporary work is not new. The construction industry, hotel trade and many other industry sectors have always covered their needs for expertise and extra capacity by taking on contract or freelance workers, flexing the numbers they employ according to demand. Some occupations have always had to accept flexible working and career breaks, coming to terms with interruptions to their work life, which have rarely been voluntary. What is new is that a way of working that was previously confined to very specific sectors is becoming far more widespread, as companies struggle to be more flexible and competitive and respond to demographic shifts.

The number of women returners, re-entering the workforce with the qualifications gained before motherhood, is expected to rise dramatically between now and the turn of the century. Many companies have already responded to women's need for flexibility in their working lives and are themselves gaining the benefit of flexibility in return. One organization which has recognized the influx of women returners as an opportunity is National Westminster Bank. Having understood the impact that a career break has on one's pension contributions, NatWest now offers women "the portable pension." With this type of pension, premiums may be paid as and when the woman is working and can afford to pay them, and stopped for unlimited times when she cannot.

AVON COSMETICS: WELCOMING RETURNERS

Paul Southworth, President of Avon Cosmetics Ltd (UK) estimates that of the new entrants to the job market over the next five to ten years, 80 percent will be women returning after child-rearing. Southworth adds: "The majority of organizations have yet to realize this fact and prepare themselves for the demands it will make on them in terms of flexibility in working hours, employment terms, location of work and use of technology."

Virtually 100 percent of Avon Cosmetics' customers are women. It is perhaps not surprising that Avon is particularly conscious of its obligation to its female employees as well as its customers. Avon is constantly working to improve its maternity (and paternity) policies to facilitate the return to work for those who wish. Key employees are offered a PC and a telephone link at home for the duration of their maternity leave. They may do as little or as much work as they like during this time. On their return to work, parents are given childcare vouchers so they may choose how best to care for their child during working hours.

Three years ago Avon set up an after-hours course, aimed at women who had been absent from the workplace for some time. The course, called New Direction, is non-profit-making (course members pay a modest fee to cover costs), and is open to all women regardless of where they plan to work. It aims to help women develop skills they are likely to need in any career, be they interview skills, assertiveness or presenting themselves with confidence. Since it started, the course has helped over 300 women; of these, 70 percent are now in employment again.

ATTITUDES TO CAREERS

Along with career independence comes the idea of the career break. This can either be within a company in the form of secondments or sabbaticals, or can be taken by individuals who see work as one option in a whole array of life choices. This begs the question, What is a career?

- What does the word "career" mean to you?

- What constitutes a successful career?

- What constitutes an unsuccessful one?

Zig-zag careers

How has your view of a career changed over the last ten years? For the latter half of the century, most people have been working in some mix of functional and divisional organization in which every job is defined and classified in a job structure which is linear and hierarchical. This was a way of ordering a world full of apparently unchanging certainties, and marked the epoch of the upward company career. In this kind of structure, managers typically saw a career as something which was closely linked to status, job title, upward mobility and "perks." For them, the very word "career" was also frequently synonymous with other things such as long hours, being "married" to the job, and the ability to be ruthless in pursuit of bottom-line results.

These job structures were usually accompanied by manpower, career and succession plans, which defined not only each person's current box, but also mapped out a sequence of moves into other boxes. Many fondly believed that the personnel or HR department were dealing with their career development, and were happy to trust the arrangement despite obvious cracks in the system. In the worst instances, people were not even consulted about plans for the future. One manager told us of his personnel department's plans to send him to its Japanese plant for three to five years *without his knowledge*. The discussions, which continued for six months, reached an advanced stage before he was even interviewed for the job or his opinion sought.

In the last few decades, market pressures have increased as customers demanded both more efficiency and more responsiveness.

This led divisional organizations to centralize some of their operations into strategic business units, and functional organizations to add project structures to their basic form. The age of the "mixed" organization had arrived, typified by the term "matrix." It was designed to be responsive to customers' needs, enabling new products and services to be brought rapidly to market by utilizing the knowledge, skills, and particularly the creativity of their people.

The flexibility this implied marked the beginning of the end of the company career. This need for flexibility has accelerated through the 1990s, and many businesses recognize that it is their prevailing job and career structures that are slowing this down. Apple Computers has never taken a paternalistic approach to employee career management. Apple states plainly in a career management brochure that it cannot guarantee lifelong employment, and that employees are responsible for driving their own development and careers. Apple's partnership approach to career management is intended to help employees identify skills and abilities, preparing them for advancement opportunities.

As new ways of managing careers arrive, we are witnessing the demise of the old structures. Gone are the years of the quick learner's fast-track sponsorship, climbing rapidly to the top of the organizational pyramid. The new contract requires self-reliance on the part of employees. This means that people must take charge of their careers. Many are discovering that this is more of a zig-zag than an upward climb.

NETWORK CAREERS IN SYNTEGRA

Syntegra is the systems integration business of BT (British Telecommunications plc). As a prime contractor, Syntegra orchestrates all the information and communications systems needed to enable its customers to make fundamental changes to the way their businesses work, so they are more effective and competitive. The organization is a catalyst: a combination of consultant, integrator and change manager.

As part of a move to recognize the shift to more networked organizations and different ways of managing people's performance and careers, Syntegra uses a framework to help people understand how careers will develop within the new and rapidly changing work environment. With this understanding, they are able to recognize and exploit the opportunities which arise, thereby taking responsibility for their own careers. The ideas are presented in a booklet which is given to people when they join.

The booklet explains the concept of the network career and gives individuals a visual tool to see themselves at the center of their personal career network. Looked at this way, careers are about multiple opportunities, parallel activity, flexible directions, conflicting pressures, interconnections, work and life and, most importantly, individual ownership.

Gwen Ventris, Organization and Resourcing Director, says: "In networked organizations, careers cannot progress in a normal way. The network career concept is a powerful way for each of us to come to terms with the changes taking place in our lives today. With new ways of looking at our careers, we can equip ourselves to make the most of tomorrow's opportunities."

The framework emphasizes that work must be seen as part of life, and places people at the center of a "network" of career influences defined as four major types: Experiences, People, Drivers and Opportunities.

As individuals we are at the center of a "network" of experiences and opportunities, whether we recognize them or not. Consciously or subconsciously, we seek to reconcile these experiences and opportunities with our personal needs, and with those factors which drive us in a particular direction or act as constraints.

Examples of career influences are: achievements, projects, skills, family, teams, anchors, values, ambitions, vision and rewards.

Our careers start with a small network with a few connections/influences, reflecting our early choices, experiences and opportunities. Over time, influences vary as opportunities arise or disappear and experience grows or becomes less relevant. People, opportunities and experiences become inextricably linked and, inevitably, our career network becomes very complex, combining many different, and possibly competing, influences. Syntegra encourages people to see themselves as part of many networks. These may be formal, like a project team or informal, like the players in a squash league. Such networks provide immediate access to information and influences of all kinds, and are very much a part of the network careers vision. In addition, Syntegra has a range of systems and tools in place to help realize network career management in practice. Examples of these are:

Career anchors

At Syntegra, people can work out their career anchor via a questionnaire, as part of a Career Anchor workshop.

Personal development plans

PDPs are essentially about increasing skill through a planned mix of appropriate training courses, self-paced learning, and work assignments. To put together an effective plan requires a realistic view of the opportunities for which we seek new skills. A network career vision, plus an understanding of our career anchors, can help to map the future and the past and provide a realistic "aiming point" for development.

Generic skills profiles

Regular skills reviews use a generic profile to provide guidance for an individual's skill development planning. Used in conjunction with a skills effectiveness framework, this provides a number of generic skills profiles which can act as signposts to guide skill development in an appropriate direction.

To be successful in a network career, it is essential to believe that success is in the hands of each individual and to:

- un-learn old notions of what a career is
- understand ourselves (where we are and how we got here)
- look for opportunities
- not measure success by status or grade
- not expect someone else to do it for us.

YOU AND YOUR CAREER

A career is clearly something which is wrapped in a very personal mantle, one person's "progression" might be another person's standstill or stagnation. Think for a moment about yourself and reflect on your own career.

- How many conscious career decisions have you made in your working life to date?
- On what basis have these decisions been made?

- Who else had input into these decisions?

- How effective have you been in implementing these decisions?

- What constraints are you faced with?

- How many of these are self-imposed?

- In what ways are you ensuring your own self-development?

- Could you exploit your present position more to develop yourself?

- How much do you rely on the actions of your HR department to steer your career for you?

- What are the implications of your answers to these questions?

The influence of technology

In 1982, Jacques Servan-Schreiber, Head of the World Center for Computer Sciences and Human Resources, suggested that technology would be responsible for 50 million job losses worldwide by the year 2000.[14] The reality is quite different.

It is not so much the numbers of jobs which have been affected as the nature of the jobs which have been created. Gone are the days when factories took on unskilled laborers in their thousands, and paid them not to think, but to carry out repetitive, physically demanding tasks. Now, people are expected to think about their work, focus on their internal and external customer needs, and be accountable for the quality of their work.

In 1986, Rupert Murdoch caused turmoil in the UK print industry with his decision to introduce new technology. Opposed by the print unions, he sacked thousands of printworkers and replaced them with sophisticated printing machinery.

The printworkers who moved with Murdoch to the new premises in London's Docklands were required to acquire high skill levels to operate the new machinery and, as a result, are now among the most highly paid in the industry. Not only this, the quality of the print has improved dramatically through the use of the new technology, in ways which would have been inconceivable under the old manual procedures.

The experiences of the printing industry have been replicated across the board. After all, how many purely manual jobs can you now think of which require no thought or information processing?

In the late 1980s, German automotive factories producing components and cars were still recruiting foreign workers, "gastarbeiter," who were unable to speak a word of German. To qualify for work, they only needed to fulfill two criteria: pass a statutory eye test and demonstrate a willingness to do shift work. The nature of the work has since changed so much through investment in information technology, that even the simplest tasks require basic computer skills and enough German to understand the commands and error messages on the machines, and health and safety signs.

A study in 1986 by McKinsey in Amsterdam suggested that by the year 2000, 70 percent of all jobs in Europe, and 80 percent in the US, would require cerebral rather than manual skills. The McKinsey report also stated that 50 percent of these jobs would require a degree or equivalent professional qualification.

The current number of school leavers across Europe continuing with their formal education falls way short of this target. In the UK around 18 percent of school leavers go on to higher education, and the figure for the rest of Europe is only slightly higher at 20 percent. A severe skill shortage over the short to medium term appears inevitable.

The failure to embrace the information age wholeheartedly will have a much greater impact on the work opportunities open to young people than on the generations before them. Competition for the educated is intensifying, and the future for the unqualified is grim. "Knowledge workers are winners precisely because a business job is only one of their options. They are winners because they can choose," observes Peter Drucker in *The New Realities*.[15]

Creating the human context

All the talk of commitment, empowerment, and taking charge of ourselves and our destiny overlooks two fundamental things. First, people are social as well as individual beings and second, before we can rise to self-realization, we have to satisfy more fundamental needs.

People have a human need for security which is not just financial or material, it is also a need to belong, to be involved with other people in relationships based on mutual trust. Our view is optimistic, but not naively so. The information age is not suddenly going to begin the age of human happiness.

"These millennial years are ushering in an age of melancholy, just as the twentieth century became an age of anxiety . . . each successive generation since the beginning of the century has lived with a higher risk than their parents of suffering a major depression – not just sadness, but a paralyzing listlessness, dejection, and self-pity and an overwhelming hopelessness – over the course of life," noted a recent book. [16]

One of the most striking and disturbing features of work is the low levels of trust and loyalty shown by people toward each other, and particularly toward their managers. People can work together every day and not reveal personal or sensitive information, or seek support in times of difficulty and vulnerability because of these low levels of trust.

Trust requires networks of communication. Three types of informal networks operate at work – chat lines, knowledge lines and trust lines. A survey at Bell Labs revealed that successful management of *ad hoc* or fluid teams relies on working all of these networks. This requires high levels of social intelligence, in addition to other skills such as an ability to feel empathy and generate rapport and commitment. These will be important dimensions of managing the new contract.

"Knowledge-based competition will demand more of us, not less, and, ironically, the requirements for committed involvement in work will increase in parallel with the insecurity associated with it," says Richard Pascale. "Rather than teach ourselves to care less, imagine that we can somehow shield ourselves from the bonding and self-identification that committed work inevitably entails, we must face a harder and more demanding truth: namely, that healthy resolution lies in inner wisdom, not external arrangements."[17]

It is these human qualities, drawing on our strength and maturity, which are essential in creating a climate that enables people to perform.

Creating a high-performance climate

ORGANIZATIONAL CLIMATE QUESTIONNAIRE

This questionnaire is designed to provide information about the climate that exists in your work team. You will be asked to respond to 20 descriptive statements. Please take your time and respond to all statements.

Please indicate the extent to which each of the following statements is true. Select the answer choice that best reflects your feelings about each statement and write the number representing that answer in the box to the right of the statement. The answer choices are:

5 Totally true   4 Mostly true   3 Somewhat true/somewhat false
2 Mostly false   1 Totally false.

Consider your work team to consist of yourself and your co-workers.

A. Performance agenda

1 I clearly understand the performance agenda, objectives and goals of my work team □

2 The objectives of the team have been clearly related to the objectives and intent of the wider organization □

3 I am clear as to what is individually expected of me □

4 I understand how my performance affects the overall success of my team and connected teams □

B. Expectations

5 The expectations for my performance are challenging yet realistic □

6 Managers emphasize the importance of constantly striving for greater results □

7 There is an expectation of excellence in the work that I do □

8 My work team is continuously challenged to deliver exceptional performance □

C. Enablers

9 I have been able to complete tasks more simply and/or with clearer results because I have been able to make changes □

10 I feel that my work efforts and time are well spent □

11 It is relatively easy to have new and innovative ideas considered □

12 I am encouraged to take calculated risks □

D. Feedback on contribution

13 I am justly recognized and rewarded for my good performance, ☐ rather than simply being criticized when things go wrong

14 I am recognized when I am doing good work ☐

15 I have no difficulty seeing the contribution that results from my per- ☐ formance

16 In my work team, people are rewarded in proportion to the qual- ☐ ity of their contribution

E. Commitment

17 I am willing to make personal sacrifices if it will enhance the ☐ achievement of my work team's goals

18 I am a member of a high-performing work team ☐

19 I take pride in my work team and its performance ☐

20 Delivery excellence is valued by my work team ☐

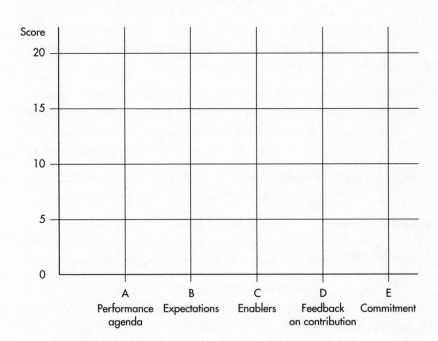

147

Scoring

Total the scores in each section and plot them on the graph above.

Enabling performance through climate

The work climate is simply defined as how the workplace feels to those working in it.

Many factors in the climate influence performance – for better or for worse. The physical setting, the inter-relationships between people, the way responsibilities are distributed, the extent to which communication is open and decision making shared, are just some of the factors that influence how people feel. The questionnaire looked at these in the following groupings:

- **Performance Agenda** – the clarity with which people perceive group goals and objectives and the individual work goals within this.

- **Expectations** – whether people believe that management hold high expectations for their performance; includes the extent to which they are encouraged to work toward challenging goals.

- **Enablers** – how far people perceive that they are free to perform their work in a manner that they feel is appropriate; includes the extent to which they are allowed to make needed changes, simplify tasks and incorporate new ideas in order to perform better.

- **Feedback on contribution** – the confidence people have that they will be recognized and rewarded for good performance.

- **Commitment** – the extent to which people feel that they are members of a high-performing team; includes the extent to which personal sacrifices will be made to deliver exceptional results.

In developing an environment for people to flourish and perform, you may wish to make some changes. Changing the climate means examining your own motives and attitudes, and having a willingness to adapt yourself to benefit relationships in your group.

Be aware of the **chill factors**, the things which can adversely affect the climate. Understand how to **assess climate** and think about the **steps to improving climate** in your work environment. The following tips and checklists will help you to do that.

CHILL FACTORS

Are you:

- communicating mixed or conflicting messages ?
- overloading some people with too much responsibility and underloading others?
- failing to recognize the unique skills and abilities of people and the work they are best suited to?
- failing to involve people in decisions that affect them?
- failing to involve yourself with the concerns of others or to communicate concerns of your own?

HOW TO ASSESS CLIMATE

1 Look at the way work is allocated: does it allow for initiative, or will some people feel boxed in?

2 Look at the organization's intent: what is its direction? Are people aware of and signed up to this?

3 Look at how your people get on: is there friction or not? Do people understand where their contribution fits in with those of others?

4 How do your people feel about you? Are you open to new ideas? Do you ignore their real motivations and goals? Do you seek contributions from everyone?

5 Check out people's responses regarding climate by giving others the climate questionnaire.

STEPS TO IMPROVING CLIMATE

1. Create a dialogue

Ask people "What is it like to work here?" Ask for ideas on how things could be improved.

2. Create a shared vision

See that people participate in forming the goals of your group, and that the overall objective is shared.

3. Make changes to the physical environment

Improving the physical work space is tangible evidence of your intentions to make things better. Do not overlook the significance of symbolic changes.

4. Create systems and processes that enable a positive climate

If you ask people to come up with ideas, make sure you set up a framework to capture them, for example, ideas bulletin board, weekly reports or regular brainstorms. Do not tell people you want a change and then not enable it.

5. Consider reassignments

When someone's aspirations correspond with what you want to be performed, then the energy put into achieving results will be high. Consider who does what. Does this take advantage of the abilities and interests of the people involved? Would someone else be more interested in performing a particular task?

Most people will feel some kind of security and trust, and will respond positively to uncertainty if they:

- have faith in the people guiding the business
- support and believe in the business direction
- identify closely with the business values
- feel they have a valuable contribution to make.

The art of managing the new contract is to create the climate for people to have high octane experiences, where they become so involved in what they are doing that they feel that it is a part of them. We have already said this is about creating a human context, but it is also about responding perceptively and sensitively to all kinds of information and subtle cues about how people feel about what is going on.

The challenge is to harmonize widely different sets of expectations with each other and with the intent of the business, harnessing energy and channeling it towards exceptional outcomes at the personal and business level. This requires emotional maturity, allowing yourself to be instrumental in enabling the achievements of others. As one leader told us: "If you take the glory, it's gone."

THE NEW CONTRACT AND EXCEPTIONAL PERFORMANCE

Some companies have recognized already that there is a desperate need to align their performance management approach to the new sets of expectations implicit in the new contract. Several dimensions are key:

- the need to relate more clearly the individual's contribution to overall company goals, as the new contract is forged with individuals and contains many expectations about performance;

From: the old contract	To: the new contract
Loyalty to the company	Commitment to the current project
Working towards "golden handshake" and company pension	Individual employee works as if self-employed
Large, traditional companies offered steep hierarchies, "automatic" promotion and guaranteed career paths	Companies striving to become an employer of choice need a social conscience and proof of investment in people
Employment for life	Employability
Pay based on seniority/longevity	Pay based on contribution
Regular promotion up the functions	Variety and challenge across the functions
Incentives based on visible evidence of career advancement, level and status within organization (larger office, car etc.)	Incentives based on personal reputation, expertise, teamwork and challenging projects

Figure 4.1 The differences between the old and the new contract

- the need to recognize the blurring of discrete job boundaries, which means that performance outcomes will be increasingly defined in terms of the achievements of project teams;
- the need to manage performance in situations where people have multiple roles and are delivering to multiple stakeholders, such that a single manager no longer has the information needed to assess outcomes;
- the need to accept that self-managing, career-independent people will no longer so readily accept the authority of others in shaping and assessing their work.

There has been a flurry of activity around these issues in recent years. One major study of organizations implementing performance management initiatives in the UK asked why the initiatives were being implemented. Apart from the obvious desire to improve performance, the next most frequently cited drivers were a desire for improved individual participation and better internal communication of the vision. If all these things are achieved, the result will be a positive culture within the organization, and a positive image of the organization from the outside.[18]

The survey also asked about the tangible benefits, perceived by the organization and individual employees. The following list shows eight of the most frequently cited benefits:

- improved retention rates
- better time management and reduced costs
- awareness of skill gaps
- helping attract better people for management positions
- assisting in restructuring by clarifying accountabilities
- increasing people's sense of personal value and self-esteem
- enhancing the individual's perception of control/empowerment
- identifying poor performers.

Taking action to address the performance agenda has helped these companies retain and develop their most valued staff, by fostering individual recognition, identifying individual strengths and building targets and objectives into the expectations of the contract.

Redefining performance in the new contract

Organizations are becoming more sophisticated; they now realize that there is more to high performance and succession planning than moving names in organizational boxes. At the same time, they are realizing that individuals would not accept the high-handed behavior which was common ten years ago. They are beginning to pay more than lip service to the fact that "talent is the only remaining scarce resource."[19]

However, it is still only a beginning. There is a huge difference between an organization saying it values people as a scarce resource, and demonstrating that it does. How can you, as an individual, tell the difference? One way is to ask people why they are leaving, why they are voting with their feet. What efforts are being made to stop scarce resources from walking away and offering their services to the highest bidder or from becoming a competitor?

One of the issues many organizations face is the absence of a common language for defining and measuring new areas of performance. The prescriptive job and reward structures we mentioned earlier, with their rigid and narrow definitions of roles, are one of the main barriers to this. To prosper in the years ahead, businesses will have to cope with thinking more broadly in terms of flexible roles and activities. These flexible roles can only be described by their relationships with other flexible roles. The situation is even more complex than this implies, because so many people now have more than one role. In the course of even half a day, an individual may well switch hats once, twice or even three times. For example, changing from leader of a design team, to trainee in client negotiations, to mentor of a new recruit.

The new frameworks must allow people the flexibility to think of performance in terms of these complexities, and as something fluid and emerging. Navigating through this context with the aid of clear accountabilities and objectives will not always be possible. The uncertainties shaping the world of work will also shape performance. We can expect to face challenges when not only the problem, but also the solution is unknown. There are a number of lessons to be drawn from the world of business operations. Here, initiatives such as reengineering and benchmarking, have encouraged a process perspective which makes what is happening and about to happen as transparent as what has already happened.

Transparency makes it much easier to influence performance and to make real-time improvement. Once you can see what is happening, you can begin to do something to change it. You can take out any unwanted steps, find better ways of sequencing them, or see where you can change the activities by exploiting technology. Then, you can identify measures to track the improvements. How can this apparent return to mechanical time and motion studies of the production era be reconciled with moves towards empowerment? There is no comparison because the person doing the studying is the person performing the task – there is no overseer or supervisor with a clipboard and stopwatch.

When looking at the outputs of the performance management process, the tendency is to focus solely on the financial results, and the goods and services sold. We believe that there is a need to consider other, more subtle outputs, such as success factors and risks, and expectations about benefits for customers and the people involved. It is often true that these can only broadly be specified, but they need to be included nevertheless.

Exceptional performance depends on the human talent that is brought to bear on the projects, the activities and processes that those individuals undertake. As we saw in Chapter 2, to deliver exceptional performance you cannot just equate people with resources and think about them in a detached way. We can no longer take the traditional route, separating people and their human interactions from the work that they do.

In managing the new contract, we have to remember its mutual basis, and be geared to meet the needs of more than one customer. At its extreme this means seeing yourself as a supplier, delivering your managerial skill and influence to the performance of those you are managing. This is precisely what upward appraisal is all about.

Managing people with the new contract

The new contract places a premium on the performance that each individual delivers. The expectation of exceptional performance goes hand in hand with the notion of employability. Harnessing the capabilities of each person in such a way that the overall result is more than the sum of the parts, requires us to frame performance more holistically than we did in the past.

You need to be "capable of working with increasingly individual-ized needs, while simultaneously retaining a strategic perspective."[20] This means understanding and interpreting the organization's intent in such a way that you bring it alive and inspire your people to buy into it. It also means recognizing that you cannot separate perfor-mance from the context of the organization in which it takes place. The aspirations and expectations of the organization and the individ-ual must be harnessed in a continuous process of mutual development. "One of the main issues is to ensure that the vision is not something people do in workshops on Thursdays – but it is some-thing you do all the time," observed one manager.

Building the performance agenda

There is a need to develop a clear performance agenda, linking individual and organizational goals. For example, at Avon Tyres, the employees' individual objectives reflect the corporate goals and are directly related to the five-year plan set out by the focus factory. Individual and team objectives relate to overall outcomes including environmental friendliness, workplace improvement, efficiency gains and waste reduction.

Monsanto Chemical Group used the concept of accountabilities to ensure that for every work assignment, individuals understand what it is about and where it fits into the strategy as a whole. People can now see how they contribute to what the organization has set out to achieve.

MONSANTO CHEMICAL GROUP[21]

In 1986, the acquisition of GD Searle signaled that the Monsanto Company had changed direction. Its future lay in biotechnologi-cally derived products and human health care. The speciality chemicals, plastics and fibers produced by the Chemical Group, which had been the core business, were suddenly peripheral – its main role now was to generate cash through an ambitious target of achieving a return on equity (ROE) of 20 percent.

The staff found the situation bewildering; one commented that she felt "as if someone had blindfolded her and rearranged the furniture." The challenge for management was to remove the blindfold, turn on the lights and let the always moving furniture become visible.

The Human Resources Group responded to this challenge by generating a new approach to managing people, an approach founded on three radical principles:

- employee performance cannot be managed, people have to be liberated and empowered to perform
- we rely on knowledge workers – developing them is the only viable strategy
- we should manage the context in which performance occurs rather than performance *per se*.

To reflect these beliefs the new approach was christened the Performance Enhancement Process (PEP). At the core was a new human resource strategy based on development. It focused on building and enhancing those competencies most critical to developing the core competency of the organization, as well as the individuals in it.

PEP has changed the nature of performance discussions. These now focus on:

- accountabilities: why a particular job exists and a listing of the fundamental deliverables which will make a difference to the company
- goals: the specific accomplishments which derive from these accountabilities
- how they may best accomplish the accountabilities and goals.

A competency model has provided a common language which anchors these discussions in a developmental framework. For example it allows people to talk about and agree the specific combination of knowledge, skills and behaviors that they will need to bring to bear on a *particular assignment*.

Figure 4.2 illustrates how the competency "customer focus" is defined using the stages model.

The stages model of career development[22]

This approach shows four stages of career development:

1. Helping and learning
2. Contributing independently
3. Contributing through others
4. Leading through vision

It is widely used to help people think about activities, skills and relationships in a broad way. It is based on the assumption that careers do not necessarily develop these sequentially. It is quite possible for a research scientist, for example, to be at stage 4, when devising a research program, but only at stage 1 or 2 in when building customer relationships.

Helping and learning	Contributing independently	Contributing through others	Leading through vision
Has basic knowledge of customers (internal and external) and their needs; is responsive to customers	Actively seeks customer input; anticipates customer's needs and effectively meets them; seeks feedback to ensure customer expectations are met	Helps others understand customer's needs; develops effective partnerships with customers; models good customer relations; seeks ways of improving customer service and building the customer base	Fosters culture and organization systems that entrench customer service as a key value

Fig 4.2 Customer focus defined using the stages model
Source: 'Performance Management in a Changing Context: Monsanto Pioneers a Competency Based Developmental Approach,' Jones T, *Human Resource Management*, © John Wiley, Fall 1995. Reprinted by permission of John Wiley & Sons Inc.

The same competency framework allows people to: self-assess their performance against the agreed profile; receive and act on 360 degree feedback about their performance; plan and assess development, and set objectives for continual coaching.

Each individual is now the chief architect and owner of their career development and performance enhancement plan. The role of the supervisor has changed – a supervisor now acts as sponsor and coach, removing barriers and providing resources and supports where required.

Monsanto's initiative demonstrates how it is possible to find a way of helping to focus on both the short and the long term. The new performance enhancement process recognized the need to manage people to deliver exceptional performance today, while developing the capability to compete in the future.

While we support the view that inputs are key measures which must not be neglected or overlooked, it is unusual to find an organization which focuses on them to such a degree. In our view, the output measures are equally important. (This theme, together with more detail on the measurement of outputs, is picked up in Chapter 6.)

The case also illustrates how Monsanto Chemical Group, in common with many other organizations, has developed a framework based on the concept of competencies and the stages model of career development to generate a common language. As a result the onus for development has been shifted from the line manager, to the individual involved.

Bringing vision to life

Bringing the vision to life can only be done by practising what you preach. To do it successfully, you have to be very clear in your own mind about what this vision is, and about how you and your people can contribute to it. Can you verbalize this now?

If you have this clarity, you will be able to work through the process described in Figure 2.9 and by working through the questions below, you will be able to translate the vision into individual actions.

FROM INTENTION TO ACTION

- What is the overall vision for your business unit/team?
- How can you translate this into goals?
- Then for each of these goals take a view on the key success factors – i.e., the few critical things you have to get right in order to succeed with this goal.
- Next, think about how you are going to subdivide them amongst your people. To do this, ask yourself the following questions:

- What knowledge and skills do we need?
- Who is available and what can they bring to the party?
- Who would be interested in this?
- Where do we need to develop competence?
- How can we create leverage with other initiatives?
- How can we build capability for the future?
- What are the risks and benefits for each of these options?
- How shall we pull this together?

Building the performance agenda means remembering that if it focuses solely on business goals and priorities, they are unlikely to be fully achieved. Success is more likely if the agenda is built and shared out to individuals in a way that takes account of their experience, capabilities, skills, knowledge, career aspirations, development needs and personal circumstances.

Your objectives need to be focused on outcomes rather than vague actions. As you will see in Chapter 6, they need to focus on a wide range of measures, such as customer satisfaction and staff motivation, as well as the traditional financial yardsticks.

The new performance relationship

Just as exceptional performance is implicit in employability, then so is a more developmental style implicit in new expectations of management.

HAVE YOUR RELATIONSHIPS CHANGED

Which of the following statements best describes your typical behavior?

Do you:	Do you:
Create and maintain a "them and us" power situation	See yourself as a partner in pursuit of a common goal
Extract obedience	Encourage autonomy and provide space for empowerment

Set performance criteria and measure how well they are met	Let people set their own performance agenda and measure their own performance against this
Focus only on maximizing "bottom-line results" at all costs	Focus on ensuring that tasks are interesting and challenging
Punish failure or below-average performance	Encourage risk taking in the name of innovation and problem-solving
Show no empathy for employees' problems or concerns	Partner in problem-solving based on shared concern and shared information
React negatively (doubt, anger, blame)	Give constructive feedback and demonstrate active listening based on fairness and understanding
Protect information and "trade secrets" from others	Share information and trust people to use it well

What does this say about you and your style?

Thinking developmentally

Managers with a developmental philosophy believe that the key added value they bring to their organizations is their ability to help people learn, grow and develop. The purpose of this learning and development – to enhance the performance of the individual, the manager and the organization as a whole – is clearly understood.

Such managers are unlikely to pigeon-hole people into high performers (As), average performers (Bs) and those who will not make any progress (Cs). Instead, they believe that everyone wants to do a good job and to be well thought of. Realizing the risk of self-fulfilling prophecies, they do not readily categorize people as poor performers. Instead, they tend to think in terms of performance issues and recognize that anyone who is under-performing is likely to be unhappy with the situation.

DO YOU HAVE A DEVELOPMENTAL STYLE?

How often do you:

- talk to your people about how you can help them develop on the job?
- see opportunities in routine work and projects you hear about through your network to develop a specific individual in a particular way?
- think in terms of As, Bs and Cs?
- communicate your positive or negative expectations through your behavior? For example by:

  - being more attentive to As than to Bs?
  - entering into more eye contact with As than with Bs?
  - giving As more positive and less negative feedback than Bs?

- criticize performance without asking yourself:

  - could it possibly be due to something you are doing, not doing, assuming or taking for granted?
  - could you be doing a better job of setting or communicating objectives?
  - are you checking for understanding?
  - has the problem arisen suddenly?

- consider whether another manager would see the same poor performance as you, and interpret it the same way
- consider whether you could be exaggerating the problem
- ask yourself how you can help the person to want to perform better

EVOLUTION AT PHILIPS SEMICONDUCTORS

Philips Semiconductors, Southampton, produces integrated circuits (ICs) for consumer applications, such as teletext and compact discs, and is part of the worldwide Philips Group. It has restructured several times since the late 1980s.

Recognizing that the company's future is dependent on its ability to meet the short-term demands of the business now, while building the capability to develop and launch new innovative new products in the future, Philips Semiconductors launched the "Organizational Evolution" in 1993. With this came the new "teaming" structure shown in Figure 4.3.

This structure aimed to strengthen the customer and business focus by ensuring that each new product development activity was run as a "bounded box" project, with clearly defined budgets and timescales and a named cross-functional team leader. The cross-functional teams (CFTs), with members drawn from different functional skill groups, report in to a product sector team (PST). Each product sector team focuses on customer satisfaction and their product portfolio. The overall needs of the business are balanced by the New Product Review Board (NPRB). Recognizing the risks of focusing exclusively on short-term business imperatives, Philips Semiconductors has kept in place a functional structure to counterbalance the new operational focus.

The organizational evolution has not stopped at structural changes, it has also meant a wholesale shift away from the command and control culture, where a person's value was based exclusively on research activity. The new organization stresses that " value can be defined in terms of depth *and/or* breadth of expertise. The business needs therefore must value specialists, leaders and generalists."

Aware that hollow statements are inadequate, the company has inculcated the philosophy of continuous on-the-job development through a program of coaching workshops. These workshops, which emphasize the need to tailor development to the needs and aspirations of the individual, have been attended by managers at all levels and have been highly successful in changing the way people think and behave.

According to Richard Phillips, who designed and ran the coaching workshops at Philips Semiconductors: "A committed manager as coach displays evidence of *all* the following characteristics:

- a true developmental philosophy
- they see learning taking place primarily on the job
- the process is focused on the learner's learning, not the coach's teaching
- their style is usually, although not always hands-off, however they are able to switch to a more directive style when needed
- they recognize that their own knowledge and skills need not limit the learning
- they need to be comfortable setting objectives and with their ability to review progress and give feedback."

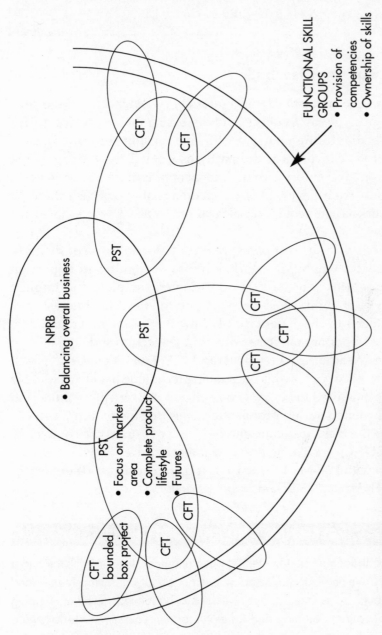

Fig 4.3 Teaming at Philips Semiconductors
Source: Philips Semiconductors

In the words of one senior executive at Philips Semiconductors, "Our company ethos promotes the view that "we must value our people as our greatest resource," consequently, programs such as coaching which support this have enabled the human resource development process to be actively realized."

Performance and feedback

Many people are distinctly uncomfortable when it comes to reviewing progress, giving feedback, and discussing the way forward. This is partly due to the manager-staff relationship set up under the terms of the old contract, and partly, as we will see in Chapter 6, it arises from discomfort with traditional appraisal systems. Whatever the reason, we believe that feedback on a continuous basis throughout a work assignment is crucial. Without feedback we cannot adjust and grow.

Obviously, your own perceptions of risk and those of the individuals with whom you work, will have a significant impact on the boundaries you draw. However, even complete and implicit trust in their ability does not abrogate the need for interest: you always need to check periodically how things are going, and here there are important overlaps with your leadership style.

Craig Weatherup, President and CEO of Pepsi-Cola North America describes how his questioning technique has changed. "My first question used to be, 'Are you going to deliver your volume and NOPAT [net operating profits after taxes] for the month?' You can imagine the messages that sent. Now the questions are completely different: 'Are we giving great customer service? How is our relationship with Wal-Mart? Where are you on coaching and support for sales?' The focus is much more on the doing."[23]

RECEIVING AND GIVING FEEDBACK

Good feedback must be founded on open and honest communication and a genuine developmental philosophy. It is not about attributing blame, and there should be no need to justify what has happened. To avoid slipping into justification, you may find it helpful to limit yourself to the following questions when receiving feedback:

- Do I understand it, or do I need a second explanation?
- Is it valid?
- Does it have a real impact on my effectiveness?
- Do I want to act on it?

Equally, when giving feedback, the guidelines below will help you to avoid attributing blame.

The feedback should:

- be factual and specific – which means supporting it with evidence (for example, a description of what was said or done when dealing with behavior)
- identify the consequences
- be balanced, looking at good things and areas for improvement
- be owned.

The all-round 360-degree view

Numerous organizations are now using 360-degree feedback to help people see the impact of their behavior on others. Research at Ashridge Management College[24] shows that companies find this method far more effective than traditional appraisals at middle and senior levels because it provides the honest and accurate feedback which is normally difficult to acquire when the person is near the top of the organization.

It can be a formal system, where tick-box competency forms are handed out to an individual's boss, peers and subordinates, and the results collated. However, if your organization does not have a formal system, you can introduce a more informal process of two-way communication.

W H Smith introduced 360-degree appraisal five years ago. Managers choose the people who will appraise them, and they are measured against their own state of objectives and the firm's required skills. "It tells the real story, it gives an accurate picture and gives a helpful list of things people need to do to improve," says one senior executive at WH Smith.

The first step is the hardest – creating a climate where it is acceptable to give feedback. Actually eliciting feedback from your subordinates or peers, and showing them you are prepared to listen and act on their feedback, requires a climate of trust and mutual respect, as well as good interpersonal skills.

Chris Bones, Human Resources Director at United Distillers (UD), used the 360-degree approach as part of a wider change initiative after the company's acquisition by Guinness. "We stressed the appraisal would not be used to review performance, and the results are confidential to the individual," he says. People participated on a voluntary basis, and so far about 100 of UD's top managers world-wide, have taken part. Mercury One to One has decided not to make the information confidential to the individual, believing that open-ness is the best approach. So far, this seems justified, with individuals saying it is the best review they have had, and managers saying it is the best development review they have been able to conduct.

Asking your team members for help in changing the way you manage ensures that they feel included in the change process, and are more likely to buy into your desire for self-development and improvement.

It is often a painful process but, if handled positively, 360-degree feedback can be a powerful vehicle towards self-development. The results can form the basis of a wide variety of personal-effectiveness measures – from routine progress reviews through to career development, skills training, coaching and mentoring.

Review at the end of an assignment

Equally important is the review at the end of a work assignment, which needs to encompass all the objectives set at the outset. The conclusions of these discussions should be used when reviewing overall performance and should form a significant input into discussions about future activities.

THE NEW CONTRACT

Many of today's managers come from a generation which expected job security, regular promotions and pension rights. In return they were prepared to pledge their loyalty, diligence and functional exper-tise. There is a great well of resentment among this generation of managers, as they feel that their organizations have let them down.

In place of the old contract there is a new, less secure arrangement, under which the employee agrees to flexibility, responsibility, accountability and commitment for the duration of the arrangement. The organization, for its part, offers constant challenge, opportunities for self-development and a salary based on merit rather than seniority. Ironically, these new expectations, allowing as they do for many variations of the new contract, may reduce the need for the brutal and total severance which has characterized recent years.

The changing expectations of individuals and organizations are summed up by Peter Herriot and Carole Pemberton: "Careers are becoming more complex sequences of actions, based on choices and constraints, which can take an individual from the core to the periphery and back again."[25]

To prosper, businesses need involvement from people which enhances the value of the product or service. This involves thinking as well as doing. People also need to feel involved in the environment of their workplace, in their product or service, and in the decisions which affect them directly. One manager said: "If people are involved, they can't use others as scapegoats, and they have to own and work with the decisions they participate in."

Much of this book is about responsiveness, the ability to exploit new and emerging opportunities. It is not only businesses that thrive in this way, it is also people. Career independence and employability are about responsiveness at the individual level. They prepare each of us to be well-positioned against the uncertainties ahead.

As human beings we fear many things, and among the things we fear most is freedom. Much of the stress and anxiety that accompanies the changing work landscape stems from this fear and our challenge in making the new contract authentic is to face it and transcend it.

References

1. Goleman, D, *Emotional Intelligence*, Bloomsbury, London, 1996
2. Wooldridge, E, "Time to stand Maslow's hierarchy on its head?", *People Management*, December 1995
3. Undy, R and Kessler, I, IPD Conference, Harrogate, 1995

4. Moss Kanter, R, "Change in the global economy: an interview with Rosabeth Moss Kanter," *European Management Journal*, Vol 12, No 1, March 1994

5. Watson Wyatt, *The People Factor – A Global Study of Human Resource Issues and Management Strategies*

6. Ibid.

7. Handy, C, *The Age of Unreason*, Century Business, London, 1993

8. Whyte, W H, *The Organization Man*, Jonathon Cape, London, 1957

9. Quoted in Tucker, B, "The New Individualists and the Human Resource Challenge of the 1990s", GDI Impuls, Nr. 2, Switzerland, 1993

10. Waterman, R, Waterman, J and Collard, B, "Toward a Career-resilient workforce," *Harvard Business Review*, July–August 1994

11. Handy, C, *The Age of Unreason*, Century Business, London, 1993

12. Quoted in *Financial Times*, 15 September 1995

13. Handy, C, *The Age of Unreason*, Century Business, London, 1993

14. Quoted in *Computerworld*, Fromingham, Mass., 24 May 1982

15. Drucker, P, *The New Realities*, Butterworth–Heinemann, Canada, 1994

16. Goleman, D, *Emotional Intelligence*, Bloomsbury, London, 1996

17. Pascale, R, Euroforum 20th Anniversary Conference, 15–16 September 1995

18. "Performance Management in the UK: An Analysis of the Issues," IPM, 1994

19. Sadler, P, "Gold Collar Workers: what makes them play their best?," *Personnel Management*, April 1994

20. Herriot, P and Pemberton, C, "Psychological Contracts: A New Deal for Middle Managers," *People Management*, June 1995

21. Jones, T, "Performance Management in a Changing Context: Monsanto Pioneers a Competency-based, Developmental Approach," *Human Resource Management*, Vol 34 No 3, Fall 1995

22. Dalton, G W and Thompson, P H, *Novations – Strategies for Career Management*, Scott, Foresmen and Co., London, 1986

23. Garvin, D, "Leveraging processes for strategic advantage," *Harvard Business Review*, September–October 1995

24. Devine, M, "360-degree feedback," Ashridge Management Research Group, 1996

25. Herriot, P and Pemberton, C, "Psychological Contracts: A New Deal for Middle Managers," *People Management*, June 1995

"In the field of group endeavor, you will see incredible events in which the group performs far beyond the sum of its individual talents. It happens in the symphony, in the ballet, in the theater, in sports, and equally in business. It is easy to recognize and impossible to define. It is a mystique. It cannot be achieved without immense effort, training, and co-operation. But effort, training and co-operation alone rarely create it."

Dee Hock, former Visa chief executive[1]

Chapter 5

◆

TEAMS OF TEAMS

In the past, *individual* performance and behavior was the focus of measurment and appraisal, and management development concentrated on individual development areas. Now there is an abundance of teamworking models for learning organizations, suggesting that learning and sharing of knowledge is best done in teams. With more and more organizations committed to teamworking, there needs to be a shift in focus from individual to team effectiveness and from individual to team development.

WHY TEAMWORK?

Teamworking means different things to different people. To some, it may involve breaking down barriers and encouraging communication and information-sharing between departments. To others, it means totally restructuring the organization around projects or business processes, and introducing cross-functional teams to run them. The teams may be permanent or temporary, they may have a leader or be self-managed.

The variations are endless, and despite the range of approaches, one thing is certain: a team approach is here to stay. Why?

- It improves quality and productivity
- It improves service
- It decreases operating costs
- It encourages innovation and flexibility
- It helps to exploit information and create new business opportunities
- It simplifies job structures and flattens hierarchies.

It improves quality and productivity
"Boeing used teams to cut the number of engineering hang-ups on its new 777 passenger jet by more than half."[2] To achieve this, Boeing reorganized its Seattle operation into over 200 cross-functional work teams, each responsible for a particular part of the plane, such as the flap or the wing. The creation of airplane integration teams to ensure good communications between, for example, the wing team and the cockpit team significantly reduced the scope for design glitches and improved the quality of the final product.

It improves service
The reporting lines imposed by Bayer corporate headquarters in Germany dictate the salesforce structure at its UK subsidiary. Historically, in the UK Polymers Division, for example, this has meant three separate business groups selling their own products independently into the automobile industry.

At the extreme, you could conceivably find three different sales people each carrying a business card sporting the Bayer UK logo, each representing a different product group, meeting the same buyer on three separate occasions to talk about the same piece of business.

With the 1994 launch of its Vision 2000 initiative, Bayer plc recognized the synergy that comes with teamworking. Ray Kaufman, director of Polymers Division, explains: "Imagine the difference if all three sales people approached the customer together, or one person represented the three product groups. That way we would be able to lock into the customer and build a truly creative partnership more cost-effectively."

It decreases operating costs

In its bid to gain a reputation with its customers for world-class manufacturing, BAe Defence Division has been totally reorganized around empowered teams. There are now integrated production teams and integrated design and development teams. These, combined with a team approach to total production maintenance and process improvement, have helped the business achieve major benefits. Between 1989 and 1995, inventory was reduced from £65 million to £12 million, and lead times from 84 weeks to 10. Productivity levels have typically increased by 35–45 percent and there have been significant improvements in cash flow.

It encourages innovation and flexibility

When Lars Kolind became President of Oticon, the Danish hearing-aid manufacturer in 1988, "he found an 84-year-old company going to sleep forever in the high-tech market dominated by giants like Siemens, Philips and Sony."[3] By 1995, new products were coming to market at an unprecedented rate, among them – the self-adjusting multi-focus hearing-aid – a world leader. Sales had grown to $100 million and Oticon held 15 percent of the world market. How was it achieved? Oticon demolished the company hierarchy and replaced it with multi-disciplinary project teams. According to Kolind, the aim was to "make everybody accept they could do more than one job and switch between different tasks and projects that would be changing all the time."

It helps to exploit information and create new business opportunities

Federal Express' philosophy "People – Service – Profits" means that everyone identifies strongly with the needs of the customer, and thinks of customers as part of the team. Says Dr Ron Ponder, Senior

Vice-president for Information and Telecommunications: "The notion of picking up and delivering a package without being able to offer the customer total information on it is totally unacceptable to us."[4]

This attitude to customers, combined with the constant search for new ways to use technology and information, has allowed Federal Express to identify a stream of new opportunities, such as those exploited by the Business Logistics Services (BLS) Division.

BLS is a high value-added business. According to Bob May, its President: "What we sell is integrated logistics solutions . . . we facilitate the thought process on how to do business in a different way. Distribution and logistics systems are very capital intensive and take a long time to build. We've found that firms have a tendency to try to make their existing systems work. But that's not necessarily the right way to go about it.

We work back from what our customer's customers want. We ask them: 'Can you help us define what you would see as superior customer service?' We prepare a flow chart for the complete supply chain and examine how much value there is at each link in the chain . . . in order to create a high-value, high-velocity system that is responsive to our customer's own evolving marketplace.

The components of a solution might sometimes seem a little mundane – a truck, a plane, a warehouse, a normal Fed Ex delivery, an information system, a process control center – but the way you link these services together becomes a unique solution for the customer."

It simplifies job structures and flattens hierarchies
In 1991 the outlook for K Shoes, an autonomous subsidiary of the C & J Clark Group, one of the UK's best-known shoe manufacturers, was grim. Faced with a declining turnover of around £100 million and over-reliance on a declining domestic market, the company introduced teamworking. Realizing the need to present a unified face to its customers, K shoes restructured the sales function. It believed its sales people should be:

- multi-talented
- commercially aware
- professional and well prepared
- skilled administrators
- conceptual thinkers

- team players
- strategic in the extreme.

K Shoes believed it had individuals who could satisfy some of these criteria, but no one who could satisfy them all. In order to introduce the notion of cross-functionality, it eradicated the posts of regional managers, senior reps and specialist reps, and replaced them with three business development teams, all reporting to one national manager. This action, combined with a move to team-working in manufacturing and the building of closer links with fewer suppliers, has been instrumental in turning the company around. By 1995, turnover was growing, with exports accounting for 37 percent of business. The future was looking rosier.

According to Robert Perkins, Head of Manufacturing, the bene-fits are clear: "Managing a business in the 1990s using traditional methods is extremely hard. Empowered teamworking spreads the workload, improves focus and accountability and allows managers to look ahead."[5]

Reflect for a moment on your own experience of teamworking.

- **Where has your organization used teams?**
- **What was the reason for introducing them?**

Given their huge potential, it is no wonder that teams and team-working have been so high on the corporate agenda since organizations in the West imported the concept of quality circles from Japan. What is surprising is the number of organizations which have yet to introduce this work practice in any consistent way. After all, teamworking has been touted as the most effective way to deliver exceptional performance for over 15 years.

Many of the managers we meet are committed to the concept of teams, and are well versed in the models and frameworks that go with effective teamworking, yet are dissatisfied with their efforts to introduce it. It seems that many of their attempts have foundered, and their initiatives have failed to realize the benefits they had hoped for. What is more, when they have succeeded with one team, they have often found it difficult to replicate the success. When it comes to teams, it is difficult to apply the learning from one situation to another. Why?

We believe that part of the answer to this question lies in the word "team" itself. It is ambiguous. Think for a minute how widely it is used in everyday language, and how many different interpretations can be put on it. There is the autocratic finance director, who will refer to the people in his department as his team, even though the only thing they share is an open-plan office and the same fear of the boss. Then there are virtual teams and global teams, not to mention quality circles, and cross-functional project and process teams.

The confusion is worsened by casual comparisons with sports teams. According to John Neal of Neal Training, there is a problem when comparing business with sports teams. A sports team by definition shares a common goal (that of wanting to win the match), but the same cannot be said of business teams. Depending on the composition of the team, members of the production, marketing and HR departments may have widely differing objectives. The production department will be interested in simplifying the production process, marketing in raising profits, and HR may be more interested in succession planning and staff development issues. In addition to this, teams might have to contend with the less legitimate issues of hidden agendas, threatened powerbases and the pursuit of short-term results for personal aggrandizement.

As this example illustrates, the very nature of teams makes teamworking difficult because they are made up of groups of individuals. It is ironic that while organizations rely on the creativity and brain power of people to secure competitive advantage, it is the very same diversity and independence which makes teamworking so difficult.

Moreover, the majority of managers have cut their teeth in an environment which places a high value on a transactional style of management, and which has favored the development of analytical skills at the expense of interpersonal skills. As a result, many feel ill-equipped to deal with the human issues which inevitably arise when people work together.

When you see these inherent contradictions combined with the ambiguities that come from this over-generalized use of language, it is hardly surprising that so many managers find teamworking elusive. Yet with increasing commercial and individual pressures, it is easy to see why so many managers put the effective management of teams high up on their list of performance management issues.

In our experience they are concerned with four particular aspects of teamworking: establishing a team atmosphere to improve overall performance; ensuring that multi-disciplinary teams work together; defining objectives and creating identification with a specific project.

We will be introducing a framework to help you tackle these issues later in the chapter. The framework will be followed by a brief look at the particular issues associated with running the most common sorts of team. However, first we think you will find it helpful to think about attitudes to teamworking in your organization. To do this you need to consider two crucial questions in relation to teams.

- What is a team?
- What baggage do teams and their members carry?

The answers to these questions will have a major impact on your efforts in using teams to deliver exceptional performance.

WHAT IS A TEAM?

While some of the benefits of teamworking are widely recognized, confusion remains over what teamworking actually involves. Yet we are all members of many different forms of teams in our social and professional lives. Whether the team is our family, sports team, operatic society or church, it has an identity and a purpose which are shared by its members. In today's business environment, teams are taking on a multitude of forms. Virtual teams, project teams and self-managed teams are but a few examples. With the variety and scope which teamworking presents, traditional definitions of teams inevitably fall short of encompassing all of today's interpretations and possibilities. They tend to exclude cross-functional teams, which do not do similar work; global teams which may not meet on a regular basis; and virtual teams may never meet. Therefore, the nearest definition we can find is that offered by Katzenbach and Smith:

"A team is a small number of people with complementary skills who are committed to a common purpose, performance goals and approach for which they hold themselves mutually accountable."[6]

177

WHAT BAGGAGE DO TEAMS AND THEIR MEMBERS CARRY?

Many people have a very skeptical view of teamworking. Sometimes it can arise from fear of the unknown and sometimes it comes from negative experience, where perhaps senior management have naively launched teamworking initiatives, without understanding what it entails. In other instances, the concept of teamworking flies in the face of deeply held personal values. For example, some might believe that teams dilute individual talent, reduce their chances of success, or that team decisions are by definition compromises, and are therefore unwilling to commit to them. Others might see teams as an "easy option", or a way to avoid taking full responsibility for their actions.

Whatever the reason, a team's success depends on its members' ability to identify where history is getting in the way of progress. The obstacles provided by historical experience come in a variety of guises:

Survivor syndrome

Since team initiatives are often accompanied by redundancies, rationalization and restructuring, those who "survive" this fate are not always particularly motivated to adopt a new way of working. The fear is great that they will be the next casualties, and might be "working themselves out of a job." Such beliefs, whether founded in fact or not, cause serious resistance to change.

Change fatigue

Organizations which have a history of embracing new ideas like teamworking, only to drop it like a hot potato when the next buzz word comes along, are susceptible to change fatigue. Their employees begin to categorize all new ideas in the same way as "another one of those change initiatives which are doomed to fail." The more change initiatives that go this way, the more severe the change fatigue. Trust gives way to acute distrust; goodwill gives way to working to rule; and enthusiasm and commitment give way to apathy and resistance to anything new.

Country club effect

According to Jeanne Wilson, Project Manager at Development Dimensions International, a lot of teams are set up as a result of the "country club effect." "This is where one vice-president finds out at the club that his cohort has established self-directed teams, and therefore, he has to have them too."[7] Such teams are unlikely to have the strength of support behind them which they need to sustain them after the initial kick-start they may have had from their country club godfather.

Quick-fix

Not appreciating that a move to teamworking is a long-term investment, there are many examples of thrifty senior management introducing small-scale, short-term teambuilding pilots. They have no commitment to taking the next step, sustaining any momentum which may be achieved, or developing the process into a company or business unit-wide initiative. Furthermore, the pilots are often allowed to fizzle out before they are properly reviewed or measured on a larger scale.

Lack of visible support

Sustained support involves managers ensuring that teams see the importance of their contribution and giving approval for achievement. It also involves managers voluntarily distancing themselves from artefacts of the old culture – the spacious office with the forbidding closed door, the reserved parking space, the separate canteen. Managers who do not live the new culture of teamworking, commitment and empowerment, risk sabotaging not only the current teambuilding initiative, but also any future initiatives.

Untouchables

Untouchables are paid-up members of the old order, who may have positions of power, or empires to defend in the old order; power which could be diminished or even totally eroded in a consensus-driven, information-sharing society. Their perceived power has been created through the old systems and structures, and has been sustained through autocratic leadership, secrecy, and often by management through fear.

If the untouchables have been successful in their creation of fear, it is likely that this fear will be carried into the new society, and fearing confrontation, empowered team members might allow their unacceptable behavior to go unchallenged. If this happens, the message sent out by the organization is clear – individual power is more important than teambuilding.

Inappropriate systems

Many organizations do not realize the impact of their performance management systems, and have tried to introduce teamworking whilst reinforcing negative patterns of behavior, through outdated reward and appraisal systems, which favor single-handed "hero" achievement. Individual bonuses or commission, annual one-to-one appraisals between boss and subordinate behind closed doors, and individuals being "sent" on remedial training courses, are all components of systems which discourage, rather than encourage, teamworking.

Neglecting the individual

Hay Consultants point out that while it is important to reinforce messages about teamworking, team performance management cannot totally replace individual performance management. [8] The contract of work is drawn up between the individual and the organization. Therefore, some recognition of the individual's performance (and this need not necessarily be financial), as well as his or her development needs, must feature in the organization's evaluation of its overall performance. Ultimately, the individual must retain his or her identity, even within the team role they fulfill.

Inappropriate leadership

Some leaders make the mistake of putting every last decision to consultation and a democratic ballot. This wastes time and gives ammunition to team skeptics who see compromise decisions as "compromised" decisions. Others make the mistake of overcontrol, imposing too many autocratic, top-down decisions, which result in team members not buying into the decisions, and not feeling confident about their implementation.

The "happily ever after" team

There is a myth surrounding teams that "we like each other therefore we are a team." This is often perpetuated by teambuilding training, where the facilitator, aiming to reduce tensions and build relationships, has downplayed the team's *raison d'être*. The result can be a team that believes getting along together is incompatible with conflict.

In this situation performance often suffers. A team based on this premise is not motivated to experiment or stretch and learn. When a team is founded on "getting along together," this often creates a barrier to moving the task forward through individual contribution. Instead, members wait until they are all together in order to agree on what needs to be done, believing that progress can only be made through the synergy of all team members working together.

Groupthink

Taken to extremes, the avoidance of conflict within the team can lead to a situation where conformity is more desirable in team members than creativity, task-orientation or commitment. More common in long-standing or permanent teams, such over-conformity can result in the team closing itself off to external influence and becoming self-perpetuating, an end in itself, rather than the means to an end. The team becomes more important than the interests of the organization or the task which it set out to fulfill, and more creative members are discouraged from contributing ideas or information which conflicts with the group's views. In the book *Victims of Groupthink,* Janis refers to this phenomenon, "groupthink," which, in its worst form, can reduce a team to little more than a "bitching session" directed at the rest of the organization.[9]

RECOGNIZING THE BAGGAGE

- Spend a few minutes making a list of the teams you are/have been involved with that are running/have run into problems.

- What baggage might be/have been in the way?

- What are the implications for you?

As you can see from this discussion of baggage, building a culture of teams requires major long-term commitment. It needs continual development and review so that everyone has a clear picture of their responsibility and role in the achievement of exceptional performance.

WHAT EXPECTATIONS DO PEOPLE HAVE?

What do individuals and organizations want from their teams? Are they seeking short-term solutions to their immediate quality issues, or long-term work patterns which will be integrated across the business? Are their expectations consistent with each other?

Some organizations seem to be locked in the 1980s, with teams introduced as a bolt-on, in a vain hope to find the Holy Grail of exceptional performance. Others, which we might term organizations of the future, are structured as teams of teams, with a matrix of cross-functional reporting lines and mutual accountability across the business. One such organization is the National & Provincial Building Society.

TEAMS OF TEAMS AT NATIONAL & PROVINCIAL BUILDING SOCIETY

National & Provincial Building Society has transformed itself from a typical hierarchically run organization into a successful, innovative process-driven one.

Management layers have been simplified from 22 to four, and all activities have been reorganized around 40 core business processes. As a result, there has been a dramatic improvement in operating profits and levels of market penetration.

Figure 5.1 below illustrates the major shifts in the attitudes of all employees through the creation of a "team of teams" environment.

Attitude to	From being seen as	To being seen as
Own role	Individual	Member of team
Success	Pay and status	Team achievement
What motivates people	Promotion and career structure	Competency development, contribution to team achievement and performance-related team pay
Organization	Hierarchy	Team of teams
Relationships	Boss-subordinate	Team-based
Goals	Unclear – related to own job and department	Clear – understand what own and other teams and organization are trying to do
Purpose of customer relationship	Sell products	Anticipate, understand and satisfy requirements over the customer's lifetime
Business change	Threatening	Essential and desirable to improve continuously

Fig 5.1 Shift in attitude of all employees through the creation of a 'team of teams' environment
Source: O'Brian, D and Wainwright, J, "Winning as a team of teams," *Business Change and Re-engineering*, Vol 1, No 3, Winter 1993

Everyone now identifies with a process team and has a role within a defined process. Job descriptions are a thing of the past. Managers are referred to as team leaders. Their role has become one of coach, facilitator and motivator. Competencies form the basis of assessment, development and reward. Appraisal is process-based, involving other members of the team alongside the line manager.

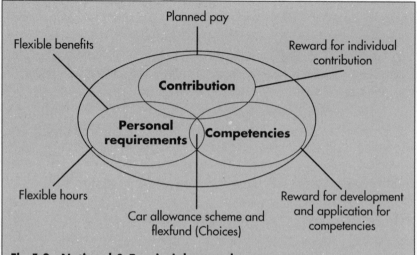

Fig 5.2 National & Provincial reward system
Source: O'Brian, D and Wainwright, J, "Winning as a team of teams," *Business Change and Re-engineering*, Vol 1, No 3, Winter 1993

As Figure 5.2 shows, reward is related to three broad areas: contribution, competencies and personal circumstances. Contribution-related rewards include planned pay and reward for individual and team contribution. Individuals also have some scope to choose from different kinds of reward – i.e. payments or mortgage subsidy. This recognizes the different motivators that people have in the different stages of their lives. The alignment to the organization's strategy and purpose is obvious and the continual focus on communication means that concerns can be voiced and dealt with.

Charles Handy introduces the concept of a "shamrock team" in *The Age of Unreason* to illustrate flexibility and change in a team of teams environment. These teams are built on the concept of a project team, and are made up of different groups of employees dependent upon the task at hand. Employees may enter and leave teams as needed, and can be engaged in a number of different projects at any one time.

Shamrock teams

Each Shamrock team has three components. The first component is a group of team members who remain the core of the team throughout its existence. These members possess the technical, problem-solving and interpersonal skills necessary to sustain the continuity and momentum of the team, address particular issues and build on new ideas.

The second component of the team comprises those specialists who are needed at a particular stage, for a particular contribution to the overall task. These people enter and leave the team as needed, and are therefore only temporary members, bringing with them new ideas, different perspectives on particular obstacles, and relevant information or resources. Being specialists in their field, they often bring with them new learning for existing team members, and their flexible team membership ensures that they are treated as "insiders" while providing a vital communication vehicle with the team's external environment.

The third component (or leaf of the shamrock) consists of temporary or part-time team members. Like the specialists, these people are also called upon as and when they are needed, for example to gather information, carry out a particular research project or prepare a progress report for the team's sponsors. Being insiders like the specialists, these people also act as team champions, carrying out public relations missions for the team's activities, gathering and disseminating information and providing vital links to opinion-formers in and outside the organization.

LUCAS DIESEL SYSTEMS

Many organizations are experimenting with teamworking models along the lines suggested by Handy. Although they do not use the term "shamrock team" as such, the new culture at Lucas involves maintaining small core teams, with trained experts being called in when required. In this way, their expertise is maximized, as they can help a number of teams at once, without becoming a member of just one team where their talent is maybe only utilized for a small proportion of the time. The core team ensures the continuity of the project and the team process, and also provides a clear focus for those temporary members of the team. A degree of standardization also results from a permanent core of members, while the disadvantages of a totally permanent team are avoided.[10]

For employees at K Shoes the concepts of job and team swapping have been embedded into the culture. Secondments offered to team members are designed to build and reinforce relationships outside the team as well as inside. Employees from suppliers are encouraged to join training courses at K Shoes, and are even invited to come into the factories and work in teams with K's own employees.

TEAMS IN NETWORK ORGANIZATIONS

Taking the concept of shamrock teams to the next stage means recognizing how much movement there can be. With relationships becoming more and more dynamic, the stability implied by the core would take a lower profile and the networks of relationships come into ascendancy. Some organizations are already beginning to think along these lines.

Digital Equipment, ABB and the World Health Organization are moving this way. They are beginning to define themselves in terms of a "constantly changing kaleidoscope of relationships between people."[11] They recognize that their organizations are made up of multiple, small units and they are now experimenting with networking strategies to create intense interdependence among these small units.

In this new environment, some believe that projects will become *the* way to deliver work and results. Success will depend on the organization's ability to assemble the right resources and to deploy them effectively.

In a world where speed, flexibility and innovation are crucial, there will be no room for remnants of the old order. The organizations which survive will be those which rewrite the rules of teamworking; those which realize, for example, that business can be lost if progress is held up by laborious resource negotiations midway through a project, caused by a vital team member being diverted onto another piece of work.

The pressure for constant innovation means that in the future, teamworking has to permeate all levels of the organization – from the very bottom to those at the very top. Paul Allaire, CEO of Xerox, describes the challenge he faces: "Now, for the first time, you must have a team at the top. We always *talked* teams, but today they really are necessary to make companywide processes work."[12]

This theme is echoed by a recent study of 550 American, European and Japanese companies, surveyed to identify the characteristics and capabilities that differentiated the companies that innovate faster and more successfully than their competitors[13].

"We discovered that none of the best known programs – total quality management, reengineering, the formation of self-managing teams, or the institution of cross-functional processes – are enough . . . Success depends on the willingness and ability of the entire senior executive group to address not just their individual functional or divisional responsibilities, but also their collective responsibility for the company as a whole."

This study goes on to explain why it is so difficult for senior management to function effectively as a team: "Besides holding divergent views of the business, top-level managers also have real conflicts of interest. However much they may need to co-operate, they also *compete* with one another – for resources, for recognition and ultimately for the top job . . . Acutely aware of the potential for head-to-head conflict, they protect their own turf and avoid attacking anyone's sacred cows. The result: major issues are left unaddressed."

The message from these quotations is clear. A culture of teamwork can only really take off if those at the top of the organization have embraced it for themselves.

We believe that in many organizations, senior executives are only just beginning to face the reality of teamwork among themselves. As a result, many of them are now personally experiencing the demands it makes. They are seeing first-hand the need to overcome their reticence to address major issues.

In our experience, the majority of managers at all levels underestimate the barriers to communication. They recognize the problems caused by being located in different places, or working with people of different nationalities and languages. However, they usually find it harder to recognize (and indeed deal with) people"s reluctance to address major issues. This is not surprising, given the "not invented here" attitudes and individualistic "not my problem" behaviors which have prevailed in the past.

Think about your own organization in the not-too-distant past: does it suffer from a production era mind-set where people from different parts of the organization, levels in the hierarchy, business units or departments are regarded with suspicion? In allowing this to happen, many organizations have created cultures that actively discourage working across boundaries.

By feeding people on this diet of unwritten rules about who they can and cannot talk to, and what they may and may not talk about, we have created psychological barriers to communication. As you will see later from our model of high-performance teams, opening this baggage and demolishing these psychological barriers to communication is crucial if you are to develop teams capable of delivering exceptional performance.

BUILDING AND DEVELOPING HIGH-PERFORMING TEAMS

Our model for team performance (see Figure 5.3) emphasizes the importance of performance management at a team level. It focuses on the task issues of purpose and performance which encompass the setting, measuring and monitoring of goals. It also focuses on the softer issues of building relationships and communicating clearly both within and between teams. True team performance is a combination of skills and behaviors which together bring out the potential of the individual members, the team and finally the organization.

HIGH-PERFORMING TEAM RATING QUESTIONNAIRE

How would your team rate on a scale of 1–5 (1=low; 5=high)?

Purpose	
1 Members can describe and are committed to a common purpose.	
2 Goals are clear, challenging and relevant to purpose.	
3 Strategies for achieving goals are clear.	
4 The purpose is aligned to the organizational strategy.	
Performance	
5 Progress is measurable.	
6 Team rewards are evident.	

7 Specific objectives are set with agreed timescales.	
8 High standards of quality and output.	
Relationships	
9 Individual roles are clear.	
10 Members are individually accountable.	
11 Members perform different roles and skills as required.	
12 Individual contributions are recognized and appreciated.	
Communication	
13 Members express themselves openly and honestly.	
14 Members listen actively to each other.	
15 Different ideas and approaches are explored.	
16 The team communicates with the wider organization.	
Learning	
17 Skill gaps are recognized and training provided.	
18 Members coach each other.	
19 The team reviews its learning on a regular basis.	
20 Team accomplishments are recognized.	

INGREDIENTS FOR A
HIGH-PERFORMING TEAM

So what constitutes an effective or high-performing team? And how do they differentiate themselves from average or under-achieving teams? Robert Perkins and Grant Ritchie of K Shoes believe the most important thing is to "develop a true love for your people, their strengths and their potential," and to "make it obvious." The most important ingredient, according to Olympic hockey coach, David Whitaker, is mutual accountability. He defines an effective team as "one that is capable of responding to dynamic situations and modifying roles to suit changing circumstances without a significant drop in performance."[14]

These are the elements which we have identified as being crucial to ensure high performance in teams:

- creating a sense of purpose
- shared goals and objectives
- measuring and reviewing performance
- team rewards

- team process
- clearly defined roles
- open communication
- sharing information
- team training
- coaching.

1. Purpose

Shared sense of purpose

It is essential that your team shares a sense of purpose which goes further than the actual "problem" which needs fixing. Aside from the end result or solution to the problem, each team member has something on a personal level to gain from the process. It is important that your team members see a future in their work. If they feel that management is sponsoring them purely as a means to a quick-

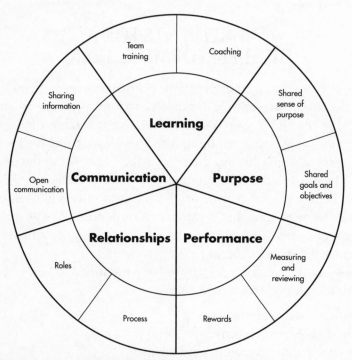

Fig 5.3 Model for high-performing teams

fix solution, team members will be unlikely to put much thought or effort into the task, and with nothing to drive it, the team quickly loses momentum.[15]

The purpose of your team is not to become a closed entity or island within your organization, but rather an effective vehicle with which to solve problems, improve processes and work in a more cohesive, integrative and mutually beneficial manner. It is important that your team understands its role within the organization, and the expectations placed upon it. Your organization, for its part, has responsibilities to the team in terms of providing resources and training, rewarding good performance and desired behavior, and supporting the team in its problem-solving processes.

TEAM PURPOSE

- Does your team have a written or unwritten purpose which is understood and "owned" by all team members?
- How long-term is the purpose?
- How do you reinforce the stated purpose?
- Are others aware of the purpose?

Shared goals and objectives

Your team is not an end in itself, but a means to an end. One of your first actions, therefore, must be to establish the goal or objective. Sometimes this is imposed upon the team – a task may evolve from dissatisfaction with the status quo shared by a number of people.

A team which does not have a clearly defined goal is not a team, but merely a collection of individuals, often with quite differing and even conflicting agendas. Holding a shared goal or objective does not mean that team members must be in total agreement about how to fulfill the objective. On the contrary, differing ideas on the prospective method or route provide a fertile basis for creativity and imagination.

Chris Bonington, mountaineer and conqueror of Everest, explains: "Starting at the beginning, in the case of a climb you have to decide on an objective, so let it be Everest, the highest mountain on earth. But we need to be more specific. How do we want to climb it? Do we want to attempt a new route, and in what kind of style?"[16]

HARVESTER RESTAURANTS – EMPOWERMENT

At the Harvester chain of restaurants, empowerment was introduced together with the concept of teamworking in the early 1990s. Everyone works in teams, and employees who have mastered all components of the team's tasks, known as "accountabilities," are known as "team experts." The whole team can be made up of team experts, and team members collect badges for the accountabilities they learn. Every team member has at least one "accountability" for the week, and these are shared out at the beginning of the week, rather than being allocated by one person for the team. The whole team sits down and works out challenging targets it wishes to aim for, as well as the rewards for achieving them.[17]

SHARED GOALS AND OBJECTIVES

- Does your team have a clear sense of direction?
- Does your team understand the reasons for its existence?
- Is your team aware of and accountable for its contribution to the organization as a whole?
- Does your team understand the goals, purpose and mission of the organization?
- Is your team committed to the goals of the team and the wider, longer term goals of the organization?

2. Performance

Measuring and reviewing team performance

At Lucas, teams set clear milestones with manageable, realistic timescales along the route to the end goal. Then the team is encouraged to gather data regarding the attainment of these milestones from various sources – questionnaires, opinion surveys, "quick hits," photographs, action logs and frequent audits.

Regular monitoring and evaluation of team performance, against preset success criteria agreed by team members, is vital to ensure that the team's objectives are met within the agreed timescale. In the absence of an evaluation system, the team has no idea about its level of output, quality standards, speed or failure rate, and is not able to review and adjust its objectives accordingly.

The most effective monitoring is carried out by the team itself. If team members have decided and committed to reaching certain targets, they will be the first to know whether these have been achieved or not. If targets have not been reached, your team will know, or know where to look for, the likely cause of the shortfall. It will be in a stronger position than any group of outsiders when it comes to deciding upon remedial action and re-evaluation of the targets. The same is true when targets have been exceeded; the team will have a better idea of its collective capabilities than anyone else, and will be able to review and amend targets for the next period.

Team measurement criteria are in place in the UK operations of Cadillac Plastics (a distributor for Bayer and General Electric). These include measures usually set for individuals – such as numbers of resolved complaints; sales activity and, more importantly, value of sales; number of new accounts; and number of items per invoice. Introducing these measures necessitated a culture change from an individualistic culture to one built round team performance. To build commitment, when targets are met or exceeded, the whole team (or, more usually, the whole organization of 22 employees), receives a sweatshirt with the particular measure emblazoned on it.

Similarly, the idea of "Families and Clans" at Lloyds Bank has been implemented with the idea of team ownership and measurement at its heart. What is important under the scheme is not how many times a day a certain action is carried out, but the level and quality of the business relationship with clients. Since this is a far more qualitative, even subjective, measure, it is important that the development of those relationships and the implementation of the scheme is left to individual managers to decide with their teams. While there is a central personnel department, its members largely act as consultants to the business. The only thing which is still carried out centrally is pay administration. Recruitment, training and development are team responsibilities.

As these examples illustrate, if your team is to become accountable for its own performance, and for setting and monitoring its own targets, it must be given the support and resources it needs. As far as support is concerned, team members need to be trained in goal-setting and monitoring techniques. If the training is carried out off-the-job, they must also be encouraged to use, experiment with and expand these techniques as soon as they are back in the workplace. In this way, team members are accountable not only for their performance, but also for the learning process they have participated in.

Once the team has been given the training and the tools for monitoring its performance, it must also be able to decide what resources are needed to achieve the goals it sets. These resources might be financial, material or human. Of course, teams should not be given free rein to hire and fire, or spend unlimited amounts on plant and equipment. It is, however, important that the team has a measure of self-control and empowerment over how best to fulfill the targets it sets itself. This self-control and empowerment is clearly dissipated if decisions about what machinery to buy, for example, are taken at a more senior level.

MEASURING AND REVIEWING TEAM PERFORMANCE

- Who sets the goals for your team's performance? Who else has input into this decision?
- How often does your team meet to take stock of its performance?
- What are the performance criteria measured by your team? Who decided on these criteria?
- Does your team usually achieve its targets? If not, what is the most common reason for this? Below-average performance by team members, machine failure, impossible targets, lack of support from senior management or something else?
- Are team members satisfied with the training they are given? If you answer "yes", how do you know?
- Can team members use what they have learnt in courses? Again, how do you know?
- Who decides on how to spend your team's budget for plant and equipment? Who else has input into this decision?
- Who is responsible for team member selection and recruitment? Who else has input?

Team rewards

An organization's reward structure sends out signals about what behaviors are desired and acceptable within the workplace. Selecting an appropriate pay structure is critical to ensure that the messages you wish to communicate are reinforced. Team-based bonuses, as opposed to individual ones, for example, might reinforce the importance of team contribution. Alternatively, a profit-related scheme encourages individuals and teams to look at their contribution to the gains of the organization as a whole. If customer focus, or the quality of customer interfaces, is your overriding priority, then a quantitative bonus, where employees are rewarded for numbers of people through the door, clearly sends out the wrong signals.

With the move to empowered flexible teamworking, British Aerospace Defence has stopped its quantity bonus for manufacturing employees. This type of bonus was "forcing" people to certify bad work in the name of speed. What is more, under the old reward scheme, the more failures and returns they produced, the more rework they guaranteed. Rework, as those in manufacturing know, is a lucrative business – and used to be factored into manufacturing costs from the outset. It pays well, ensures jobs, and apart from anything else, forces the organization and ultimately the customer to pay for the same work twice.

Even in organizations where teamworking is seen as desirable, some senior managers still tend to reward and recognize individual actions rather than team actions. This is still very common, for example, among sales people, where the belief abounds that the sales "team" needs individuals who are willing to go it alone, act proactively and take risks. The macho image of the sales person, driving single-handedly, single-mindedly and ruthlessly to hit his or her monthly sales target, is a hard one to dispel. The same endeavor and ambition, if invested in teamworking and team targets, could result in even greater success, both for the individuals involved and for the organization as a whole. This might be encouraged by rewarding individuals for achievements other than financial results, for example, sharing customer information for the good of other sales people and the business as a whole. Alternatively, a team could be rewarded on the results produced across several geographical sales areas or across a group of products, which would necessitate inter-teamworking.

A reward system which is gaining more and more momentum in the 1990s is the concept of skills or competency-based pay. This is used to encourage flexibility, with team members paid according to the number of relevant skills they possess and the level of competency they have attained in those skills. Many organizations are moving towards simpler grading systems, with fewer grades, and sets of desired competencies for each grade. As employees gain competencies at the desired level from the list, so they can augment their flexibility within the team, and their earning power. The more competencies a team member possesses, the more flexibly he or she can be employed within the team or the organization as a whole, and thus the more he or she is worth to the organization. Competency-based pay is particularly successful when implemented in organizations with cross-functional teams or cell manufacturing. As well as becoming more flexible, team members enjoy more job satisfaction and greater employability, within or outside the organization.

TEAM REWARDS

- To what extent are targets based on teamwork in your organization? Could this be increased (for example, by introducing opportunities for joint problem-solving)?
- How important is the level or quality of customer interaction? How is this measured within your team?
- What team behaviors do you need to reinforce through the reward structure?
- What level of team performance do you wish to reward (immediate team, department, whole division)?
- How will individual contributions to the team goal be assessed?
- How important is it for team members to be recognized individually?
- Are the performance measures explicit and understood by all team members?
- Do you encourage frequent, honest, constructive feedback so that there are no surprises when bonuses are paid out?

3. Relationships

Team process

Process refers to the softer side of team development and performance. It is concerned with the way in which the team operates, how people are relating and working together. It determines whether a team operates to its full potential using the resources of all its members.

The specialist knowledge and expertise required by your team members will depend on what kind of team you have, and its objectives. A cross-functional team must, by definition, include a representation of the different functional stakeholders involved, while a firefighting team set up to analyze a particular production or quality problem may not require the presence of marketers or finance specialists.

What is clear, however, is that no individual team member can bring all the skills or technical knowledge necessary for your team to be successful; least of all you as manager. When teams begin working together, or even holding discussions about the task at hand, they soon realize that different people see the same task from different perspectives. At this point it is crucial that you and your team members understand the value of these differences of opinion, and are aware of your interdependence within the team. Derek Pritchard of the Hay Group says: "Much of the art in making teams work effectively is getting the right mix of capability and balancing it with the contribution required."

TEAM PROCESS REVIEW

The following is a list of questions which you may like to use to kick off a process review discussion at your next team meeting:

- What do I like/enjoy about working in this group?
- What do I dislike about working in this group?
- What could be done to improve how this group works?
- What form does leadership take in this group?
- How could I/we be different?
- What prevents me/us from working to my/our maximum ability?

197

Team roles

As well as having a function within the team (such as financial expertise or marketing experience, for example), each of your team members also has a particular team role. It is important that you as team leader recognize and value, not discourage and suppress, the individuality of your team members and the differences in the way they like to work. When Chris Bonington selects his mountaineering teams, he does not merely look for good climbers. He needs people with good organizational or man management skills, some who are prepared to lead and shape the team, and others who will take on more of a passive, supporting role.

CLEARLY IDENTIFIED TEAM ROLES

- Do I have a balance of the necessary roles in the team? Could one person take on more than one role?
- Does each member understand the importance of team roles and recognize their own?
- Do all team members understand what they need to do in order to collectively succeed?
- Do team members understand their individual contribution to the success of the team, and the team's contribution to the success of the organization?

4. Communication

Open communication

Having clear goals and objectives is obviously not enough if these are not known and understood by all team members. Effective communication systems must be in place, and more importantly, open communication must be " role-modeled" by you as the team leader. This implies an ability to communicate with your team members individually, showing sensitivity to their strengths and weaknesses, and with your team as a whole. Quantity and quality of communication between your team members is probably one of the most significant attributes which could differentiate its performance.

Team meetings are your team's forum, a chance for debate, coordination and self-monitoring. For this reason, a clear structure and communication are particularly important, though often difficult, in team meetings. Some members will contribute more than others – this is human nature. The quality of the contributions will also vary considerably, but it is essential that everyone is encouraged to contribute and communicate their ideas and opinions. Those who are not encouraged to participate from the start, and participate in every part of the process along the way, will not fully "own" the project, and will never be a true advocate or champion for the cause. For Jacqueline Henshaw, Operations Manager at Lucas, the most important thing is not to *tell* people something has changed, but to explain **why** the goalposts have moved.

When Robert Perkins, Head of Manufacturing, and Grant Ritchie, Head of Wholesale Division, together prepared to introduce flexible empowered teams into K Shoes in 1991, they committed themselves to "the most comprehensive communication process ever undertaken in our business." Rather than briefing the workforce, they took on the task of selling their ideas through debate and discussion. "We met them in groups of between 30 and 50 in the morning, afternoon and evening. We met them during formal presentations and discussion groups in our conference center, in our canteens and in the local pubs, in fact, wherever seemed appropriate! We sought to share the reality of our situation and to excite them with the opportunity for the future and cajole them into becoming advocates for change."

Speaking with the benefit of hindsight, both men agree that this "pre-positioning" paved the way for smoother negotiations later on in the change process. Of this comprehensive communication drive, they say: "While it was expensive in terms of time, resources and cash, it paid itself back many times over."[19]

TEAM COMMUNICATION

- Do you hold meetings frequently enough? Or too frequently?
- How much thought goes into deciding who needs to attend the meeting?
- Do you consider and publicize the agenda enough in advance? Do you make a certain team member responsible for each item?
- Are people open, are they able to express their feelings without fear of recrimination?

- Do you listen to each other?
- Is everyone encouraged to contribute in meetings? How do you ensure this?
- Are you available to your team members outside meeting times? How "open" is your open-door policy?
- Do you operate in a climate of mutual trust?
- Do you devote enough time in meetings to reflecting on the process, checking for understanding and motivation, and ensuring that morale is high?
- Is there enough time at the end of meetings for a question and answer session?
- Do you work through conflict together?

Sharing information

If teamworking is a new concept in your organization, and reward and recognition have traditionally encouraged the "lone ranger," then the uncertainty caused by teamworking may create fear, defensiveness and an ostrich mentality. At best, team members will only work within the area which remains "safe" for themselves and their career. They will not take risks and share their more creative or innovative ideas for fear of stepping out of line. In order to avoid this, your team members and those outside the team must be made to feel secure in the knowledge that this new way of working is desirable and supported by senior management, and above all is here to stay. If there is any threat that teamworking is merely the flavor of the month for a senior manager who may soon depart, the team initiative will not succeed.

In order for individuals or the whole team to take risks, they have to be given a certain amount of information, and need to be updated as and when new information becomes available. The necessary information might include subjects which under the old style of working were taboo, not to be shared outside the four walls of senior management meetings, or not considered important, or even understandable, for employees lower down the hierarchy. Your team's performance at best can only ever be as good as the information and resources the team has to work with. A team which has been given a vague task or objective, indeterminate deadlines and vague success criteria, or a team which is isolated from the rest of the organization in terms of human, financial or material resources, will not succeed.

John Smythe, Corporate Communications Consultant with Smythe Dorward Lambert (SDL) talks of a "two-way vertical and lateral communication process involving every level of employee in an organization." Information must be diffused "osmotically" within the organization. An organization where this happens is Mars UK. Here, employees receive a pay rise every time the company achieves a predetermined rate of growth, which has been publicized throughout the organization. As a result, it is quite possible for employees to receive pay rises every couple of months. What is important is that employees receive the information in a form which they can understand and relate to their own contribution.

Communication can use formal or informal methods. Formal methods might include regular publication of the company newspaper, newsletter or information bulletins, electronic mail systems and regular team or product group meetings. Informal communication can be an impromptu meeting or memo on a specific issue, or a widely publicized open-door policy.

Just as you expect your team to be creative, you too should experiment with methods of disseminating information to them. The information your team needs might best be communicated in the form of a factory visit to another plant, or even organization, which is already practicing whatever it is you expect of your team. Lucas Diesel Systems found this very effective, organizing both internal and external visits for whole teams. Alternatively, a presentation by a visiting speaker or even external consultant, for the whole team plus other stakeholders, would deflect the emphasis on you as the leader.

Open communication is not only important within the team, product group or the organization. Close links with external stakeholders, such as suppliers, customers, unions, even competitors and the local community, are also vital to ensure that all possibilities are explored and all opinions aired.

MANAGING UNCERTAINTY AND SHARING INFORMATION:

- Does your team receive the same information as you do? How do you ensure this?

- Does the information disseminated to your team add value to them?
- Is your team briefed formally as a team, or individually on an *ad hoc* basis?
- How is information communicated to your team? Is there a better, more effective way of doing this?
- How is this information updated? How often?
- Who decides what resources are needed by your team? Who has input into this decision?
- Is your team clear about its role within the organization?
- Are members confident of the team's future existence, regardless of the nature or sensitivity of the results it produces?

WHITBREAD MAGOR BREWERY – TEAM COMMUNICATION

The Whitbread Magor Brewery realized early on the route to culture change and empowerment that communication and getting people talking about change was of the utmost importance. It introduced four types of formal gathering:

- the site joint negotiating committee
- departmental implementation groups
- functional review groups
- teamwork training sessions.

Some of the meetings are held off-site and some are facilitated by external facilitators, trainers and by a former shop steward, which has helped the process of acceptance and buy-in.[20]

At Stew Leonards' Dairy in Connecticut, for example, customers are invited in on a regular basis to give Stew and his team feedback on anything from service delivery on the checkouts to the price of smoked bacon. Customers give advice on the layout of display cabinets, the variety of products on offer and what they would like to see on special offer.[21]

BAe DEFENCE – INFORMATION SHARING

Before its organizational restructure in 1989 into flexible manufacturing teams, British Aerospace Defence had a less than
flattering record for employee communication. Mainly downwards, via unions or the company's grapevine, information
was kept to a minimum, and senior management was
shrouded in a "cloak of secrecy," according to David Aspey,
Head of Manufacturing. The "information is power" culture
was very strong, as illustrated by the management's "unoffi-
cial motto:" "Tell them nowt and not a lot of that!"[22]

Plans of the restructure were communicated to employees
from Day 1, and reviewed frequently. A site newspaper was
created, there were daily team briefings, a regular monthly cascade of information, as well as a 24-hour cascade in the case of
urgent messages. The new motto for management became
"Management by walking the shops," and many of the old
artefacts of the "them and us" culture between workers and
management disappeared.

5. Team learning

Training

Training in its broadest sense is vital at all stages of a team's existence. Equally as important is the need to involve the team in the
decision process regarding its training and development needs.
Training can take on a number of forms, from the familiar in-house
or external seminars and workshops, to more task-focused coaching and team-based on-the-job training.

Team training must begin at the teambuilding stage, and must
be perceived by those involved as an ongoing process, rather than
a discrete event. It is a process which needs to be reinforced, nurtured and reflected upon constantly. The most successful teams,
whether they are theatrical casts, football teams or orchestras, continue to train together and learn to work together more effectively,
as well as carrying out their work.

There are a number of training and development opportunities open to you and your team members. One might be a team workshop run by an external consultant, in which a constructive climate is created for team members to air their ideas and views, and come up with a team action plan. Another is a series of team training sessions based on particular issues such as problem-solving, decision making and project management.

LUCAS DIESEL SYSTEMS – TEAM TRAINING

Lucas Diesel System, introduced a five-point team training plan which was linked to the new vision of empowered flexible teams:

1. initial launch
2. building confidence
3. leading from the back
4. treating each new activity as a training opportunity for the team
5. asking the team what they want.

Team training needs to be as task-focused and tailored as possible for the best added value to your team. Training merely for the sake of training, or to fulfill some spurious "training days" target, does not add value to you, your team or your organization. Rather than revolving training around the question "why teamworking?," or around exercises to "get to know each other," your team training sessions should have a clearly defined and well-communicated theme. This may be a particular set of interpersonal skills, performance evaluation skills or achieving a certain standard in a technical area. Making your team accountable for what they learn (in terms of performance results following the learning process) will ensure that the training session is taken seriously, and that weaker team members are coached and brought up to speed by those who have mastered the subject faster.

It is not always imperative for every team member to possess the same level of expertise in a particular field. The team as a whole may need to provide all these skills by selecting experts in the particular fields. On the other hand, it may be desirable for the rest of the team to have a level of awareness of the knowledge areas where they are not experts. In this case, training in a particular technical field can be carried out by more proficient members of the team in the form of coaching (if other members are required to reach a certain level of proficiency) or presentations (if knowledge and understanding of the process is sufficient for other team members).

Sending cross-functional or production teams on training courses is one element of team training. Another is the example set by the top management team. Training is important for individuals and teams at all levels and stages within your organization, and the top management team can act as a useful role-model in this area. If the top management team communicates openly about its own training and development, this sends the right messages down the organization regarding the importance of continuous learning.

TEAM TRAINING

- Are team members involved in the decisions regarding the amount and nature of their training?
- Are they content with the training they receive? How do you know?
- Are team members trained in the skill of coaching? Are they encouraged to use this skill within the team?
- How often is "number of training days" used to measure training?
- And how about "average number of training days per employee" being used as an organizational measure?
- How do you as team leader monitor the effectiveness of external training courses?
- Who generally facilitates learning in your organization? An external consultant? A specifically trained internal consultant who knows the business?
- Are teams actively encouraged and supported in putting their new knowledge and expertise into practice? How?
- How open is your senior management team on its own team training goals and achievements?

NORTEL – EMPOWERMENT AND DEVELOPMENT

Nortel backs up its empowerment strategy with consistent employee development opportunities. It realizes that in order for employees to be empowered, they must have the knowledge and skills necessary to understand the processes they contribute to. For this reason, a career structure has been put in place for diagnostic, technical and process operators, as well as for managers and engineers. NVQs, recognition as trainer/assessors and professional and management qualifications may be attained. For middle and senior managers who are empowered and enabling their teams to become empowered, Nortel has introduced the Enlightened Leader's Program, which consists of three elements:

- unlocking potential
- facilitating managers
- situational leadership.

Nortel has committed itself within its People Contract to: "Provide opportunities for all people to fulfill their potential both as individuals or as members of a team within the NT organization."[23]

Coaching

Coaching is an element of training which can and should be carried out on a regular, frequent basis. As David Whitaker, Olympic hockey coach says: "Coaching is not about taking over when the going gets tough, or even about offering solutions. Rather, it is about encouraging the team to find their own solutions and having the courage of their convictions in implementing them."[24] If Whitaker's team needed to look to the bench for answers in a hockey match, they would never improve their game or come up with solutions for themselves. First, the team would not have responsibility for the outcome of the match, and second, if the coach (as a former player himself) were to provide all the answers, they would probably be the answers to yesterday's problems. In other words, in a truly empowered team, the coach belongs on the bench, the team on the pitch.

What the coach can do to encourage the team, is to provide the vision. However, living out the vision must be done by those who own it – the team players. The coach does not need to know what it will look like when they get there, or even how to get there. Whitaker talks of the empowering coach providing direction, not directives. The empowered team creates everything twice – once in vision, once in reality.

This model of high-performance teams applies to all types of team. However, given the huge range of teams in today's organizations, it is as well to recognize that different aspects of the model will present specific issues to different types of teams.

WHAT TYPE OF TEAM DO YOU WANT TO CREATE?

Much has been written extolling the virtues of self-managed or cross-functional teams. But how do you know whether this is right for you? And how do you go about setting up such a team?

The type of team you choose will impact upon your organization in a variety of ways. The pay structure you implement, for example, will depend upon such things as the nature and permanence of the team, its level of decision-making power, and the role of the individual within the team.

It will therefore be necessary to define the role and status of your team within the organization. For example, some organizations build a matrix structure of numerous, co-existing, long-term, cross-functional teams within the traditional hierarchical structure. Others consist of a group of employees, all with fairly generic "roles," who are committed to one or more project teams for the duration of those projects.

In this section, therefore, we look at the particular issues that are likely to arise when working with:

- cross-functional project teams
- self-directed teams
- global teams
- virtual teams.

Cross-functional project teams

These teams are set up to achieve a particular goal which can range in scope from the very narrow, "find out why pump C keeps on overheating," to the very broad, "extend our operations into Eastern Europe." Team members are recruited for their particular expertise. Depending on the project, this may be on a full- or part-time basis.

This approach presents a particular challenge in organizations where the culture is attuned to functional working, and where the performance management systems focus primarily on contribution to the "home department."

AVON COSMETICS – PROJECT TEAMS

Avon Cosmetics has used project teams to meet a particular threat in the marketplace, to come up with a business plan for a new market or product. What is important for members of project teams, according to Paul Southworth, President of Avon Cosmetics Ltd, is the fact that project teamwork is recognized and rewarded as special in a variety of ways.

At the end of a project there is always a big "Thank you" to the whole team, and partners are also recognized for their support during the project. A team process is sponsored and supported by a particular vice-president, who is responsible for reporting the team's progress back to the board. Ownership of a project by a particular vice-president is important not only for the status of the project itself, but also for the standing of the team members. He or she may identify particular stars within the team for individual recognition or inclusion in a future team. This creates an important message for employees, as it casts aside the anomaly of teams taking precedence over individual achievement.

Self-managed teams

Self-managed or self-directed teams have no formal leader, but base their decisions upon a consensus style of management: often this includes sharing or rotating the leadership function. Team members are responsible for typical management areas, such as recruitment, budgetary control and appraisal, as well as scheduling work, problem-solving, resource planning and customer intimacy.

Those who have traditionally held line management posts often act as liaison officers between teams, or between a particular team and the senior management. They might be charged with securing the resources or senior management support for a particularly high-risk solution proposed by the team. They may also add value as facilitator or coach.

K SHOES – EMPOWERED TEAMS

The senior management team at K Shoes realized its empowered teams initiative was on the right track when, over several months, the confidence of the teams began to grow sufficiently for them to question the norms, clash with supervisors and managers, and break down the physical and mental barriers to success. While this was in the long-term interests of the organization, the pressures and the pain felt by supervisors and line managers were unbearable for many, and they left.

Of those who stayed, Perkins and Ritchie comment: "By now our employees were so excited by the concept of empowered teamworking that we had taken the lid off Pandora's box, and there was no way they would allow us to put the lid back on again." The implementation of empowered teams at K Shoes and the focus of accountability on to team members have allowed managers to do what managers in general are paid to do – look ahead and plan the strategy.[25]

Many managers, brought up in a culture of control, find it exceedingly difficult to let go of the reins they have been used to holding tightly. Thus they feel that the phrases "self-managed" and "self-directed" imply that there is still a place for them to "direct" and "manage" their people; it indicates that their traditional transactional leadership styles may still be appropriate.

As an effective alternative, we suggest thinking in terms of "self-propelling" or "self-driven" teams, as these phrases make no reference to the behaviors we aim to discourage.

Global teams
More and more organizations are coming to realize that to compete in global markets requires global, multi-cultural teams which may

span continents, subsidiaries and parents, suppliers and customers. They are expected to set the organization's international culture and values, and pave the way for a more extensive global integration of their organization with its partners abroad. Percy Barnevik, Chief Executive of ABB, sees them as a vital source of competitive advantage for any organization which wants to become a player in the increasingly competitive global arena.

Research comparing performance of multi-cultural teams with that of mono-cultural teams, suggests that the former tend to be either extremely effective or extremely ineffective, whilst the latter tend to be more average.[26]

It is not enough to send prospective team members on a language course, or simply insist they give up old judgements and stereotypes in the name of multi-cultural integration. Such teams require substantial investment in terms of training and development. Sufficient time must be allowed to develop both the team and the technology for long-distance communication such as electronic mail, telephone, fax and videoconferencing.

To succeed, international teams must make more of an effort to communicate, share information and seek and give feedback on a regular basis. The communication should include not only status reports on the team's objective, but also review sessions on team processes.

As communication is often in a foreign language and relies more on technology than face-to-face meetings, it is essential to realize the extent to which personal nuances and important non-verbal communication are lost. It is therefore easy for impatience, misunderstandings and hasty prejudgments to set in. Consequently, the frequency and quality of communication must compensate for this.

Although we have said that language and inter-cultural training is not the total solution, it is nevertheless important. High-level language training can help to reduce the gap between team members who are able to work in their mother tongue and those who are less proficient. Equally, it is crucial that team members appreciate the way national culture can affect individual and group behavior, level of commitment, approach to rules and regulations, importance of consensus within a group and openness towards feedback, to name but a few.

Failure to do this can mean, for example, that some find progress cumbersome, whilst others feel it is too fast. Splinter groups may then be formed by those who are left behind. The result can be side-talking and disinterest in the team objective, leading in extreme cases to a "them and us" situation, mental "opting out" and the sabotage of team efforts.

Virtual teams

A virtual team is a group of people working closely together on a particular project in scattered locations, who meet rarely, if at all. They are very dependent upon technology, and communicate, for example, by telephone, fax, E-mail or videoconferencing. They may also be linked by shared software, known as groupware, which enables members to work on, swap and update project information simultaneously.

There are several reasons why there is a marked increase in the existence of virtual teams: globalization of markets, customers' demands for shorter lead times, increasing numbers of people working from home, and the need to tap expertise which may be involved in other projects (and therefore unable to attend meetings in distant locations).

Perhaps you, like other managers, are wondering how to get high performance from a team whose members never actually meet? What about the issues of team training, teambuilding and team roles? Can teams really be expected to become task-focused without concentrating on their team process?

PRICE WATERHOUSE – VIRTUAL TEAMS

At Price Waterhouse, virtual teams spend maybe two or three weeks working together for a particular client. As it would be unrealistic to gather all the team members together in one location (with a staff worldwide of 45,000 in 120 countries), they manage team processes and synthesize information electronically. Having a highly sophisticated groupware product (before the advent of the Internet), Lotus Notes, was paramount to the success of PW's virtual teams. One manager from Price Waterhouse told us: "Of course it is essential that the corporate culture encourages information sharing, a shared methodology and a common language."

Lotus Development Corp (now part of IBM) manufacturer of Lotus Notes, believes, on the other hand, that preteamworking introductions are crucial because "it's important to develop some level of trust and relationship before you can move into electronic communication."[27]

If it really is impossible for the team to meet, a culture needs to be in place which encourages information sharing. At an American consulting group, if a piece of information that a consultant puts into the shared database is utilized a certain number of times by his or her colleagues, he or she receives a bonus. Similarly, systems need to ensure that team members are accountable for keeping abreast of the information placed on the database.

Research in America seems to indicate that E-mail actually increases people's level of communication – firstly it is cheaper than telephoning, and secondly it cuts down the amount of time spent playing "telephone tag." Since E-mail communication is easy and inexpensive, more information can be disseminated to a wider audience, thereby involving more people in decision making.

TEAMS OF TEAMS

In this chapter we have looked at:

- The growth of teams and why they are vital to success in today's business environment
- Why it is so difficult to develop effective teams
- How to identify some of the problems and issues individuals and organizations impose on teams
- How, despite these difficulties, it is possible to build high-performing teams
- A model for achieving high performance
- The various types of teams we can expect to belong to.

Teamworking is now an everyday part of our management experience. It requires regular review and development to bring out clearly the potential of the team and its individual members, but when this is achieved the motivation and commitment it generates can bring with it exceptional results.

References

1. Quoted in Schlesinger, L Eccles, R and Gabarro, J, *Managerial Behavior in Organizations*, McGraw-Hill,New York, 1983
2. Dumaine, B, "The Trouble with Teams," *Fortune*, September 5, 1995
3. Piper, A, "Denmark – what a way to run a company! Oticon," *Mail on Sunday*, 11 September 1994
4. Lovelock, C, "Federal Express: Quality Improvement Program: Creating Value and Building Barriers to Competition" in *Competing Through Services: Strategy and Implemention, Cases and Text*, Prentice Hall, New Jersey, 1994
5. Perkins, R and Richie, G: "Using Empowered Teams to Improve Existing Operating Systems," Paper to the Empowered Flexible Teamworking Conference, London, June 1995
6. Katzenbach, J R and Smith, D K, *The Wisdom of Teams: Creating the High Performance Organization*, Harvard Business School Press, Cambridge, Mass., 1993
7. Quoted by Caudron, S, "Are self-directed teams right for your company?," *Personnel Journal*, December 1993
8. *People & Performance*, a publication by the HayGroup, London, 1994
9. Janis, I L, *Victims of Groupthink*, Houghton-Mifflin, Boston, 1972
10. Henshaw, J, "Motivating Teams – Getting Through the Difficult Patches and Improving Productivity and Pace," Paper to the Empowered Flexible Teams Conference, London, June 1995
11. Hastings, C, "Building a Culture of Organisational Networking," *International Journal of Project Management*, Vol 13, 1995
12. Quoted in Garvin, D, "Leveraging processes for strategic advantage", *Harvard Business Review*, September–October 1995
13. Hout, T and Carter, J, "Getting It Done: New Roles for Senior Executives", *Harvard Business Review*, November–December 1995
14. Whitaker, D, "Coaching the Team: Getting Them to Operate Efficiently and Problem Solve," Paper given to the Empowered Flexible Teams Conference, London, June 1995
15. Gustafson, K and Kleiner, B, "New developments in team building", *Industrial and Commercial Training*, Vol 26 No 9, 1993
16. Bonington, C, "The Heights of Teamwork", *Personnel Management*, October 1994
17. Pickard, J, "The Real Meaning of Empowerment", *Personnel Management*, November 1993
18. Pritchard, D, "People and Performance," HayGroup Publications, London 1994
19. Perkins, R and Ritchie, G, "Using Empowered Teams to Improve Existing Operating Systems," Paper given to the Empowered Flexible Teams Conference, London, June 1995
20. Hughes, C, "Overcoming the Problems and Pitfalls of Introducing Teams into an Established Culture," Paper given to the Empowered Flexible Teams Conference, London, June 1995

21. Taken from the video by Peters, T and Waterman, R, *In Search of Excellence*
22. Aspey, D, "Effective Training and Development to Build Empowered Teams," Paper given to the Empowered Flexible Teams Conference, London, June 1995
23. Rowden, A, "Using Empowered Teams to Cope with Flexible Workloads and Patterns of Demand," Paper given to the Empowered Flexible Teams Conference, London, June 1995
24. Whitaker, D, "Coaching the Team: Getting Them to Operate Efficiently and Problem Solve" Paper given to the Empowered Flexible Teams Conference, London, June 1995
25. Perkins, R and Ritchie, G, "Using Empowered Teams to Improve Existing Operating Systems," Paper given to the Empowered Flexible Teams Conference, London, June 1995
26. Adler, N, *International Dimensions of Organizational Behavior*, PWS – Kent Publishing Co. USA, 1990
27. Quoted by Geber, B, "Virtual Teams," *Training*, April 1995

"There is a theory which states that if ever anyone discovers exactly what the universe is for and why it is here, it will instantly disappear and be replaced by something even more bizarre and inexplicable. There is another theory that states that this has already happened."

Douglas Adams[1]

Chapter 6

♦

PERFORMANCE THROUGH PEOPLE AND SYSTEMS

To succeed in the information age we must create systems which change people's jobs in a way that compels them to behave differently. This requires adopting an integrated approach which optimizes performance at individual, team and business unit level. This has repercussions on the way we address areas such as measurement, feedback, pay and development.

CHALLENGING TRADITION

Organizations increasingly recognize that in an ever-changing business environment they need to ensure that everyone is pulling in the same direction. This requires multiple communication channels putting out the same messages. With this changing emphasis, performance management systems are acquiring a new role as a crucial mechanism for translating vision, mission and strategy into meaningful objectives at individual, team and business unit level.

This realizaton has led organizations to reassess old approaches. Do their policies and procedures in areas as diverse as business planning; pay and rewards; performance review and assessment; succession planning, career development; and training and development send out consistent and mutually reinforcing messages? Or are they separate entities transmitting confusing and conflicting messages?

Clearly, to perform effectively individuals need to understand what is expected of them, what they will be rewarded for and what they have to do to progress. Performance systems must actively support managers in their new transformational role and link to all facets of the Prism.

Most people intuitively feel that this broader approach to performance management makes sense. Yet discussion of the practicalities of making it work is fraught with difficulty, not least because for many people the phrase "performance management" immediately raises the specter of the formal annual appraisal. This event is rarely seen in a positive light. So first, we suggest you stop and reflect on your views. Consider two questions:

- **What do the phrases "performance management" and "performance management systems" mean in your organization?**
- **What images do these phrases conjure up?**

The majority of managers we speak to see performance management systems in a narrow context. They talk about an irrelevant annual ritual, which is often uncomfortable for those on the receiving end and for those charged with its execution. They see the systems as self-propagating and divorced from reality. The main output is paperwork, ostensibly required by the organization for formulating strategic plans, but which is usually filed to gather

218

dust from one year to the next. The outputs only become relevant to the individual where they relate to pay and promotion.

In some organizations such comments may be justified. But we believe there is a place for performance management systems in building sustainable competitive advantage and in driving organizational change. To fulfill this role, **the systems have to add value**.

Added value does not emerge simply by introducing metrics and performance-related pay (PRP). While these aspects of performance management are important, they have often been overemphasized, and indeed their success can be questioned. Figure 6.1 shows the new, broader picture, which is concerned with framing, discussing, guiding, developing and delivering performance. It requires internal consistency, whether looking at the level of the business unit, team, individual or the organization as a whole. It overlaps with processes and policies in areas as diverse as strategic planning, rewards, staff communication and recruitment. It links to all facets of the Prism, and requires you to think in terms of shaping a dynamic, active set of relationships, processes and decisions.

From:	To:
Static systems designed and owned by personnel departments to support managers in a stable environment	Dynamic systems developed and owned by people in the business to support managers in turbulent times
Prescriptive and bureaucratic systems imposing "one right way to do things"	Systems are facilitative, aiming to help managers enhance performance and leaving some room for discretion
Systems as separate entities	Leverage comes from seeing the connections between systems
Treating individuals as the primary cause of variations and focusing on appraisal once a year	Systems which encourage continuous learning and development
	Focus at the level of the individual, team and the business as a whole, and seeing the impact on the organization itself
	Systems as powerful communication tool – reinforcing strategic intent and continuous development of culture and capability

Fig 6.1 The changing face of systems

Organizations of any scale will want to build coherence and control into these activities by developing them into a formal performance management approach.

We expect that you will be using formal systems which may have some, or all, of the shortcomings described. Our objective is to help you find a way to use and develop these systems so that they help you actively manage the performance of your people in an integrated way.

YOUR PERFORMANCE MANAGEMENT SYSTEMS

- What formal systems are in place for managing performance?

- How do they operate?

- What constitutes good performance in your organization?

- What aspects of performance do they measure?

- How do you get feedback on your performance?

- How do you give feedback to your people?

- What constitutes good performance for your people?

- How integrated are the performance management systems you use?

- What happens to the paperwork once it has been completed?

- To what extent do you think they add value for you as a manager?

SYSTEMS OF DISCONTENT

Perhaps the biggest complaint about performance management systems is that they are supposed to be objective. Ever since the 1920s, people have recognized that subjectivity and emotion are unavoidable when evaluating and assessing what people are achieving in their work. Yet, in spite of this obvious shortcoming, organizations have persisted in denying that the subjectivity and emotional content exist. Instead they continue to develop formal systems which they describe as "objective." In addition, they frequently use this as a way of determining how individuals should be rewarded, while denying that appraisals are linked to pay.

The failure to acknowledge obvious truths has a lengthy history. According to Peter Scholtes, a consultant who taught with quality guru Deming, the modern appraisal has its roots in an 1840 Wisconsin railroad accident.[2] Industrial management was then in its infancy, and management systems were largely adaptations of the models used in the military and the Church. At the inquiry, the company recognized that accidents were likely to happen in the future and wanted to be sure that it knew who to blame. To this end, it decided to specify the responsibilities of each employee, though it worked on the assumption that "the system" itself was correct.

These two assumptions – that "the system" is correct, and that organizations want to attribute blame – have been with us ever since. In the minds of many they are two of the unwritten tenets of performance management. It is only with the coalescing of ideas about leadership and total quality that we have begun to realize just how pervasive and insidious these assumptions are. They are so deeply entrenched, and the root cause of so much cynicism, that disproving them is a major challenge in most organizations.

Deming asserted that the manager's role is not to control people but to learn, with people, to control "the system." In doing so, he was the first to recognize the problem and to point out that tackling it requires a fundamental shift in perspective. For all the

AMERICAN EXPRESS: FROM EXPANSION TO SHRINKAGE

American Express enjoyed huge success in the 1960s and recorded year-on-year double-digit growth in profits throughout the 1980s. All of its business lines grew in terms of numbers of customers and revenues. With a series of acquisitions, the company expanded to become a financial supermarket.

In Europe it was organized geographically. Each country was a market in its own right, with an autonomous general manager. Even so, to an outsider there was consistency of customer service and quality, achieved through a brand which really meant something to front-line customer service staff who were managed quite differently from the rest of the organization. Quality initiatives focused on them: they had standards, measurement, and *ad hoc* customer service training. Unlike the rest of the organization, if customer service had a problem which required additional resources, its needs were met.

In fact, the whole organization was internally focused. Business planning was done by senior management who concentrated on setting profit and growth targets and then worked these back to customer targets and employee investments. These goals were cascaded down the business and sometimes included middle managers. None would be set for the levels below. The cascading process often ran late, so some people did not have any goals until three months into the financial year.

A senior manager from American Express Europe describes how the goal-setting process worked: "Typically I set my goals as an action plan, so that my success could be measured at the year-end. The goals would then be put on one side until review time. For the review you would tick off the action points you had completed. In reality, the results of the actions didn't matter. In fact the only firm measure of achievement was keeping to budget and meeting your revenue targets. The process was symptomatic of a highly political organization where there was very little listening to customers or employees. Rewards were dependent on your personal relationship with your boss. The same applied to promotions: only 40–50 percent of senior level positions were advertised. The rest were filled through political networking. It depended on relationships, and people just tended to be placed. To be honest – it lacked integrity."

This apparently integrated approach and focus on customer service sustained the growth until 1992, when things came to an abrupt halt. In the words of one former executive: "It was a case of the incredibly shrinking franchise."

Market share, revenue per merchant, card profits and share price were all falling, and there were well-publicized problems – merchants were actively urging cardholders to use bank rather than Amex cards; well-known restaurants and hotels were refusing to take Amex cards because they could not justify the higher discount rate; and competitors were closing in.

These factors, combined with the worldwide recession and a change in people's lifestyles, meant that the fundamental flaws in both the product and the way the organization was run could no longer be ignored.

enthusiasm for TQM and quality, such a shift has proved beyond many organizations.

CHANGING THE MIND-SET

Aspects of the American Express story may be familiar. Organizations which approach performance management in this way are commonplace. They are locked into the view that the manager's role is to control the workforce, and with this comes another assumption – that the primary motivator for most people is their pay packet. The challenge of today's business world is to shed this "production mind-set."

This means that managers have to let go of many of their most deeply held values and beliefs about the way organizations function (see Figure 6.2). They have to replace their traditional hierarchical and inward-looking philosophy with an obsessive commitment to adding value for customers. To support managers in this task, organizations have to fundamentally redesign their performance management systems to ensure that they communicate appropriate messages.

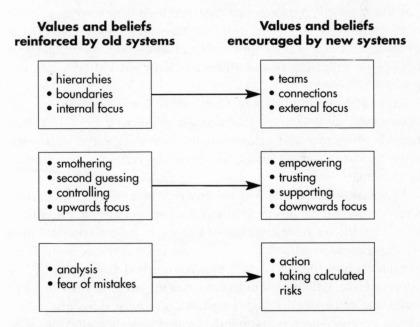

Values and beliefs reinforced by old systems	Values and beliefs encouraged by new systems
• hierarchies • boundaries • internal focus	• teams • connections • external focus
• smothering • second guessing • controlling • upwards focus	• empowering • trusting • supporting • downwards focus
• analysis • fear of mistakes	• action • taking calculated risks

Fig 6.2 Performance systems and organization culture
Source: Patel, S, "Shedding old habits," *Directions* April 1995

One manager we spoke to summed up the challenge: "The new systems must change jobs in a way that forces people to behave differently."

It does not matter whether an organization arrives at this new orientation through total quality, business process reengineering or some other route. To survive in the future, performance management systems must demonstrate that organizations understand Deming's assertion that management is about learning to control "the system." Indeed, given the speed of environmental change, they need performance management systems which go one stage further and support managers in an even broader role: **to learn, with their people to continuously develop "the system" in such a way that it reflects and anticipates the ever-changing environment.**

The implications on systems are profound. It calls for a total rethink of the traditional approach to measurement and feedback, and supporting this with changes in areas such as rewards, training and development.

Measurement and feedback

For many people performance measurement is synonymous with Management by Objectives (MBO). Others may not recognize the phrase MBO, but will recognize its features – one-to-one dialogue between a subordinate and superior about individual goals and goal attainment.[3]

MBO aims to move away from subjective judgments of efficiency and achievement, toward an "objective yardstick that records efficiency and achievement immediately and automatically." It was in use in General Motors in the 1920s and is a product of that era.[4]

However, while its ideal of objectivity is still relevant, its narrow focus on measuring results to assess the performance of individuals brings problems. In many cases it has led to organizations where people are able to articulate goals, but are often unaware of the need to consider how these goals will be accomplished. Consequently key questions, like whether an individual has the necessary resources or skills, are often overlooked. In addition, where skills are talked about, the discussion is frequently limited to technical skills, even though missing "soft" skills, like collaboration and co-operation, may be a prerequisite to achieving the desired results.

224

Situations like this have caused a particular problem in organizations which have created close links between an individual's achievement of results and their pay. Think, for example, of the marketing manager who is constantly churning out new promotions to reach targets, irrespective of whether the production unit has the flexibility to meet the constantly changing schedules. These linkages can work against the organization, by encouraging people to ignore the fact that accomplishing their goals prevents someone else from doing the same. In such cultures it is common to find that people either do not realize the need to ask for help from others, or feel unable to ask for it. Clearly, this is incompatible with the current move towards empowerment.

Organizations need not, and should not, lose their focus on results. However, they should balance their focus on "what is achieved" with a focus on "how it is achieved." This means introducing a set of objectives and measures which encourage co-operation across different business units and functions, which are consistent throughout the organization and ensure there is an appropriate organization architecture.

AMERICAN EXPRESS: FROM SHRINKAGE TO EXPANSION

In 1993 Harvey Golub, the new American Express Chairman, embarked on a major divestment and reengineering program, which resulted in a new European and global structure. This was rapidly followed by the introduction of a vision – "To become the world's most respected service brand" – and a new approach combining total quality and performance management. This approach, christened American Express Quality Leadership (AEQL), aimed to "change the way the organization works and individuals behave."

In Europe, three new businesses, with their focus on products, replaced national markets. The new businesses are Consumer Services Group (CSG), whose products include the famous green and gold consumer charge cards; Travel Services Group (TSG), whose offerings include packaged Amex products such as corporate charge cards, management information systems and business travel; and Establishment Services Group (ESG), which is responsible for signing up service establishments, such as hotels and restaurants, to accept Amex products. It has also meant centralizing many processes in Brighton, UK.

The annual strategic planning process now drives performance management. The three businesses have to seek clear alignment across countries and markets when setting their five-year plans. So, for example, if CSG decide that Germany, Italy and the UK are the key markets, then ESG, whose role is to support CSG and TSG, must follow suit. Decision making is international, there is no place for autonomous national barons.

Once the businesses are aligned, goal setting begins to make sure that people at all levels know what is required to support the business. Everyone from board members to associates who work on the front-line is set employee, customer and shareholder goals. The goal setting is far more sophisticated than in the past. One executive contrasts the old and the new approaches: "We are focused to a point where we know what results we are looking for. We are seeking alignment of results – not alignment of action points. Goals are objective and measurable. For example, my goals relating to employees are very specific about improving certain scores on the annual employee survey. I also have goals relating to customers and goals about improving consolidated leadership scores in certain teams."

Everyone is measured on performance against their goals, and this drives bonuses. In 1995, bonuses were split with 25 percent relating to employee goals, 25 percent to customer goals and 50 percent to shareholder goals. In addition, all those in a leadership role were evaluated and rewarded according to their performance as a leader. Everyone with responsibility for managing others, including the most senior people, have been through intensive leadership training every year for at least two years. This training, which is mostly run by senior leaders, stresses that "leadership is about providing followers with what they need to do their job, when they need it, in a form they can use." It is positioned as an integral part of the quality drive, and includes use of an upward feedback tool which links leadership competencies to the Amex values.

Feedback, which is totally confidential, comes as an intensive 30-page report which focuses on the three key areas shown in Figure 6.3. It includes numerical data to allow comparison with a typical colleague and anonymous comments. After spending about half a day reflecting on it, individuals work with an independent counselor to formulate action plans to change their behavior. To ensure that people can take their action plans away and use them immediately, the training events include role plays which cover the same three areas.

Individuals are urged, but not compelled, to share their action

"Live the Values"	*"Strive for Credibility"*	*"Match Style with Need"*
• Clients and customers	• Competence	• Assess readiness, then match style by:
• Quest for quality	• Character	– directing
• People	• Composure	– guiding/coaching
• Integrity	• Courage	– supporting/participating
• Teamwork	• Care for people	– delegating
• Good citizens		

Fig 6.3 Feedback on leadership competencies
Source: American Express

plans with their direct reports and colleagues. After two years the feedback has become accepted and institutionalized, and has created a new climate of openness. Most people now voluntarily share the results with their boss, and are happy to incorporate their action plans into their goal setting.

There is a new leadership language. People are no longer frightened to admit they lack the competence to do something. Now, self-disclosure is allowed. According to one manager: "People will say, 'I'm at readiness level one, I don't feel I can take that on.' Or, 'I'm at level three, I need more support.'"

Seeing senior people, from the European President down, trying to change their behavior is a very powerful message which is reinforced again and again by the sight of senior people running the leadership training events. At the same time, running these events is powerful for senior people – it reminds them how strong the old mind-set is, and emphasizes why changing the culture is crucial for future success.

"For some people the feedback is traumatic, especially the first time round. Most people know some of their problems and live with them," says one European manager. "Their reaction is 'I expected it.' But the parts of the feedback that really hit home are those areas which you are blissfully unaware of. When it comes to behavior change, we find three camps: those who are really determined to make it part of their agenda; those who do it for a while, say four months, and then let it go; and those who think 'the feedback's wrong' and do nothing about it.

Then the next year comes around. There are some who started out like Attila the Hun and have genuinely changed, there are others whose feedback has got worse, and others who have just not got better. In the end they have either got to change or leave. We all know of people who have left because they do not feel they can match where the culture is going."

With operating profits up 18 percent in the first year, the progress is appreciated on Wall Street. American Express's share price had almost doubled by mid-1995.

XEROX: USING SYSTEMS TO REDEFINE THE BUSINESS

In 1981, with increased competition from Japanese rivals such as Canon, Xerox Corporation's annual profits fell by almost 50 percent to US$600 million. Xerox reacted by embracing total quality and transforming its organizational and management philosophy.

With the transformation came a new set of ranked performance measures: customer satisfaction; employee motivation; market share and return on net assets; and a new "policy deployment" process to ensure coherence and alignment across the business.

These four parameters are reflected in the day-to-day objectives of every employee, and performance against them is measured relentlessly. For example, customer satisfaction is monitored in a number of ways. An external agency conducts a twice-yearly survey to compare perceptions about Xerox to perceptions about its competitors. In addition, following every product installation, the purchaser is involved in two face-to-face surveys: one completed at the time of installation, the other 90 days later. This information, supplemented with qualitative data from regular focus groups, forms the basis for continuous improvement efforts.

The same attention is paid to surveying employee motivation. An external agency is employed to gather information which identifies sources of employee dissatisfaction, and compares Xerox to other companies. Senior management use this information as the basis for investigating and eliminating the causes of employee concern.

By the late 1980s, Xerox had extended the use of surveys to teams, by introducing the management practices survey. This survey, an upward feedback tool, was an addition to the annual appraisal process. It asked employees to rate their managers' performance on 27 different dimensions reflecting the company's goals.

The survey results were collated by a member of the local Xerox quality group, and used in conjunction with the manager's self-assessment to build a picture of the overall situation in the work group. This picture, which included observations about areas of agreement and disagreement and judgments about goal congruence, were then fed back to the manager *and* team in order to help the manager understand how they operate.

According to Paul Leonard, who worked as a quality consultant at Rank Xerox UK during this period: "When this first started, there were some severe bloodbaths: dictatorial managers, defensive managers, employees too intimidated to say anything. So for the first five years, each of these sessions were facilitated by someone from the quality office who was seen as impartial. We are now running these sessions without the help of a facilitator, although groups can still request one."[5]

Since changing its philosophy, Xerox has gone from strength to strength. Having restored its position as the world's leading supplier of photocopiers, it has embraced process thinking and begun to redefine the very nature of its business. It now aims to establish itself as "The Document Company" – operating in a consultancy role and helping clients to make their document creation, transmission and storage more productive.

This relentless search for improvement has meant innovations in terms of promotion and pay. Managers are now assessed regularly against a comprehensive list of criteria. Each one could be "a knockout factor in promotion."[6] The list is unusual in putting attributes like "business and financial perspective" and "overall technical knowledge" at the bottom, while "inspiring a shared vision" and "developing organizational talent" are near the top.

The method of calculating bonuses, which had been linked strongly to customer satisfaction for some years, has been further refined to encourage co-operation and teamwork. The old method, which was to add together three elements – one related to your individual performance rating, one related to your division's performance and one to the company as a whole – has gone.

Now, a factor related to performance against corporate objectives is multiplied by a factor related to your division's performance and your individual performance. So it no longer makes sense to achieve 100 percent of your goals if the company achieves only 80 percent – as you would score only 80. Suddenly there is a real inducement for managers to embrace team thinking and to consider the needs of other departments and divisions.

According to Paul Allaire, Xerox CEO, bonuses are no longer viewed as "a virtual entitlement."[7] Managers have seen variations of from 35 to 250 percent of target. This size of variation encourages a new attitude to risk and focuses them on the drivers of performance.

Lessons from American Express and Xerox

Both American Express and Xerox use multiple measures to link explicitly the external environment, overall business goals and internal culture in a way which ensures every individual employee understands their role in meeting the company strategy.

The measurements are entirely consistent with the philosophies of both organizations. They focus on "what needs to be achieved" and "how it is to be achieved" and link into pay and promotion. These strong messages have built a culture where measurement is a way of life. Overall processes, activities within processes, people, behaviors and end results are all measured – yet there is no sense that it is done to attribute blame.

American Express changed its structure and focused on building leadership skills aligned with its professed values, in order to develop the capability to succeed in the future. Its initiative also demonstrates how the innovative linking of 360-degree feedback to the quality initiative created scope for leverage.

The Xerox case shows how measures can be used in conjunction with technology, to give people at all levels access to information which is vital to running the business. This attitude has built an environment where self-managed teams flourish, whether they are dealing with customer complaints over the telephone, working as service engineers on customer sites or internally on cross functional projects.

The Xerox workforce is highly flexible and no longer reliant on a lengthy annual appraisal cycle to judge performance. Increasingly, self-managed teams receive feedback directly from the customer, and take corrective action without having to wait for the intervention of a boss. Indeed, the idea of feedback is becoming redundant. As more information becomes available and measures evolve, people are learning to operate much like the driver of the car in Figure 6.4 in a feedforward rather than feedback mode.

They no longer need to wait for something to have gone badly wrong before they can react to a situation. Appropriate measures are helping them react to what is going wrong, and they are learning to anticipate where things might go wrong before they have become problems. So, like the car driver operating in feedforward mode to avoid costly bangs and scrapes, when people are armed with the right information, they can avoid running into so many unanticipated problems.

With the management practices survey, Xerox recognized an area that organizations often overlook – teams need systems to help them diagnose and deal with issues about the way team members actually work together. Again, the concept of feedforward is applicable.

In our experience, people underestimate the effort required to build these competencies. They seem to believe they will come as if by magic, once teams are put into place. However, at Xerox some groups still need help from a facilitator five years after the technique was introduced.

Given the inexorable move towards network organizations, we believe that organizations will have to focus on this area in the near future in order to realize the benefits of teamworking in terms of responsiveness and flexibility.

Fig 6.4 Feedback or feedforward?
Source: Durcan, J and Oates, D, *The Manager as Coach*, Financial Times/Pitman, London, 1993

THE BALANCED BUSINESS SCORECARD

An alternative approach to developing consistent measures

In contrast to the approaches adopted by Xerox and American Express, some organizations are choosing to use the balanced business scorecard (BBS)[8] to help focus on a broad range of measures and to develop consistency.

The BBS framework allows managers to translate the organization's vision into objectives which people can understand and act upon. It provides an instant snapshot of performance in four key areas (see Figure 6.5) and represents the information in a way which is easy to understand and interpret. The same areas apply to all organizations, and at all levels in an organization.

However, the measures in each area will vary depending on the particular organization and its mission. In addition, the measures for a particular organization will vary according to the level you are looking at. So while the BBS for a business unit will have measures which relate to the organization's mission, the BBS for a team will relate to the team's goals and the BBS for an individual will focus on their objectives.

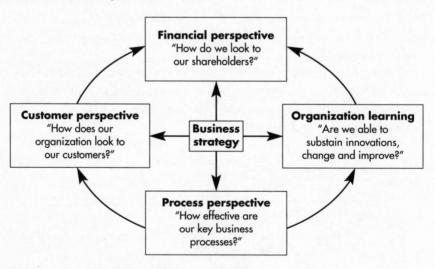

Fig 6.5 The balanced business scorecard
Source: KPMG

232

Developing the measures is a crucial process, which must involve people from right across the organization. Although it typically takes up to two years to set up the measures and really begin to see the benefits, this time-consuming process should not be cut short, as it develops alignment and a common understanding of the strategy throughout.

As you can see from Figure 6.5, a BBS rosette encourages managers to focus on the traditional short-term financial results *at the same time* as the three other areas which are crucial for securing long-term performance improvements. Aligning strategic intent and internal capability requires people to think in terms of the things which must be done today, in order to achieve the results of tomorrow.

According to a consultant from KPMG, when the BBS was first introduced, it reflected the production mind-set and was financially oriented. The other measures were introduced to enhance the financial aspects. "It has moved a long way since then. We now realize that balance is of the essence. To really manage performance you *must recognize that all four areas are equally important.* The trick is to filter the strategy at each level, and to derive consistency between the measures. Ideally, there should be no more than four to five measures in any of the quadrants. It takes a while for people to feel comfortable with so few measures. When the scorecard is first introduced, their automatic response is to measure everything, and they often drown in a sea of data. However, once they begin to understand the relationships between the measures, they can really start to make progress."

The measures on a BBS rosette are a dynamic improvement tool. They need to be reviewed every three to six months. Once performance has begun to level off, the measure should be changed to encourage another step improvement in performance. For example, an IT department, concerned about computer uptime, would be advised to change measures once uptime had reached, say, 95 percent of working time (see Figure 6.6). Going for the extra 5 percent would require a massive investment of staff and resources, which would not produce real customer benefit.

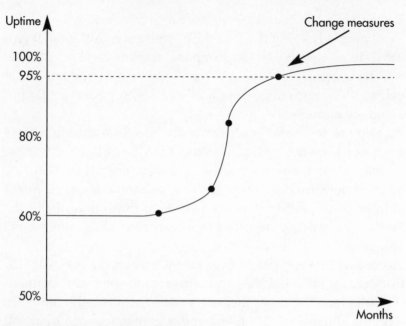

Fig 6.6 When to change measures

THE BALANCED BUSINESS SCORECARD AT FSC

FSC (standing for financial services company and the pseudonym for a real, major financial services corporation) has used the BBS framework to maintain and improve its position as market leader. The scorecard provides a measurement system to help its people understand and follow through two key facets of its strategy:

- to increase the speed of credit assessments from several days to less than five minutes
- to maintain a focus on customer loyalty at all points in the distribution chain.

FSC's scorecard in Figure 6.7 shows the measurements used to monitor progress against its key success factors. The "traffic lights" in Figure 6.8 show a detailed snapshot of FSC's progress against some of its organizational development measures in mid-1995. This style of presentation allows managers to interpret information even more rapidly than the more traditional graph.

Financial: to be effective in the market • trading performance • customer balances • bad debt/asset • sustainable growth	Organization development: commitment to outstanding performance • executive teamwork and development • staff first choice • staff training and development • staff turnover • benefits based on EVA • product innovation and new markets
Customer: to provide value for customers • first choice in chosen markets • first choice for business partners • first choice for end users	Business processes: to be robust and compatible • direct marketing developments • risk assessment • debt management • portfolio management

Fig 6.7 Key success factors for FSC
Source: KPMG

The scorecard also helps them to take a holistic approach and to see complex cause and effect relationships between measures from each of the four quadrants. One set of relationships is shown in Figure 6.9. This illustrates how improved staff training will improve credit response time, risk assessment and staff turnover. The improved response time will increase benefits based on employee value added (EVA), and improve trading performance. The trading performance will be further improved by improved risk assessment.

The same relationships would show the impact of problems. For example, slow credit response times would directly affect benefits based on EVA and trading performance.

At FSC the scorecard has brought the vision to life by facilitating discussion, at all levels of the organization, about performance, based on facts rather than opinion.

235

Commitment to Outstanding Performance

KEY SUCCESS FACTOR	RATING		CURRENT ACTUAL PERFORMANCE	PERFORMANCE BENCHMARK	COMMENTS	YR END OUTLOOK
	CURRENT	PREVIOUS				
1. Executive teamwork and development	●	●	Action plans in place and under way	Investors in people audit complete and action plans in place by 3rd quarter		●
2. Staff first choice	○	○	Action plans complete and under way to achieve 1995 targets	Action plans to achieve investors to people award to be in place by 3rd quarter Staff surveys to be completed and action plans for improvement in place by year end		●
3. Staff training and development	○	●	2.04% yld Q3	3.25 - 3.75% (Group guideline)		○

● Performance level achieved
○ Within performance range and under review
○ Outside acceptable performance level
● Performance information not yet available

Fig 6.8 Progress on organizational development measures
Source: KPMG

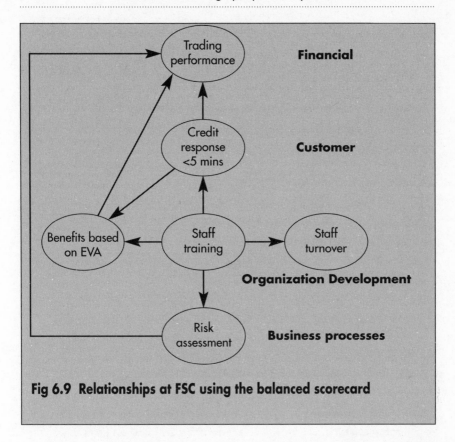

Fig 6.9 Relationships at FSC using the balanced scorecard

It is important to note that introducing the scorecard does not guarantee a truly integrated approach to performance management. The measures chosen reflect the organization's culture and the value it puts on its people. For example, one multinational company used the following statement to determine the measures to include in the organizational development quadrant:

"Our commitment to outstanding performance means giving people the right training, interesting jobs, rewards that reflect the value of their work, making them attractive to our competitors and helping them to find new employment."

From this statement came measures relating to training, job satisfaction, rewards and employability. At the other extreme, there are examples of organizations which focused the organizational learn-

237

ing quadrant on measures relating to innovations in products, markets, and technology, but totally omitted the human dimension. As you can imagine, this obvious lack of alignment transmits uncompromising messages about the value of people in the organization. In addition, it has an adverse effect on other initiatives which relate to people management and aim to deliver exceptional performance.

As you can see from the three cases we have looked at, the whole area of measurement and feedback is undergoing fundamental change. The key trends are summarized in Figures 6.10 and 6.11.

From:	To:
Focus on "what is achieved" primarily in financial terms	Focus on "what is achieved" and "how it is achieved". Monitoring of overall processes and activities within processes, results, competencies and group processes
Measures which disconnect financial results from the market and organization context	Measures which explicitly link the external environment, internal culture, day-to-day activity and overall business goals
People management is unrelated to business results	People management is a crucial activity which must be measured in order to improve teamworking and build leadership skills
Narrow measures relating to a particular function	Broadly based process and cross-functional measures to obtain a "balanced" view
Reactive measures to understand "what has happened in the past"	Proactive measures to create rapid feedback loops, increase learning and manage "what may happen in the future"

Fig 6.10 Key shifts in measurements

From:	To:
From boss to subordinate	From many sources including peers, subordinates and customers
Primary focus on "what was achieved"	Concerned with "what was achieved" and "how it was achieved"
Limited feedback on personal style, frequently subjective and unsubstantiated	Comprehensive feedback on personal style, objective and substantiated
Feedback used to explain and justify rewards	Feedback used to develop the individual and reinforce the business needs through reward strategy

Fig 6.11 Key shifts in feedback

In the next section we will be exploring the new emphasis on customers. Before moving on to it, you might like to reflect on your own organization's attitudes to measurements and feedback.

MEASUREMENT AND FEEDBACK IN YOUR ORGANIZATION

- What aspects of performance are routinely measured to assess you and your people? (You might find it helpful to make a list using the headings of the four BBS quadrants.)

- What links can you see between these measures and:
  - the external environment?
  - the internal culture?
  - day-to-day activities?
  - overall business goals?

- Which measures are proactive, helping you build future capability?

- Which ones are reactive, helping you to understand what has happened in the past?

- How do you receive and give feedback on personal style?

- Overall, where and how do you think your organization could improve its use of measurement?

FOCUSING ON THE CUSTOMER

Focusing on the customer means recognizing that you cannot rely on your product alone to build sustainable company performance. Service is becoming an increasingly important differentiator. It is a key consideration when debating how to secure customer loyalty, and as soon as it enters the equation, you have to re-examine the way you think about purchasing behavior.

Think of your own experience as a consumer. How often have you made a telephone call to get some information or to query some aspect of a bill, only to be bemused by the response at the other end? It does not take long to realize that no matter what your business, you are dealing with constantly evolving customer expectations and perceptions, rather than isolated product purchases. These perceptions are shaped by a stream of individual incidents or crunch points – moments when the customer comes face-to-face with the company through direct or indirect contact and consciously, or subconsciously, evaluates the quality. In the words of Ford Ennals, Marketing Director at British Airways: "No matter how attractive the product, if people think badly of the way they are handled at the check-in desk, or their baggage goes missing, their overall impression will be tarnished."[9]

The framework in Figure 6.12 is useful in highlighting the differences between organizations successfully embracing the ideas of service quality, and those which are not. Successful companies understand the need to look constantly at customer expectations and the behavior and expectations of staff.

Mike Havard of the Decisions Group, which specializes in telemarketing, describes the challenge:

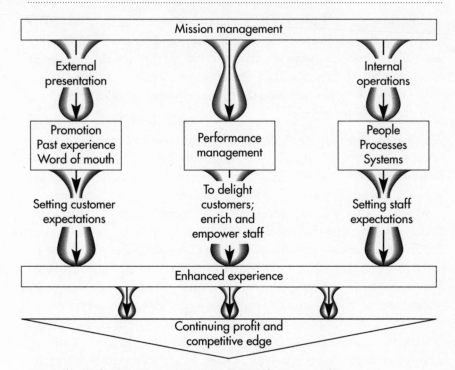

Fig 6.12 Peformance management to enhance quality

"You need to deliver consistent messages across advertising and what the consumer experiences over the phone. It's a continuum. You can do great damage to a multi-million pound above-the-line campaign with just a simple conversation."[10]

To get the balance right, an organization must treat the external presentation and the internal operations as two inter-related areas, and strive to achieve new levels of consistency between the two. It requires:

- thinking in terms of exceeding customer expectations and enriching staff jobs through empowerment
- active mission management to imbue a sense of mission throughout the organization
- recruiting the right staff and training them to ensure that they not only understand what the customer expects, but that they gen-

uinely want to meet those expectations and that they have the appropriate supports in terms of systems and processes to do so

- feedback mechanisms which track the quality levels perceived by customers, and facilitate the adjusting of internal operations to ensure that they are constantly developing to reflect changing customer requirements.

As soon as you take the holistic view and treat internal operations and external presentation as two closely related entities, you start thinking in terms of the links between what the customer experiences and what happens internally.

In doing this you are adopting a "process view" of the world. Suddenly, you see the need to re-examine the way the different departments and business units think of themselves and the way they inter-relate. You realize how much of your time is taken up with activities which add no value. Activities which involve, for example, sorting out problems which should not have arisen in the first place, or rectifying delays which have crept in, in spite of your best efforts.

It is no longer good enough to stick with the old way of doing things because that is the way it has always been done. Instead, every role must be redefined. You either work directly at the customer interface, or you support someone else who does. Once you understand where you fit in the customer-supplier chain, you can begin to identify where the existing ways of doing things limits your ability and your organization's ability to provide a quality service to both external and internal customers.

Sadly, many managers have failed to understand the challenge in these terms. They are locked into a mind-set which treats the internal operations and external presentation as separate entities. Consequently they are often very slow to recognize and act upon the loss of customers – with dire results.

CUSTOMER FIRST AT NORTEL

Nortel no longer considers itself an equipment supplier, but a provider of integrated networks for information, entertainment and communications. This $9 billion company operates globally. With the launch of the Customer First strategy in 1995, Nortel World Trade, its sales and marketing arm has publicly stated its belief that: "Customer satisfaction that is ahead of the competition is absolutely key to winning market share and increasing profits."

Customer First aims to ensure that by 1997, 95 percent of customers are so satisfied with Nortel's service that their loyalty is assured. In financial terms, the company hopes this will translate into a 30 percent growth in sales. To meet this challenge, Nortel has changed its approach to managing performance and customer relationships.

Like Xerox, Nortel has recognized that delighting customers and satisfying employees drives market share and delivers value to shareholders. This shift in perspective has meant replacing the purely financial key performance measures – earnings, cash flow and return on assets, with a new set – customer satisfaction, employee satisfaction and return on assets.

In operating terms, achieving these targets means paying a new level of attention to the customer's needs. A senior executive describes the difference: "It means listening to the customer with both ears, as opposed to with one ear and a mouth. It means new account teams defining with the customer a few metrics which relate to specific aspects of the service which that particular customer values. Examples of these measures include on time in full delivery, delivery with supporting documentation and minimum levels of dead on arrival equipment. These measures will then be the focus of regular reviews with the customer."[11]

This focus on the customer is being extended to every employee, including those who are not in customer-facing roles. Everyone will be set customer satisfaction improvement objectives – something requiring considerable innovation for people in support roles. For example, a human resources manager, who only has internal customers, may be expected to forge links with a human resources manager in a customer organization such as British Telecom.

Progress is being monitored by worldwide customer surveys which gather data annually through interviews with every customer. Loyalty will be taken as assured if the customer says they would definitely repurchase from Nortel and that they would recommend Nortel to others.

To ensure that the Customer First strategy is given appropriate priority, 25 percent of the senior management bonus plan is related to achievement of the improvement targets. This component can drop to zero for any manager who fails to achieve a certain threshold.

The Nortel experience illustrates how the search for step-function improvements in performance has led the company to redefine "the system" itself. It has meant creating a totally new set of key performance indicators for business as a whole and then cascading them down and across the whole organization. The new indicators, with their focus on three crucial perspectives – customers, people and financial criteria – are demanding that everyone approaches their work in a completely different way and that this translates into new behaviors.

HOW CUSTOMER-FOCUSED ARE YOU?

Think about yourself, your job and your staff.

- Who are your key internal/external customers?

- What do they rely on you to deliver?

- How many of your staff would give the same answers to these two questions?

- How much of your time do you spend *listening to your key customers* speaking about their expectations and needs?

- How often do you think about balancing external presentation and internal operations?

- How do you incorporate the external/internal customers' perspective into the systems you use to manage?

- How do your performance management systems reflect the link between employee and customer satisfaction?

THE PLACE OF PAY

The idea of systems which integrate across all facets of the Prism is still very new. Indeed, in 1991 a survey of 1,800 employers in the UK looked at the effort organizations were putting into integration within just one facet of the Prism – systems and measurement.

While the survey found some examples of organizations that were trying to do this, its authors found no examples of organizations that had done so successfully.[12]

The survey also found that where organizations were trying to integrate their systems, the majority were doing so by linking their appraisal system to their reward strategy through some kind of PRP scheme, ie profit sharing teams or individual bonuses, merit pay and share options. A few were taking an alternative approach and focusing on development activities such as training, coaching and career planning as the central theme for integration. Organizations in this second group recognized the importance of remuneration, but saw it as an enabler rather than the key driver for performance improvement.

Interestingly, the survey did not find any correlation between the existence of a PRP scheme and the performance of the organization as a whole – the experience of several organizations in the survey indicated that it is possible to achieve significant improvements in business performance without a PRP scheme.

PRP is undoubtedly a useful tool, but in the past too many organizations have used it as the main plank in their performance management strategy, without realizing its limitations. For example, many have selected one of two basic approaches. Some focus exclusively on high performers, while failing to consider how they can motivate those whose performance will never be ranked above average. Other organizations focus primarily on the average performer and largely ignore the needs of the high performer. Neither of these approaches is satisfactory. Organizations must take into account the needs of both groups, and move away from the single recipe for all.

They also need to recognize that the kinds of rewards which motivate vary enormously from person to person, and even vary for a single person at different stages in their life. Companies like Avon Cosmetics are dealing with this through flexible benefits schemes, which make it easier to manage individual needs and expectations. At Avon Cosmetics, employees have an annual opportunity to "flex" or change the composition of their benefits. They can choose different levels of holidays; life assurance; pensions; permanent health insurance; private health care or extra cash.

Schemes like this are not enough on their own. Too many organizations rely on their pay and benefits package to motivate their staff, despite the fact that there is plenty of evidence to suggest that it can act as a distraction.

Philip Sadler points out in *Managing Talent*, that this is a particular issue for knowledge workers.[13] Think, for example, of the research scientist who channels his or her creative efforts into gaining a bonus or promotion with minimum effort, rather than completing the job they are paid to do – be it understanding more about genetic finger-printing or developing a new polymer. At a more down-to-earth level we hear constant complaints about sales people who sacrifice margin because their incentives are based on volume.

This emphasis on material reward can lead to a short-term focus on results, at the expense of a long-term focus on corporate health. Organizations need to recognize the existence of other motivators – such as professional pride – and build these into their performance management systems.

LEVI STRAUSS: ENERGIZING PEOPLE

In the early years Levi Strauss was a family-run business and its product, jeans, essentially sold themselves. Then, in the early 1980s, the situation changed. Denims fell out of favour, international competition hotted up and recession hit hard. Large numbers of employees were laid off, and in the middle of the decade there was a $1.66 billion leveraged buy-out.

Under the leadership of Bob Haas, the challenge was to turn the company around. In 1987, the management team addressed two key issues: the kind of company Levis should be, and the history it needed to leave behind. Haas explained the reasons: "You can't energize people or earn their support unless the organization they are committing to has a soul."[14]

Haas set out to discover the company's soul. Levis produced an Aspiration Statement and, at the same time, a new pay structure was introduced. It put a new focus on the "how" of management. One-third of each manager's rise, bonus and other financial rewards, was linked to their ability to manage aspirationally. The new structure was aimed at changing the way the business operated. It was no longer appropriate for people to consider their rewards before needs of the business. Instead managers were encouraged to create an environment where people would take the business forward because it felt right and because they wanted to do so.

To assist with this transition, Levis introduced 360-degree feedback and an educational program centered on leadership, ethics, understanding and valuing diversity. It has also made self-directed production teams responsible for setting their own production goals and for delivery of the finished product. This innovation has had a significant effect on the time it takes to have jeans ready for shipping once sewing has started. The overall time has been reduced from six days to one.

Levis is now able to compete on the basis of customer responsiveness rather than lowest-cost production. As a result, notwithstanding the relatively high labour costs, in the period from the buy-out to 1992, Levis' after-tax profits increased almost sevenfold to $360 million.

The Levis example shows how, by embracing a new mind-set, an organization can demonstrably cut all links with its old way of thinking. The oft-repeated phrase "a fair day's work for a fair day's pay" no longer applies in the new environment, where people are really empowered. With the creation of self-directed teams, people are motivated to put in an exceptional day's work. The staff are now engaged and committed to a degree which could not have been anticipated under the old regime, and this is without the carrot of a PRP system based on piece work. In the new organization, there is still a place for PRP. However, its role, to reinforce the messages about developing people to develop the business, is far more subtle.

From:	To:
• Pay seen as primary motivator	• Motivation seen in terms of personal growth and financial recognition
• Pay dissociated from business needs	• Pay used to reinforce strategic imperatives by linking to broad business needs
• Primary links to outputs i.e. financial results	• Link to inputs (skills, competences) and full range of outputs
• Incentives fixed and "go with the grade." Focus on visible status (car, title...).	• Incentives flexible to match what individual values

Fig 6.13 The changing place of pay and rewards

As we saw in Chapters 1 and 2, the emphasis now is on building capability. At Levi Strauss it has meant linking across all facets of the Prism and redefining "the system" as a whole by finding new ways of focusing on the customer.

THE PLACE OF PAY IN YOUR ORGANIZATION

- What themes are the focus of performance management systems in your organization – pay, development or both?

- What aspects of performance are linked to pay, benefits or incentives?

- What are the strengths of your organization's approach?

- What are its limitations?

- Overall, how effective is this approach in improving performance?

DEVELOPING PEOPLE TO DEVELOP THE BUSINESS

Levis emphasized development in order to develop its business. It is equally important to recognize that in this age of downsizing and delayering, individual development and the acquisition of a "portable CV" are important considerations for staff because they are working in an environment where job security is no longer guaranteed.

Many organizations are seeing this link and incorporating skills acquisition into their reward and recognition strategies. This trend puts a new pressure on line managers – their staff now expect them to be interested in their development as individuals and well informed about the options available in addition to all their other responsibilities. To help manage these transitions, an increasing number of organizations are introducing competency frameworks like the one described in Chapter 4, and personal development plans, as key elements of their performance management systems.

FAMILIES AND CLANS AT LLOYDS BANK

In recent years Lloyds Bank has piloted a revolutionary approach to career development with the 1,200 staff of its independent financial services division, Lloyds Private Banking (LPB). This new approach is a competency-based initiative known as Families and Clans.

Like most organizations in the financial services sector, the nature of the work at Lloyds Private Banking has been changing rapidly. With the flattening of hierarchies, career structures along with guarantees of promotion have disappeared. At the same time, the division has radically changed its primary business focus from estate management (giving advice on trusts, wills and death duties) to managing the assets and investments of living clients. The business has grown dramatically, and new technology has been introduced.

This has necessitated fundamental changes in the organizational structure and staff profile. LPB has moved to smaller units and cascaded decision making down to lower levels. It has reduced the number of senior management positions and created more junior managers. Historically, the youngest managers were around 40, they had an in-depth knowledge of specific legislation areas such as death duties, and a clear career path to follow. Now the youngest managers are under 30, and their skills are in more general areas, such as building client relationships and selling. They are frequently ambitious, yet there are limited senior management positions to aspire to.

The introduction of Families and Clans was driven by the thought that if Lloyds was continuously taking things such as career prospects and promotion opportunities away from staff, it needed to start putting something back. This "something" was needed to offer new ways of managing the workforce, and to help people think more broadly about their jobs and roles. The aim was to discourage people at all levels in the organization from waiting expectantly for a guaranteed upwards promotion every two years, and to encourage them to think in terms of sideways moves to broaden their base competencies and skills.

A key part of the change at Lloyds has been the scrapping of the 120 prescriptive job descriptions which detailed what each job holder had to do and how they had to do it. These have been replaced with about 25 generic role descriptions which focus on the nature of the work to be done.

The role specifications are described in a comprehensive Families and Clans documentation pack which is accessible to all. The documentation sets out the core responsibilities, competencies and skills associated with each role. It also groups the roles into different "Families", or areas of work. There is a total of six Families in LPB, each covering a specific and clearly differentiated area. Examples include investment and operational support.

This integrated approach has allowed people to see links which would previously have been unheard of. For example, secretaries can become relationship people, and relationship people can move into investment banking. The same approach is used to link the different Lloyds business units, or "Clans." For example, people now speak about the "LPB Clan" and the "Offshore Banking Clan."

The Families and Clans terminology has created a sense of how the individual parts of the organization fit into the whole. This new broader outlook is reinforced at every level by people moving between Families and between Clans. It has also allowed people to think about the roles they would like to move into, and the competencies they need to develop to do so. Employees are encouraged to complete a personal development plan (PDP) to help them work towards a particular role. They are also encouraged to discuss it with their manager, although this is not forced upon anyone. The PDP is there for those who wish to take advantage of it. Some, like this staff member, actively develop themselves: "I wrote my PDP and discussed it with my boss. Now I have it in my head, I know where I want to go. In the past you were expected to stay in your pigeon-hole, and to be happy with your performance. Now they think about you differently – you can be interested in moving on, without appearing pushy or ambitious. When you see an advert of interest, you can find out about it and prepare for it."

Others are less ambitious, and have realized through completing a PDP that they are ultimately responsible for their own development: "I've done a PDP but I don't refer back to it – I should, but I don't give it the priority."

The PDP sits alongside, but separately from, a new appraisal process. The appraisal process, which is used for all managerial staff, focuses on meeting business objectives and performance in the current role. It begins with boss and subordinate setting objectives and specific performance criteria to be assessed in the future. These criteria include observable behaviors, which relate clearly to the Families and Clans role specifications.

Measurement now focuses on key areas, such as relationships with clients, achievement of budget and business targets, team development and personal development, rather than how many times a day a particular function is repeated. This allows far more flexibility. For example, the system recognizes that quality of service determines the quality of the client relationship. It also recognizes that all clients are different, and that employees must be given the freedom (within the bounds of legality, and stopping short of anarchy) to treat clients as individuals in order to assure customer satisfaction.

There is generally an informal quarterly or half-yearly review of progress. This allows discussion of where performance is "above track, on track and below track," and appropriate action to be taken well before the formal review at the year-end. In contrast to the old approach, this joint development of performance criteria has resulted in joint ownership of targets. As a result, both parties have a clearer understanding of expectations, and there are fewer surprises. At the year-end review, individuals receive a rating related to their 'whole job" performance, which is directly linked to their pay rise.

After successful pilots in LPB and other areas, Families and Clans is being extended to employees in most parts of Lloyds Bank.

The language of Families and Clans has enabled Lloyds to make changes which relate to each facet of the Prism and change the way people think and behave. People can now live the new culture without constantly referring back to the old. The new language has moved the organization from the left-hand side of Figure 6.2 to the right-hand side. The old hierarchies, boundaries and internal focus have largely been replaced and there is now an integrated approach to the different facets of people management (see Figure 6.14)

It is interesting to note that the word "training" does not appear anywhere in this diagram. Instead, the focus is on personal development. This change in language reflects a fundamental shift in the nature of training and development activities.

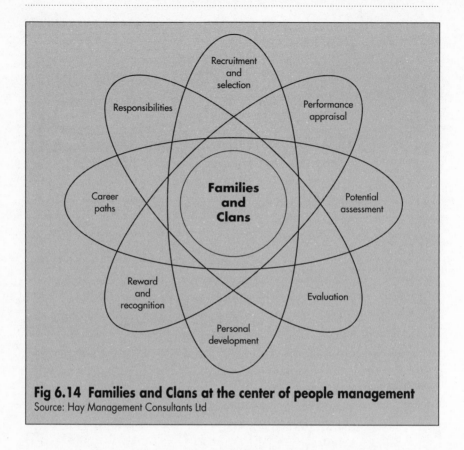

Fig 6.14 Families and Clans at the center of people management
Source: Hay Management Consultants Ltd

THE CHANGING SHAPE OF TRAINING

Alongside other innovations, organizations are becoming increasingly sophisticated in their approach to training. Figure 6.15 traces the evolution through three distinct phases. In the 1970s and 1980s the majority of organizations adopted the fragmented approach, and tended to regard training as a perk or a cost rather than an investment. Courses were typically "offered" to the organization at large through a catalog put together by the training department. No one took responsibility for ensuring that the individual learnt something of value during the course, and no one expected to see any real benefit as a result of their attending it.

With the drive for development we described in the previous section, leading organizations have moved to a focused approach. They

From fragmented	Through formalized	To focused
not linked to organizational goals	linked to human resources needs	training, development and continuous learning are necessities for the organization to survive
ad hoc selection	linked to appraisals	linked to organizational strategy, team and individual goals
training perceived as a luxury or waste of time	training viewed with skepticism; development through career planning highly regarded	training is a competitive weapon
carried out by trainers in training department	carried out by trainers; line managers involved through role of appraiser	responsibility for development rests with line managers
emphasis on knowledge-based courses	emphasis on knowledge and skill acquisition	emphasis on reinforcing organizational values, acquiring skills and knowledge
focus on training (discontinuous) not development (continuous)	training is off-the-job, but through career development the value of on-the-job learning gains recognition	emphasis is on-the-job development, learning is a continuous activity
no attention to transfer of learning	more concern to link to individual needs and facilitate transfer of learning to work	concern to measure the effectiveness of training and development activities.

Fig 6.15 The changing shape of training
Source: Barham, K Fraser, J and Heath, L, *Management of the Future*, Foundation for Management Education & Ashridge, 1988

now regard training and development as continuous processes which focus on "learning" rather than "being taught." No matter whether it takes place on or off the job, there is an increasing demand for clear links to individual, team and organizational goals.

These organizations are changing their mind-set along the lines set out in Figure 6.2. Like Levi Strauss, Xerox and American Express they are recognizing that the development of people management and leadership competencies are crucial in securing long-term success. As a result, they are devising innovative training programs and feedback mechanisms which enable them to put a new priority on developing these competencies.

ATTITUDES TO TRAINING AND DEVELOPMENT IN YOUR ORGANIZATION

- Do people in your organization think in terms of training, development or both?

- How would you characterize your organization's approach to training, fragmented, formalized or focused?

- How has it changed over recent years and how does this affect your job as a manager?

- To what extent have you taken responsibility for your own career development?

- What aspects of the existing systems encourage you to think about role broadening, upwards promotion, continuous development (of you, your people, your part of the business?

- How do you discuss roles and expectations with your people?

- What systems are in place to help you?

PERFORMANCE THROUGH PEOPLE AND SYSTEMS

Delivering exceptional performance means challenging the traditional performance management systems and adopting a new mind-set. As the examples demonstrate, there is an immense gulf between hollow statements of intent and uncompromising messages about behavior, which are reinforced at every level.

To succeed in the future means developing dynamic systems which link across every facet of the Prism. Systems which:

- encourage changes in behavior and attitude
- view development as part of the reward strategy
- genuinely add value for managers by helping them:
  - link strategic intent to day-to-day activities
  - incorporate objective feedback from multiple sources, including customers, peers and subordinates
  - focus on " what is achieved" and " how it is achieved"
  - optimize individual, team and organizational performance
  - actively develop capability and manage long-term performance.

References

1. Adams, D, *The Restaurant at the End of the Universe*, Millennium Miniature Editions, London, 1994
2. Caulkin, S, "Appraisals miss targets," *The Observer*, 17 September 1995
3. French and Drexler, "A Team Approach to MBO: history and conditions for success," *LOD Journal* 5, May 1984
4. Drucker, P F, *The Concept of the Corporation*, The John Day Company, New York, 1946
5. Geanuracos, J and Meiklejohn, I, *Performance Measurement: The New Agenda, Using non-financial indicators to improve profitability*, Business Intelligence, London, 1993
6. Trapp, R, "Will Xerox reproduce its success?," *Independent*, 5 May 1995
7. Garvin, D, "Leveraging Processes for Strategic Advantage," *Harvard Business Review*, September–October 1995
8. Kaplan, R and Norton, D, "The Balanced Scorecard – measures that drive business performance," *Harvard Business Review*, January-February 1992
9. Simms, J, "High flying rebel," *Marketing Business*, Issue 3, September 1995
10. Stevens, M, "Dial M for branding," *Marketing Business*, Issue 3, September 1995
11. "Using customer measurements to drive business performance," paper presented to the Business Intelligence Conference, "Business Performance Measurement," March 1995
12. *Performance Management in the UK – An Analysis of the Issues*, Institute of Personnel Management 1991/92
13. Sadler, P, *Managing Talent*, FT/Pitman, London, 1993
14. Waterman, R., "Riveting Aspirations," *Independent on Sunday*, 17 April 1994

"Change is a door that can only be opened from the inside."

Tom Peters[1]

Chapter 7

◆

OWNING THE FUTURE

Owning the future is about seeing where you are today from the perspective of the future you want to create; and taking action now to make sure that you can bring that future to fruition. Renewal, at the business and personal level, means recognizing that we are in the process of becoming, as much as we are in the process of being. Paradoxically, both resistance to and promotion of the inevitable change this implies comes from people. If we are to transform exceptional performance from wish list to reality then we must replace fear with fun, anxiety with anticipation, creating the excitement and challenge to be all we can be.

RENEWAL AS A HUMAN PROCESS

Owning the future is not about detailed and precise future planning or the relentless pursuit of top-down programmatic change. These classic managerial approaches to managing change simply are no longer sustainable. Accepting this and realizing that the questions, never mind the answers, will rarely be obvious releases energy. It gives us permission to be unclear. Uncertainty and doubt are the parents of new knowledge; without them, we cannot move forward.

Owning the future is about sustainable learning and growth. It demands drive and determination to release and realize potential, building momentum and commitment along the way. Everyone needs to feels involved, having some say in the constant redefinition of the part that they play, without losing the overall sense of moving in the same direction.

The pace is already being set by some of the world's biggest corporate names. Intel, ABB, Toyota and Motorola have already signed on. So, too, have some of the companies who fell from grace at the turn of the decade. Having learned the hard way some of them are renewing and delivering faster growth. IBM, for example is looking good again – throughout 1995 its share price improved and so did its earnings. Revenue growth is better than in the last ten years, as IBM reduces its dependence on old technologies and moves into higher growth segments.

AVOIDING THE PITFALLS OF FASHION AND FADS

The image of the Performance Prism helps us to remember that there are many sides to managing performance and that these sides need to be brought together holistically to deliver truly exceptional results. Andrew Campbell of the Ashridge Strategic Management Centre reminds us that developing direction, or intent, is underpinned by insights, which enable us "to see ways of creating value that are superior to those of competitors."[2] Superior insights generate advantage even if this is only short term, and this, he says, is why companies are readily prepared to embrace a variety of management ideas, because they are used as processes for developing insights.

"It is for this reason that fads are so faddish. Companies scramble to cover the processes used by competitors. Whether it is total quality management, benchmarking, process reengineering, strategic planning, empowerment, core competence analysis or some other concept, managers are right to experiment with any new solution, even if it only has a low probability of being more than snake oil. The penalty of being late on to a new way of generating insights is severe," says Campbell.

There is never anything wrong in trying out new ideas, as long as you recognize there are no long-term solutions. The trouble with the abundance of managerial fads is that there are usually several groups of people simultaneously trying to generate insights in a fragmented, incoherent and sometimes competitive way. This diffuses knowledge and focus and confuses people who quite understandably display signs of change fatigue, and are tired of what they see as yet more management jargon.

While the talk at senior levels is of change, and while the plethora of initiatives can generate lots of new activity, benefits may not be realized, and emotionally most people hope that, post-fad, things will be just the same.

What we set out in this book is a philosophy of performance through people which sees organizations as human systems, with success depending on creating a human context for performance: the human organization. Richard Pascale[3] hits on an important aspect of this when, influenced by his experience of Japanese management, he cautions us to be aware of the difference between doing and being, in Japanese *Ki* and *Kokoro*. Pascale explains: "The way in which this comes to root in business is that it would not occur to the Japanese just to do a management technique – such as total quality management. Of course, they would also 'be' quality. By contrast they view their Western counterparts as precocious children – always chasing after the latest management technique and striving to distill it down to a recipe for doing."

This reminds us of a business manager in the UK, who for years promoted total quality in his firm and set out to make people aware that this meant more than a quality program. He used to begin many of his discussions with the story of the day that the BSI first came to award the firm with the BS 5750 (ISO) 9000, the UK quality standard. Everyone involved in the award presentation nervously recognized that poor products were still being shipped out of the door. From that moment on he resolved to change things, to walk the talk and not just talk about it.

Very often we "do" management change, investing in initiatives and allocating some of our best resources to them, yet these change programs run as parallel activities in the business. Many programs run for years and, like tumbleweed, they thrive without taking root.

Generating insights for advantage is important, but not every insight is relevant. To know what is relevant, we first need insights about who we are, who we can be. This means fundamentally understanding the kind of value proposition you are pursuing and binding all thought, energy and resource to that pursuit. Research into market leaders[4] demonstrates the importance of this focus. Leaders like McDonald's, Wal-Mart, Intel, FedEx and SouthWest Airlines are set apart by the sophistication of their operating models, which build coherence across structure, systems, processes, management and culture.

PAINTING A TOTAL PICTURE

The necessary process of change is renewal from the core, from the heart of what the company intends to be. Owning the future takes more than graffiti, more than a splash of change here and a splash of change there. It is about seeing and creating the total picture and coloring the whole organization accordingly.

If your value discipline is one of operational excellence, then be operationally excellent, and if you are thinking about empowerment or reengineering or flexible pay, then think about it from the standpoint of operational excellence, and not in isolation. If your value discipline is customer intimacy then everything you do must create greater intimacy. If you are about to refashion reward schemes around new performance accountabilities, or are about to introduce new types of teams because you think you want greater cross-fertilization of ideas and information sharing, then, before you get started, ask and find out how this will help your relationships with customers, how it fits in to the operating model as a whole. When you have found out, tell everyone involved so they understand how what you are doing relates to who you are and who they are. In that way people will not *have* to do it for you – they will create customer intimacy because they believe in customers and can see it makes sense.

THE TOTAL PICTURE MEANS YOU TOO

Building a total picture means taking a holistic view of managing the organization's performance. A more integrative view does not mean taking on everything at once, it simply means seeing what you are doing in terms of the bigger picture, the whole context of performance.

This means that managers and senior executives need to rise above their own divisional, functional and team perspectives and interests, so they can be agents and catalysts of renewal for the business as a whole. This also means rising above the day-to-day detail which managers prefer, so that time is taken for the future to be understood. Future-gazing is not just about the visions of work we might have while lying awake at night. It involves bringing key people in the business together to discuss emerging patterns and trends, seeking new and discontinuous connections across the parts. It involves identifying horizontal and zig-zag paths forward, not just the classic linear lines of action we see in most work breakdowns. Leverage needs to be across the whole, rather than within the various parts.

It is people who run companies, not processes or operating models. Getting it done better, faster or differently, requires action and intervention which connects strategy to capability. On a day-to-day basis, many managers are disconnected from strategy and get bogged down in the problems of their slice of the action, the area of capability they are managing. More importantly, all of us find it difficult to transcend our local and personal allegiances.

Building alignment is as much about personal change as it is about business change. One reason why many change activities fail to deliver benefits is that they are signed off by managers whose interests lie elsewhere. Change projects can fail because they bump into functional, divisional, or personal politics. Before getting started, it is essential to build a shared change agenda to ensure commitment and ownership by the people in key positions. Often these people perceive they will be losers not winners in the change game.

While this is often not the case for them as people, it may be the case for their current set of interests. These interests may well be becoming redundant or superseded by change in the outside world. Today's functional managers are in many respects like yesterday's hand-loom weavers. In the end, local resistance and rebellion will not change the course of the future, but it can certainly slow a company down. As Hout and Carter's research into 550 global companies observed: "Improvement stopped because senior managers did not recognize the myriad ways in which they were hindering the reengineering effort. Put simply they were good at championing change but poor at changing themselves."[5]

The first and hardest lesson of renewal is that change begins with you, and the Prism model can help you do this.

THE PRISM IN PRACTICE

Over the next few pages, we show how the Prism framework can be used as a practical tool at the outset of any planned change. By considering the impact of any particular program on other parts of the business, and other facets of the performance process, you will see how interlinked the pieces are, and can take steps to build alignment from the start. Exceptional performance will only be possible when leaders are in agreement with intent and work to link capability to direction, aligning the performance of people and teams through integrated human and business performance systems.

Even something as apparently straightforward and simple as introducing personal development plans to emphasize a more developmental approach to managing performance, for example, will impact upon the role of managers or leaders, on existing training and development systems, and on the organization's current appraisal system. It also begs the question, "Personal development for what?" Development at the individual level needs to be looked at from the performance context as a whole.

If other inter-related facets are ignored or not drawn into the change process, full benefits may not be realized and the chances of long-term gains are reduced. Linkages are not just practical, they are also intellectual and emotional, and without them change can easily be discredited, with those involved building barriers to guard their existing interests, rather than opening their minds to new ones.

We have chosen three topical examples of the kinds of change many managers are currently trying to make to illustrate the Prism in practice. Recognizing, including and utilizing the interlinkages between the Prism sides will help you to build the coherence required for success.

- **Developing a networked culture**
- **Leading for empowerment**
- **Implementing 360-degree feedback at local team/departmental level**

These initiatives represent examples which are intended to spark your thought processes in relation to your own team, unit or organization. The examples barely touch the surface of the possible changes that can be made to build exceptional performance. They may or may not be the best place to start in your organization or your team at the present time.

For each of the examples, we flag other related changes which will need attention as part of building alignment. At the very least this means raising questions in the other parts of the business affected by what you plan to do.

In this way the Prism can be used as a mapping tool, so that all sides may be explored together and the possibilities for alignment fully realized.

As you work with the Prism in practice, think about your own organization, and the outcomes you might generate if you were to go forward with any change of this kind.

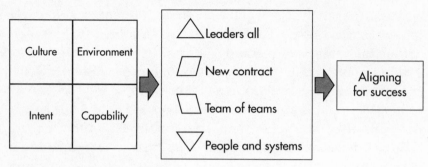

Fig 7.1 Aligning for success

BUILDING THE HUMAN ORGANIZATION

1. Developing a networked culture

Many companies aspire to a more networked operating style. This implies dissolving barriers and borders, whether geographical or structural, and creating an open-plan world where people and products, ideas and information flow freely in the absence of border controls. This is the world of virtuality – virtual time, virtual teams, and virtual enterprise.

The common experience is that virtuality is virtually impossible. Borders and mental barriers tend to remain steadfastly intact. The psychological border police can remain on patrol even when the formal walls are down.

It is one thing creating a networked organization in theory, quite another when it involves changing corporate culture. Managers who have been involved in attempting cultural change know that it is not as simple as generating a list of values and publishing these with a copy on everyone's wall. In fact this may be the worst thing to do. Cries for culture change need to be probed more deeply. They are cries for changes in behavior, usually phrased in the negative, with a focus on what is currently wrong. We hear "people round here treat information as power," or "the culture stifles creativity" or "the company is risk-averse and we have a culture of blame." None of these cries has much meaning in isolation and as a group are unlikely to be sufficient drivers for change in their own right. They need to be assessed in the fuller context of performance. What is the company trying to achieve and what are the behaviors and beliefs that will support this?

The trouble is that people tend to believe that their behaviors and beliefs are helping the organization achieve its objectives. This may have once been right or may still be right from a particular point of view. Until you have explored this more fully and increased receptivity to a different way of behaving, then attempts to change culture will fail to deliver.

The role of leaders in making culture change successful cannot be overemphasized. When the business is in trouble, the CEO often carries the can – as we have seen in recent years at IBM, Apple Computers, American Express and General Motors. New ways of doing things often develop very rapidly with the arrival of a new CEO. Change can be accelerated by new appointments from either inside or outside. Notable examples in recent years are Jan Carlzon of SAS, Jack Welch of GE, Sir Colin Marshall of British Airways, Sir Michael Edwards and Graham Day of Rover. It is the newness of these executives which makes them an asset for changing culture. Being untainted by history, without allegiance to existing players, they are outside the status quo and can more readily introduce and endorse new ways of operating.

But the days of the CEO as lone hero are over. They may take the headlines or take the blame, but it takes teams of like-minded people to deliver change. It is essential to move quickly to build critical mass in the new way of thinking and operating. Efforts must be made to bring the entire management population on side, instilling zeal and a sense of responsibility. Tough decisions may need to be taken, but it is better to face this sooner rather than later.

This group in turn needs to influence other people in the business and a campaign plan or overall style of change needs to be agreed to keep efforts aligned. Styles of culture change can range from the aggressive to the conciliatory, with more or less consensus-seeking and involvement.

As the example of Syntegra shows, culture change takes place as part of business change. It is not an end in itself. It is interwoven with the other three dimensions in the base of the Prism, and has profound implications for the remaining facets.

SYNTEGRA: DEVELOPING A NETWORK CULTURE

Syntegra is the systems integration business of BT (British Telecommunications plc), and was created in 1989 from the consolidation of over 40 disparate businesses. There was no shared culture, values or mission, except for some common behaviors typical of a Civil Service-type organization. Skills analysis in 1988/89 showed many manifestations of negative culture, like a reluctance to share information, time being spent blocking the progress of others, isolated and poor decision making, and a "bullying" management style.

In 1990, Bill Halbert became Managing Director and developed a vision to become one of the world's leading professional services organizations. The achievement of this objective necessitated a major change program, which included organization culture and design. As Gwen Ventris, Director of Organization and Resourcing comments, "It required the assessment, formulation and implementation of both strategic and operational change and this had to be a continuous and interactive process."

It was recognized that to be effective, the business needed to:

- Recognize the importance of the individual
- Develop individuals
- Develop fluid networks and teams
- Develop higher levels of skill in decision making
- Accept a collaborative and non-partisan approach to creativity
- Experiment, make mistakes and learn
- Develop an organization and resourcing strategy as a key element of Syntegra business strategy.

The main goal has been to develop a project-oriented team culture that will facilitate the flexible deployment of people on customer assignments. This approach was developed to avoid conventional development problems like the classic pigeon-holing where people are locked into specific jobs or functions and under-utilized because of where or for whom they work.

This was achieved through a resource management system, coupled with high levels of expertise and decision-making capability. In line with project demands, individuals are assigned to projects appropriate to their skills and capabilities or development needs. At any one time, a person could be engaged on several projects and be functioning quite differently on each one.

This has been working for over three years now and is very effective in enabling the continual development of people's capability and work experience.

Syntegra's culture has completely changed the fabric of the business. Psychological resistance to change has eroded: change is now expected as the norm. There is now a common culture and values more consistent with Syntegra's market environment, including:

- customer focus
- self-sufficiency, individual contribution and collective responsibility
- remuneration according to individual contribution and market value
- flexibility of approach
- imagination and creativity applied to problem solving
- meritocracy, team orientation and minimal hierarchy
- open, honest communication and extensive involvement in business issues of all its people

The transformation program comprised many different projects, covering the whole business to ensure alignment, such as skill effectiveness, resource acquisition, a team-building program and self-managed learning program for new graduates.

Syntegra is organized and operates in a way that underpins and supports its values on a daily basis. For example, "Choice" is a sophisticated flexible benefits package plan offered to all its people, enabling them to tailor their rewards package to their personal circumstances.

From being a loss-making entity in 1989, it is now a profitable organization. The nature of the business has changed, and the work Syntegra does for its customers is far more complex, requires greater skill and involves taking significant calculated risk. Syntegra has extended the concept of integration to include not just technologies and information management, but organization and people as well. This approach clearly draws on experience that Syntegra has developed from its own experience. Some customers have chosen to do business with Syntegra because its culture serves as an ideal model for where they would like to be.

What we learn is that we need to look at all the factors involved, so that all the potential levers for change can be pulled together, building an unstoppable momentum. See Figure 7.2 for areas to consider.

THINK ABOUT THE CONTEXT OF YOUR OWN ORGANIZATION

■ Your teams

- Is energy and understanding present in your team to embrace the networked approach?
- Would you pilot work in your group?
- Are there internal or external role models to illustrate value of initiative?
- Are teams used to being fixed and stable?

▲ Leadership

- Are you and others believable role models of the new network style?
- What do you and others really feel about the direction of change?
- If you feel negative what are you going to do?
- What can you personally do to recognize desired behavior?

▼ Your systems

- What behaviors currently rewarded/supported by existing systems? What needs to change?
- Can you impact upon/adapt reward systems in place?
- Have you developed benchmarks (customers, suppliers, competitors) for this change?

◢ The contract

- What does change imply for individuals in your area? Are they used to networking?
- Do contracts of employment emphasize/ formalize new ways of working?
- Are there barriers to change or resistance? How will you pre-empt problems?
- Is there jealousy between in/outsiders? How would you deal with this?

▦ The organization

- Do you have a clear vision for the future?
- What are the drivers for change internally and externally?
- Is this initiative the right approach?
- Are you prepared for the costs of change and the knock-on effects?
- Is there commitment to the change from senior management?
- How can you get buy-in throughout the organization?

■ Teams of teams

- Identify the change implied for how teams will work
- Use successful teams as role models
- Build support and communicate reasons for the change
- Pilot new approach in one or two areas, and communicate the lessons to other teams
- Build picture of ideal team to demonstrate business and personal benefits of change
- Find role models for new culture and transfer them, or their knowledge into key teams to raise teams' status

---

▲ Leaders all

- Leaders must show flexibility and commitment, they must be overt sponsors of change
- New leaderships' styles need identifying with participation by all in this process
- Degree of change required, new values and desired behaviors must be clearly role modeled by leaders
- New leaders may need to be recruited
- Champions and informal leaders will need to be encouraged
- Leaders who cannot sign on may need to be removed

▼ People and systems

- Develop performance criteria based on new behaviors and reward these when they are demonstrated
- Build support and communicate need for change, using formal and informal systems
- Develop frameworks which support multi-teaming
- Pilot new scheme in one or two areas, communicate success to other teams

---

▟ The new contract

- Assess skills already present and those needed to ensure success
- Barriers to change and resistance likely at beginning, so anticipate and prevent from taking hold by managing expectations during transition
- Assess the implications for the core and periphery supply of skills. Will all contracts be the same?
- Introduce new and relevant contracts quickly to seal what has changed

---

▦ The organization

- Are you aware of the extent of the change?
- How will your customers be affected?
- Is networking important to the successful achievement of the organizational strategy?
- Communicate the change in culture clearly to everyone
- Make sure the vision is clear and explicit
- Respond to market conditions
- Make sure the initiative reflects the strategic intent of the organization

---

Fig 7.2 Potential levers for change

2. Leading for empowerment

The empowered organization conjures up new ways of operating. Employees, freed from the shackles of over-controlling management, are able to take initiatives, make decisions and accept responsibility. They interface with clients skilfully and confidently, and in so doing, provide the highest quality of service.

With such promises, the concept of empowerment has been adopted by many companies with varying degrees of success. A US survey found that while 64 percent of respondents believed their companies were encouraging empowerment, 86 percent were of the opinion that business leaders failed to practice what they preached.[6]

Empowerment is often seen in terms of leadership. The theory is that by giving up power, leaders actually gain more power and can lead the organization more effectively. However, the whole idea of giving up power is alien to many leaders whose very success has been built on acquiring and using the relevant power bases available to them.

The problems associated with empowerment are not just personal ones. They cover every aspect of the organization and impact on every facet of the Performance Prism. Empowerment will only work if it is aligned with the culture, purpose and values of the organization, the base of the Prism. It also needs to be aligned with the sides: not only do the performance systems and team structures need to be aligned to the notion of empowerment, but as Phil Lowe, Consultant with Harbridge House, points out, the whole contract between employer and employee needs to be redesigned: "There is two-way traffic at work: the individual is given autonomy and ownership in return for a commitment to act in the interests of the organization; the organization gets more out of each individual in return for supporting and training him or her to increase his or her ability to perform effectively."[7]

So what are the issues at stake to ensure that empowerment is aligned to every side of the Prism? These will be explored through the example of Novotel which demonstrates how empowerment can work to enhance customer service.

BACK TO THE FUTURE WITH NOVOTEL

In 1993 Novotel launched its "Back to the Future" program: an all-encompassing project which meant a new and enlightened approach for Novotel worldwide. The project was aimed at improving the quality the company offered to its clients and rebuilding the success it experienced in the 1960s and 1970s.

Back to the Future has three elements: a new company image, massive investment (with a complete overhaul of the older hotels), and a new approach to management which would give unprecedented autonomy for the general manager of every hotel and ensure the empowerment of their staff.

The empowerment program provided that each general manager be made "Maître de Maison." He/she was empowered to run the hotel exactly as he/she saw fit. The Novotel operations manual, which told general managers in minute detail how to run their hotel, was abolished. They still have to work within the boundaries of design, logo and menu features, but besides this they have freedom to innovate as they see fit.

The previous lengthy reporting lines have been removed so that the hierarchy now consists of three levels, the general manager, his direct reports and the Chairman.

As Guy Parsons, Sales and Marketing Director, points out, "centralized control has been replaced by decentralized guidance." Head office functions now act in a consultancy capacity, and while general managers are encouraged to solve their own problems, they can also seek the advice of more senior general managers as mentors. They work together to solve common problems.

The staff, too, are encouraged to act in the spirit of "maître de maison" and solve customer problems as they see fit.

To provide the necessary development, Novotel has introduced three new training programs under the umbrella of School for Life, and encourages managers to take responsibility for their own development.

The results from the "Back to the Future" project are measurable in that Novotel receives fewer complaints, occupancy has risen by 19 percent in the last 12 months, and profit has risen by 15 percent since last year. Customer satisfaction has increased, and so too has employee satisfaction and retention.

> The change to empowerment has not merely been a leadership issue. It has attacked the old cultural values, encouraging autonomy when once rigidity was favored. It has attacked the structure of the organization, flattening and decentralizing it. It has worked with systems, creating new roles and career paths. It has worked with the individual needs and the new contract, which encourages development and initiative, and finally, it has encouraged the hotels to work as teams to meet customer needs and helped them to acquire the skills to do so.
>
> Change, therefore, is at every facet of the Prism, and for empowerment to work, this has to be the case. Old rigid hierarchies will find it hard to make the shift unless they take on board the consequences at all levels and in all areas of the business.[8]

So what are the issues at stake to ensure that empowerment is aligned to every side of the Prism. Figure 7.3 gives some examples of these issues.

THINK ABOUT THE CONTEXT OF YOUR OWN ORGANIZATION

◼ Your team

- What are the boundaries to empowerment? How do you decide these, and what criteria do you use?
- Do you confront issues of individuals who are unwilling to take on greater responsibility and accountability?
- How can you encourage the team to take on responsibility and accountability?
- How can team members support each other?
- How can you fully utilize the skills of all team members?

◼ The contract

- How can it "sell" empowerment as opportunity and encourage individuals to meet challenge with positive regard?
- What are the boundaries to be set?
- How can it change mind-sets within teams, and gain support for empowerment?
- How can it gain credibility within teams, and how to show wholehearted support for empowerment?

■ **Teams of teams**
• Provide team training in how to work together and manage the new responsibilities
• Regular feedback and review in the team is essential
• Empowerment must fit in with team's objectives and capability
• There needs to be trust inside and outside
• The team needs to use all its resources and skills
• Be sure that the boundaries to empowerment are clearly defined

▟ **The new contract**
• Recognize and understand barriers on individual level – fear of something new, fear of taking risks, fear of reprisals, job insecurity
• Appropriate training is required so that individuals are equipped to take responsibility for own actions
• Clear boundaries to empowerment need to be established
• Individuals and teams need to be supported in taking on more accountability

▼ **People and systems**
• People will need help to measure and monitor their own performance
• Rewards to encourage empowerment and mutual accountability within teams need to be established
• Systems must be set up for regular feedback, from internal and external customers
• Accurate information for decision making must be available and accessible on a regular basis

▦ **The human organization**
• Information on purpose, values and strategic intent of the organization must be available to understand how empowerment fits in
• It must be clear to all that culture is changing from command and control to decision making being passed down line
• There needs to be a clear message from senior management that risk taking encouraged and failure allowed in empowered environment

▲ **Leaders all**
• Leaders must be ready to give away power
• It is important to recognize the notion of "leaders all"
• Training and coaching must be provided
• The new leadership style must be more transformational
• People need to be aware of the new leadership competencies

Fig 7.3 The change to empowerment

▼ Your systems

- Do they build competencies to ensure empowerment is correctly received and carried out?
- How can you reward empowerment?
- What systems are in place for preventing abuse, such as managers who prefer "dumping" or abdicating rather than empowering?
- How do you measure progress? Are there other organizations to benchmark with?

▋▋ Your organization

- Does it ensure that the senior management team are prepared to empower people and be empowering?
- What systems are in place to ensure information-sharing and good communication, both upwards and downwards?
- Does it make sure the initiative is credible?
- Does it ensure that the hierarchy does not stifle empowerment?

▲ Leadership

- Are leaders prepared to give power to others?
- Do they really know what is meant by empowerment?
- Are they aware of the skills and competencies they need?
- Is there sufficient training and support?

3. Introducing 360-degree feedback at local level

The idea of 360-degree feedback is growing in popularity. It is a valuable way of gaining feedback from many sources including peers, subordinates, customers and suppliers. It is an ideal way of measuring competences and getting feedback on some of the softer issues such as management style, communication and teamwork.

Yet its impact is often not fully understood. It is not a tool to be used in isolation or in place of other organizational initiatives. The instrument itself must be based on behaviors and competencies which the organization wishes to develop and reinforce. It must therefore be aligned with the purpose and values of the organization.

It is important to decide whether it is being introduced as a development tool, and, if so, the appropriate training must be available to help people to improve their performance. Alternatively, it may be used to measure and reward performance. If so, it could be linked in with the reward systems or the appraisal process.

Whatever the approach, training needs to provided to those who are administering and giving feedback to the individuals involved.

The repercussions on all facets of the Performance Prism are evident, and if one area is not considered, the whole initiative will fail. An example of this is one organization we came across which introduced 360-degree feedback as a development tool. While time and effort was spent designing the instrument, they failed to train the managers who would be giving feedback. The result was that in one area the analysis was posted up in the department in the form of a league table! That was not the right way to gain support for the idea or develop the managers involved.

Any form of 360-degree feedback will have a significant impact on the individuals involved and on their work patterns. Such an initiative would place far-reaching demands on the organization's internal systems, on the overall culture, and on any other initiatives, such as TQM for example, which might be being implemented concurrently. Even introduced at team level, it would send out waves of repercussions on other parts of the organization.

Yet, despite these warnings, it has been shown to be a valuable tool, as the Tesco example in the case study illustrates.

360-DEGREE FEEDBACK AT TESCO

Tesco, the UK supermarket chain, first considered a competency approach to management development and training in 1990, aware that the future would be bringing with it new and different challenges. A considerable number of managers had reached senior management positions at a very early age. The organization was considering the option of delayering, and wanted to develop a picture of what the manager of the future would look like. They also wanted to make sure that they could retain and motivate their most promising managers. With these ideas in mind they designed a tailor-made competency model which included 17 critical success factors.

The competency framework has been creatively used in a new approach to developing divisional directors. They receive an in-depth development review followed by development workshops. As a basis for the review, a 360-degree analysis questionnaire was designed which gave the managers a way of matching their own perceptions with that of their boss, peers and subordinates.

The processed questionnaire contains detailed information about the individual's strengths and weaknesses, seen from a range of viewpoints. This is fed back to the individual by a trained facilitator, who first visits the director and spends a day analyzing the report. The facilitator then works with the individual's boss to prepare him or her for their role in coaching and guiding the person. This will help them to think of practical ways to improve performance. In addition to coaching on the job, development workshops have been designed and a self-development center was set up to enable managers to implement their plans.

Finally, the facilitator brings together the boss and the individual. Agreement and commitment is sought and the individual can move on with a clear picture of what they need to do to continue their development and enhance their overall performance.

Using 360-degree feedback in this way accessed all sides of the Prism and its alignment with all the facets guaranteed its success. As Ken McMeikan, Management Development Manager, points out, "The management style that competencies encourage has enabled a culture shift to take place within our organization." The managers who have been through the personal development process are grasping the advantages of self-development and now want to pass the benefits on to their own teams.

The Tesco approach illustrates alignment. The competencies were developed in response to the organization's needs, reflecting its purpose and strategy. It was based on a clear picture of what the manager of the future should look like, and it reflected the contract and responsibilities between the employer and employees. It has also linked into the organization's systems as the competency model is used not only as a developmental tool but also in selection and recruitment.[9]

This case and all 360-degree interventions raise some important alignment issues: some of these issues: are listed in Figure 7.4.

■ **Teams of teams**
• The team must buy into the process
• Avoid the danger of the process taking focus from the actual task
• Be aware of the fear factor involved
• Team members feel threatened or confused by intervention and this may affect performance
• Consider the implications of 360-degree feedback within cross-cultural groups
• It must be seen as positive and developmental

▲ **Leaders all**
• Rejection of "the leader owns decisions about people's performance" without being threatening
• 360-degree feedback threatens power structures and organization's "untouchables"
• HR department needs to be perceived as advisor/facilitator, not owner of change
• Create "feedback is OK" climate – by setting example
• Specific leadership qualities needed – counseling, listening, coaching, willingness to accept feedback

▼ **People and systems**
• It is important to decide whether the initiative should fit in with the current appraisal system
• Is it a tool for development or assessment?
• Measurement of the impact of your intervention is important to ensure effectiveness and credibility.
• A system for allowing regular meetings and feedback in an unthreatening way is paramount

▦ **The human organization**
• 360-degree feedback could offer a realistic opportunity for organizational and personal renewal
• A "mistakes are OK" culture is essential
• Extensive training in counseling and feedback skills will be needed for teams and individuals alike
• An open culture is vital to encourage and support self-development based on the feedback people receive

▬ **New contract**
• A visible and accessible support system is vital for individuals who undertake to act upon the feedback they receive – support might include financial assistance, time for learning, independent and confidential counseling services, or reward and recognition for successful self-development
• The process must be managed positively
• People must be encouraged to be open

Fig 7.4   Alignment issues

NOW THINK ABOUT THE CONTEXT OF YOUR OWN ORGANIZATION

■ Your team

- How could you ensure enough trust within the team to ensure that the initiative is handled positively?
- With temporary teams it is important that the team members have enough information to give feedback on
- Would you start such an initiative informally, via a pilot team?
- How would you prevent any dip in performance/motivation which may occur at beginning, when people are still unsure?

▲ Your leadership style

- Will there be buy-in from individuals and team leaders?
- Will you need a champion within the department/team to start the ball rolling?
- How can you set an example? Through informal encouragement of upward feedback to you in the first instance?
- How and when will you implement team training? What form will this take?
- Are you aware of your own areas for improvement before implementing such a step?
- Can you demonstrate the necessary open-mindedness and willingness to accept and work on the feedback you receive?
- What about leaders and team members who do not buy in?

▼ Your systems

- Is there currently a part of a larger initiative, for example TQM or Investors in People, to which you could link your initiative for greater credibility and alignment?
- Would you need to run an "official" pilot scheme? How far would you involve the HR department/senior management team – for advice? Facilitation? Direction and ownership?
- How can you monitor the initiative and stop any abuse of the system?
- What systems will be needed to encourage and support self-development and working with the feedback?

▦ Your organization

- Are you clear about the purpose and objective of the initiative and sure that it is not just a fad?

- How can you build the capability for 360-degree feedback? In your department and ultimately across the organization?
- Are there people who can champion the process?
- Will it be part of a wider culture-change initiative?
- Would it be valid to encourage an organizational audit as well, so that individuals can link their feedback to career development?

■ The contract

- Where can people go who are shocked or unhappy with the feedback they receive – will there be access to an external counsellor/facilitator?
- Does it monitor the progress and provide support?
- Does it ensure that the feedback is well managed?
- Does it provide development opportunities for people to implement any action plans?
- Does it work to remove the fear factor?

THINKING ABOUT ALIGNMENT

Before moving ahead with a particular initiative ask yourself:

- **Why is the initiative being implemented?**
  Is it for clear strategic reasons? Does it have a business goal in mind, and how will the initiative help you to achieve it? Beware of initiatives which are fashionable or experimental. They need to be tied to a clear purpose, so that employees can understand what is happening and why a change is taking place. The results and progress can be more easily measured and the initiative will gain greater support and commitment throughout.

- **Is the initiative really in alignment with the organization's purpose, values, culture and strategy?**
  Performance initiatives often fail because they are not aligned to the real values of the organization. It is essential to look beyond bland mission statements and discover what the organization really wants.

- **Where is there potential for confused messages and contradictions?**
  It is essential to look for any potential sources of confusion and contradictions. Mixed messages are often factors in the failure of innovations in performance management. If areas of confusion are highlighted, it is

essential to make changes that will develop synergy in performance management across the organization. This may mean changing direction, dropping the initiative or approaching it from a different angle. Alternatively, it may mean changing some other aspect of the Prism.

- **What can be done to get people on board?**
  Gaining the support and involvement of others is time-consuming and often expensive. What is the cost of training and communicating to all employees? How and when can they become involved in the decision-making process? How can people be enabled and supported in working with the new initiative?

- **Is this best route for the organization to achieve its goals?**
  Any initiative must complement and support other performance management processes. It may be that changes to other areas of the Prism are required to enhance the effectiveness of the initiative. The initiative must be aligned with all the facets of the Performance Prism, and looked at in terms of cost–benefit analysis.

Many organizations implement initiatives, often at great expense, which are neither relevant nor clearly thought through. The result is a slow, painful and confusing process for the employees and one which does not bring benefits to the bottom line, or to the people involved.

Organizations which have achieved success in implementing change have done so by aligning initiatives in a complementary way, and checking for consistency across all the facets of the Performance Prism. When this happens, they are really aligned for success, and both the organization and its individual members have a greater chance of delivering exceptional performance.

THINKING ABOUT IMPACT

Before getting started with what you plan to do, think through the likely impact and work out how you are going to deal with this. Ask yourself the following:

- What can you impact directly? How?
- What can you impact indirectly? How?

- Who else can make an impact? How will you get them involved?
- Who will be:
  - supportive?
  - neutral?
  - resistant?
- How will you rally support and handle resistance?
- What are the opportunities for successfully introducing the change you are seeking?
- What are the barriers and constraints?
- Are you clear of the outcomes you are seeking?
- What would be the key indicators of success?
- How will you track progress?
- Can you list some milestones or targets which would enable some early wins?
- Are you sure you want to do this, have you thought through the personal change implications?

THE CHANGING NATURE OF CHANGE

The classic view of change management leads us to think we are dealing with an extraordinary rather than an ever-present phenomenon. Success in managing change, we are told, relies on a three-stage process of unfreezing, changing and refreezing, once the desired change has been achieved. There is an underlying assumption that there is a desirable steady state. This is no longer the case – if it ever was. Change is neither monolithic nor a one-off occurrence. It, too, is changing.

If what we already know is unlikely to be enough, what should our responses be?

The only thing that can reduce uncertainty is information, information which will guide the choices we make, as we navigate through uncertain times. Managers have always been paid to reduce uncertainty, to stabilize situations and keep things under control, so what will be different in the future? The mechanistic, scientific style of management, which has dominated the industrial age, sought to eliminate uncertainty by the analytical reduction of the unknown. This produced myriad analytical approaches which plotted the course of the future on the basis of what happened in the past. Change has been extrapolated, often in neat linear progression, 5 percent more inflation over the next three years, 7 percent increase in market share in the next five years, and so on. What managers have rarely challenged are the assumptions about economic and industry conditions on which the present, and such extrapolations, are based.

Within such a paradigm, the need for anything more than incremental adjustment is seen as a kind of blip, an unlucky force majeure, which we must react to and live with, and then resume life as normal. How did that happen, we say as we tighten our analysis, revisit our calculations and build contingency in case it should happen again.

But what if the future is not like the past, what would we need to do then? What if there is no neat list of answers, no handbook, no five key points to remember, no formula for success? What we would have to do is abandon our quest for repeatability, for regulation and control, and trust our human responses, the will to keep searching, asking questions, gleaning insights and experimenting with our hunches.

Acquiring new information depends on openness, with oneself and with others. In practice, managers can no longer completely trust their experience and the information this has yielded: they must develop external eyes and ears to keep abreast of what is shifting around them. This requires humility and eagerness, being prepared to say that we do not know, but that we will certainly try to find out. These are the qualities of good students, of the young, of the philosopher, of the artist, anyone with a quest to break new ground: if we are to find ways of delivering exceptional performance, again and again and again, then they must also become the qualities of managers as they grapple with the changing nature of change.

References

1. Peters, T, "Liberation Management," Alfred A. Knopf Inc., New York, 1992
2. Campbell, A, "Mission, vision and strategy development," in *FT Handbook of Management*, Pitman Publishing, London, 1995
3. Pascale, R, in *FT Handbook of Management*, Pitman Publishing, London, 1995

4. Treacy, M and Wiersema, F, *The Discipline of Market Leaders*, HarperCollins Publishers, London, 1995
5. Hout, T M and Carter, J C, "Getting it done: new roles for senior executives," *Harvard Business Review*, Nov–Dec 1995
6. "Empowerment, a Leap of Faith", *Management Training*, August 1993
7. Lowe, P, "Empowerment, Management Dilemma, Leadership Challenge," *Executive Development*, Vol 7 No 6, 1994
8. Adapted from Parsons, G, "Empowering Employees – Back to the Future at Novotel," *Managing Service Quality*, Vol 5 No 4, 1995
9. Ward, Peter, "A 360-degree turn for the better," *People Management*, 9 February 1995

"It is easier to act ourselves into a better mode of thinking than to think ourselves into a better mode of acting."

Richard Pascale[1]

Chapter 8

◆

TURNING VISION INTO REALITY

This chapter is designed to help you to deliver exceptional performance by turning your vision into reality and putting the Prism into practice. It is an iterative process. It is not about analysis paralysis, but action. It is not about thinking what you want to do, but acting and getting started.

Two underlying themes are woven throughout the book. The first is that of **change and renewal**, where people are central to the achievement of exceptional performance. The second is that of **alignment** – pulling all performance initiatives together, whether existing or new, and managing all facets of the Performance Prism in an integrated way.

With this in mind, your action-planning process should be a map which involves people, and, ideally it should be created with the very individuals who can help it to succeed. Your action plan should also be aligned with the other sides of the Performance Prism in order to achieve long-term sustainable success.

For this reason the action-planning process has been divided into three parts. The first is **reflection** to provide you with an opportunity to look back at what you have learnt from the book and reflect on the issues facing you and your organization.

The second part is **planning to act**, deciding how to achieve the outcome you want and setting timescales so that you can be ready to implement your plan and monitor its progress.

The third part is **alignment,** checking whether your ideas are aligned with the other sides of the Performance Prism and whether you can gain support from other sides of the Prism.

REFLECTION

To give some focus to your ideas, first reflect on your learning from *Delivering Exceptional Performance*.

What are the key points and themes you recall from each chapter?

Chapter 1: Performance through people
Key points and themes

- _____

- _____

- _____

● _____

● _____

Chapter 2: The human organization
Key points and themes

● _____

● _____

● _____

● _____

● _____

Chapter 3: Leaders all
Key points and themes

● _____

● _____

● _____

● _____

● _____

Chapter 4: The new contract
Key points and themes

● _____

● _____

● _____

● _____

• _____

Chapter 5: Teams of teams
Key points and themes

• _____

• _____

• _____

• _____

• _____

Chapter 6: Performance through people and systems
Key points and themes

• _____

• _____

• _____

• _____

• _____

Chapter 7: Owning the future
Key points and themes

• _____

• _____

• _____

• _____

• _____

Now, think about your own situation.

What changes has your organization gone through in recent years (e.g., downsizing and a move to flatter structures, and the use of process teams) and how has this affected performance?

- _____

- _____

- _____

- _____

- _____

What are the specific performance problems facing you?
These may be similar to the issues discussed in Chapter 7, or they may be specific problems such as how to motivate your team, how to deal with a team member who is underperforming or how to manage your career. List the issues – e.g., how to develop my current team to take on greater responsibility and accountability – below.

- _____

- _____

- _____

- _____

- _____

The chances are that your particular areas of concern will relate to changes which are already taking place in the organization. It may be that your organization is still trying to achieve alignment and a new equilibrium. It is important to remember that *you* as much as anyone are part of the change/alignment process and *you* as much as anyone have a role in making the future work.

Once you have gone through this reflection process, it is appropriate to apply these ideas to your reality by moving from **reflection** to **planning to act**.

PLANNING TO ACT

You can start anywhere you like. It may be easiest to start with an issue which is small and for which you can guarantee success. Remember success breeds success, and as your confidence grows, you may feel ready to tackle some bigger performance issues facing you, the people you work with and the organization.

We have worked through an example to illustrate how the process works (see Figure 8.1). The example is concerned with how to improve teamwork, or more specifically, how to improve team performance so that the team can take on greater responsibility and accountability. We explored factors that could help to achieve this goal, and also the things that could get in the way. We then looked at how to overcome these, and from that developed actions and timescales so that there was a clear path forward. Notice how important it was to involve other people. The quality of the end result lies with their commitment and enthusiasm.

Now take one of your own issues and, using the framework (see Figure 8.2), work through the various steps of the action-planning process.

Now you have your action plan it might be useful to check it off against the Performance Prism model in Figure 1.4 to see if you can find other ideas and ways of supporting your issue.

In the example of improving team performance it is possible that ideas from all sides of the Prism could enhance the process. For example, it is important to develop the appropriate **leadership** style which encourages greater responsibility and accountability in team members. There may be issues concerned with the **new contract,** such as career development, life after the team, and measuring and reviewing performance, which will influence team performance. It may be possible to exploit the **systems** to their full potential to benefit and motivate the team. For example, there may be the opportunity to be flexible around rewards or to influence the appraisal process. Finally, it will be important that the team sees their role within the wider purpose and strategy of **the organization**. Presenting the broader picture can often engender greater commitment.

Issues	What are the helping factors	What are the hindering factors	Who can help	Actions	Timescale
To improve team performance so that the team can take on greater responsibility and accountability	• Some enthusiastic members • A major project to work on • Support of senior management • Some clear targets and timescales	• A couple of demotivated people • Tight timescales • Lack of resources in some areas • New team who have not worked together before	• The enthusiastic members • Training dept for team development • Senior management to secure resources • The team to set targets and accountabilities • Me – to make my role clear and act as coach and support	• Discuss plans with the team • Meet with senior management • Establish the team purpose • Set targets, goals and review dates with the team • Design appropriate team development event with training dept • Outline my role to the team and gain their support	• Jan team meeting • Jan 10th • Jan team meeting • Jan team meeting with regular review dates • Jan 15th • Jan team meeting and ongoing

Fig 8.1 Achieving exceptional performance – an example of planning to act

Issues	Outcome	What are the helping factors	What are the hindering factors	Who can help	Timescale

Fig 8.2 Achieving exceptional performance – planning process

So, you can see that the three-part action-planning process, reflection, planning to act and alignment, can help you to be more creative when seeking solutions to your performance problems. Hopefully, it will accelerate your journey into the knowledge era with greater confidence and with less confusion, enabling you to deliver exceptional performance from yourself, from others and from the organization of which you are an essential part.

The Kobe disaster described at the beginning blew apart the lives of the people who were involved. They had to piece together their belongings and move through their grief and despair into a new world.

The parallels with the challenges facing managers and organizations may appear obscure, but should now be more obvious than they first appeared. Managers have to rebuild. They have to go through the trauma and the fear – and they have do so voluntarily, spurred by their own commitment to developing themselves and their organizations. It is a sizable and never ending task. But, the process of healing and renewal is a natural one, and can clear the way for new ways of living and growing into the future. And only if new ways of living, working and growing are discovered, will managers and organizations learn to thrive in the uncertain times ahead.

References

1. Pascale, R, *Managing on The Edge*, Penguin Books, London, 1990

INDEX

◆